Modern Witchcraft—A Reli

Modern Witchcraft is not a dead ⸺ ⸺ handed down from antiquity. We now know that all religions begin as new religions, the history of Gardnerian Witchcraft reconstructed in *Crafting the Art of Magic, Book I* can be seen as archetypal, as throwing light on the way that many other religions have evolved. In this book, author Aidan Kelly has subjected the Gardnerian movement to a rigorous historical analysis, clearly distinguishing its foundational myths from its actual history. This is the manner in which all major religions must be studied if they are to speak to the needs of mature, sophisticated adults in the modern world. Judaism, Christianity, and other world religions have stood up to this type of examination quite well, and have in fact been strengthened by it. Insight says that the Craft can stand up to it also, that it need not be sheltered from the lancet of analysis and the searchlights of comparative religious scholarship.

Before now, no other book has solely relied on historical evidence to reconstruct the history of modern Witchcraft. All other books on this subject have suffered from the severe limitations of the author's own viewpoint, and from assuming the truth of unverifiable (and often simply false) statements made by the movement's detractors and even its various founders and leaders.

Crafting the Art of Magic, Book I presents:

- The first serious, full-scale study of Gerald Gardner's life as researched by a trained and respected historical scholar.
- The first publication of the complete and accurate text of the Gardnerian Book of Shadows as it evolved from 1949 to 1961.
- The first reconstruction of the evolution of the Craft as a new religion from its beginning in 1939.
- The first reliable, accurate history of modern Witchcraft.
- The first biography of Gerald Gardner based on fact, not fantasy and hearsay.
- The first true examination of what the Craft is really all about: where it came from and where it is heading.

About the Author

Aidan Kelly is unique in being both a founder of two of the largest Witchcraft organizations in America (the New, Reformed, Orthodox Order of the Golden Dawn, founded in 1967; and the Covenant of the Goddess, founded in 1975) and a respected scholar in the field of new religions. He is an active member of many academic associations, including the Group on New Religious Movements of the American Academy of Religion, the largest and most prestigious organization devoted to the study of religion.

Kelly earned his Ph.D. from the Graduate Theological Union, Berkeley, California, considered to be one of the best graduate ecumenical seminaries in North America, and has taught religious studies and humanities in half a dozen major educational institutions. In addition to writing and editing, he is a director of the Santa Barbara Centre for Humanistic Studies, a research institute which publishes reference works and scholarly monographs in religious studies and related subjects.

To Write to the Author

We cannot guarantee that every letter written to the author can be answered, but all will be forwarded. Both the author and the publisher appreciate hearing from readers, learning of your enjoyment and benefit from this book. Llewellyn also publishes a bimonthly news magazine with news and reviews of practical esoteric studies and articles helpful to the student, and some readers' questions and comments to the author may be answered through this magazine's columns if permission to do so is included in the original letter. The author sometimes participates in seminars and workshops, and dates and places are announced in *The Llewellyn New Times*. To write to the author, or to ask a question, write to:

Aidan Kelly
c/o THE LLEWELLYN NEW TIMES
P.O. Box 64383-370, St. Paul, MN 55164-0383, U.S.A.

Please enclose a self-addressed, stamped envelope for reply, or $1.00 to cover costs.

Llewellyn's Modern Witchcraft Series

Crafting the Art of Magic, Book I
A History of Modern Witchcraft, 1939-1964

by
Aidan A. Kelly, Ph.D.

Title: Crafting the art of magic

Author: Kelly; Aidan A.

ISBN
875423701

1991
Llewellyn Publications
St. Paul, Minnesota, 55164-0383, U.S.A.

FIRST EDITION

Library of Congress Cataloging-in-Publication Data:
Kelly, Aidan A.
    Crafting the art of magic / Aidan A. Kelly.
        p.   cm. — (Llewellyn's modern witchcraft series)
    Includes bibliographical references.
    Contents: bk. 1. A history of modern witchcraft, 1939-1964.
    ISBN 0–87542–370–1
        1. Gardner, Gerald Brosseau, 1884-1964. 2. Witchcraft—History—20th century. 3. Magic—History—20th century. 4. Paganism—History—20th century.   I. Title. II. Series.
    BF1571.K35 1990   90-26467
    133.4'3—dc20   CIP

Llewellyn Publications
A Division of Llewellyn Worldwide, Ltd.
P.O. Box 64383, St. Paul, MN 55164-0383

ABOUT LLEWELLYN'S MODERN WITCHCRAFT SERIES

Witchcraft is a word derived from an older word, *Wicca* or *Wicce*, which comes from a root meaning "to bend." Thus, those who practiced the craft of the Wicca were able to bend reality to their desires: they could do magic.

Today, Witchcraft is different from what it was eons ago. Witchcraft is no longer robes and secret rites. As the Aquarian Age—the New Age—approaches fruition, the mystical secrets of the past are being made public. The result is a set of spiritual and magical systems with which anyone can feel comfortable. Modern Witchcraft—Wicca—may be the path for you.

Llewellyn's Modern Witchcraft Series of books will not only present the secrets of the Craft of the Wise so that anyone can use them, but will also share successful techniques that are working for Witches throughout the world. This will include philosophies and techniques that at one time were considered foreign to "the Craft," but are now being incorporated by modern Wiccans into their beliefs and procedures.

However, the core of Wicca will stay the same—that is the nature of Witchcraft. All of the books in this series will be practical and easy to use. They will all show a love of nature and a love of the goddess as well as respect for the Masculine Force. You will find that this series of books is deeply rooted in spirituality, peacefulness and love.

These books will focus on Wicca and Wiccans today, not what was done a hundred, a thousand, or ten thousand years ago. They will help you to expand your horizons and achieve your goals. We invite you to follow this series and look toward the future of what some have called the fastest growing religion in the world, a religion that is personal, non-judgmental and non-institutional, natural and magical—that brings forth the experience of the sacredness of ALL Life. Witchcraft is called "the Old Religion" and it is found present in the oldest myths and artifacts of humanity. This series will help you see what it will develop into tomorrow.

Other Books by the Author

History and Other Explorations: Selected Poèms, 1968-74
Moving Into Space: Myths and Realities of Extraterrestrial Space
    (co-authored)
The New Healers: Healing the Whole Person (co-authored)
Secrets of Life Extension: A Practical Guide for the Use of
    Life-Extension Therapies (co-authored)
The New Age Encyclopedia (co-authored)
The New Age Almanac (co-authored)

Forthcoming

Crafting the Art of Magic, Book II: Witchcraft in America,
    1964-1990
Religious Holidays and Calendars: An Encyclopaedic Handbook

CONTENTS

Introduction

In the two volumes of *Crafting the Art of Magic*, I intend to explain the history of the Gardnerian Witchcraft movement. In this first volume, in addition to giving some background information, I cover the period from the movement's beginnings in 1939 to Gardner's death in 1964, and the treatment will be as objective as possible. In the second volume, I will bring the history down to the present; and there I will have to tell the story differently, because in 1967 I became a character in that story.

Since the publication of Gerald Gardner's *Witchcraft Today* in 1954, the religion of Gardnerian Witchcraft has blossomed, carried by Gardnerian initiates and admirers throughout the Western world. By several different methods (circulation of the largest Neopagan periodicals; attendance at national festivals; number of coven contacts in the Mensa POWSIG contact list), we can calculate that there are now roughly 5,000 covens in the USA, and perhaps several hundred thousand people involved in this movement. Roughly 10-20% of the members are fully initiated and trained to function as clergy; that is, there is a sense, used by the members, in which "Witches" (particularly the ones who have been trained in a coven) are the clergy, "pagans" the laity, of this religion. This is no longer a tiny, timorous movement. If there are in fact 200,000 practicing Neopagans in the USA and Canada, that's five times as many as there are Quakers; that's more than there are Unitarians, or Buddhists. Hence it is time for a serious history of the movement, one that can serve as a basis for theological reflection.

Within the Neopagan movement, the term "Gardnerian" usually refers to persons who can trace the lineage of their initiation along an acceptable pathway back to Gerald Gardner (all kinds of hot current topics are hidden just under the surface of this definition, but we'll get to them in Volume II). All other Witches are considered to belong to other traditions (called Alexandrian, Druidic, Dianic, Fairy, etc.), which are supposed to derive from ancient polytheism independently of Gardner. *Please* notice that I am not using the term in this sense. Instead, I call all Neopagan Witches Gardnerian Witches, because, as far as I can tell (and I will be telling the tale here of how thoroughly I have looked), all the current activity derives from widespread imitating of Gardnerian practices, and from no other source. There were a few covens around that predated Gardner, but they had an utterly different theology from what the Gardnerians propose; objectively, they were not practicing the same religion.

I need to explain here, at least briefly, what questions I was asking, and how I went about trying to find answers to them, so that you can evaluate for yourself how reliable those answers may be. People have been telling stories about the Gardnerians for the last five decades—Gardner himself, various Gardnerians, friends and foes, scholars and journalists—and I have found that almost all of these stories have been, in large part, fantasies. In contrast, I have been working since 1971 to ferret out the hard, verifiable facts of Gardnerian history. I need to explain how I was able to discover those facts, so that you will be able to see that what I am writing here is history, not more guesswork. (Those with no patience at all for this sort of thing will now turn to Chapter 1 anyway, though I wish they wouldn't.)

I suppose someone might ask why I can't just let the facts speak for themselves. That won't work because, contrary to our modern myths about how science works, fact does not exist independently of theory. What you perceive as fact depends on what theory you're operating with, and your choice of theory depends on your own personal history. And you cannot operate without theory, or you wouldn't be able to perceive at all. (Now, this is getting into some high-powered psychology that I also cannot discuss here, but for an extremely readable survey of what recent psychological research has discovered about how our perceptual systems actually work, see Goleman.) For this reason, I must summarize some of my own history here, though I will be giving it in more detail in Volume II.

I first became curious about claims that Witchcraft had survived into modern times in 1954, when I came across a book called *Witches Still Live*, by Theda Kenyon, in the Marin County branch library in Tamalpais Valley. For the most part the book is a hodge-podge of Frazer and folklore, but it opens with a summary of Leland's *Aradia*. This "Gospel of the Witches of Tuscany"—with its talk of naked meetings and free love beneath the full moon, and rebellion against the oppressive overlords—was very heady stuff for a repressed teenager in the 1950s, and I placed it high on my list of Fascinating Topics to Be Investigated As Soon As Possible.

I first found Gerald Gardner's *Witchcraft Today* in the San Francisco Public Library in 1958. (In those innocent days, books on the occult could be left on open library shelves and yet not be stolen.) I recognized that this was a Witchcraft of the same general type as in the *Aradia*, and I was intrigued by Gardner's claims that it had survived from the Middle Ages into this century, and that he had been initiated into one of the last surviving covens. I took careful notes on all the fragments of information about what was done in rituals that Gardner seemed to let slip in the book.

I was now quite focused on Witchcraft as a topic of great interest, and began searching out relevant books. This was not as easy as it sounds: most of the books on "Witchcraft" in the libraries were about medieval persecutions, and so had nothing to do with the survival of paganism that Leland and Gardner described. The most important books I found during the next decade were Margaret Murray's *God of the Witches* and Robert Graves' *The White Goddess* in 1961, and Elliott Rose's *A Razor for a Goat* in 1965.

In the fall of 1967 my friend Sarah asked me to help her write a "Witches' Sabbath" for a class on creating ritual at San Francisco State. Thus began the work of creating what we came to call the New, Reformed, Orthodox Order of the Golden Dawn. (The name was intended to be mildly funny. The major reason for choosing it was that I was studying Yeats for my Master's Orals; I knew that Yeats had been the Grand Master of the Hermetic Order of the Golden Dawn, and it was obvious to me that the magic used by the Craft was derived from the HOGD system.) The work of creating the NROOGD occupied me and many friends for much of the following decade; I will not discuss that here, since it is well-summarized by Margot Adler, in her Chapter 7, and since I plan to describe it in detail in Volume II. Here I need to make only one point: what enabled us to create the NROOGD, that is, to reinvent a very Gardnerian sort of Witchcraft for ourselves, was the fact that more and more information about Gardnerian rituals and practices was being published in the late 1960s. Having been able to construct the NROOGD rituals out of fragments of information about Gardnerian practices, I began to wonder if perhaps Gardner had not done much the same thing: constructed his "survival" out of the fragments of data that can be gleaned from Margaret Murray and other sources.

After 1958 and on through the 1960s, there had appeared a steadily growing stream of books that dealt with Witchcraft in general and Gardnerian Witchcraft in particular. Most of these were written by Gardnerians, who accepted all of Gardner's historical claims as being simple fact. There were other Witches who disputed Gardner's authority, and who claimed to belong to similarly surviving covens, quite independently of Gardner. Until 1979, Doreen Valiente seemed to be one of the most important of these independent Witches. In complete contrast, most of the scholars who touched on Gardner dismissed his claims out of hand, and asserted that he must have made the whole thing up, but they did not present any sort of evidence or argument to support this assertion. A few scholars, such as Elliott Rose, took a more moderate position, and conceded that Gardner might have had some data from an older coven or covens, but Rose, for example, doubted that such data went back past about 1875.

Now, as long as no independent evidence was available, any opinion about what Gardner did or didn't do had to remain merely an opinion. An argument from probabilities cannot be convincing, because history is full of things that were highly improbable but happened anyway. It is not inherently impossible that a few rural British families might, as they claim, have maintained some sort of pagan religious tradition into this century; likewise, Gardner could have concocted everything out of whole cloth. Just as a sidelight on British history, it would be interesting to know what really happened. (Perhaps more importantly, it would also be helpful to have a dependable history in order to evaluate the historical claims now being made by feminist leaders.)

There was one way in which, at least in theory, Gardner's

claims might be tested. In their books, Doreen Valiente and various writers who were clearly Gardnerian (such as Buckland and Crowther) had argued that Gardner had not begun from scratch; that instead he had augmented the fragmentary traditions of the coven he was initiated into, building them up into a viable system, as recorded in the Book of Shadows, which he then used to found new covens during the 1950s; and that, despite his eclecticism, he was preserving the essential concepts and practices of an ancient religion. Hence by 1970 I was wondering what had constituted the traditions of the older coven into which Gardner said he had been initiated, and what Gardner's contributions had been. I thought it might be possible, by careful critical analysis, to distinguish Gardner's additions to the Book of Shadows from the older body of data with which he was working. But exactly to what might such an analysis be applied?

The problem here is that the "Book of Shadows" is more a concept than an object. It is supposed to be handcopied by each Gardnerian Witch after she or he has been initiated, and therefore exists—even in this era of xerography—only as a family of manuscript traditions. The situation is exactly analogous to what a person faces in trying to do New or Old Testament textual criticism, since the Bible also survived into modern times in the form of many families of manuscripts whose readings differed in thousands of places. In 1971 I was already beginning the studies that led to my being in graduate school in Berkeley from 1974-1980, studying Christian origins as a historical problem; and that is why it occurred to me that I could apply the methods of textual and literary scholarship (which were actually invented by the first Neopagans, in Italy during the Renaissance) to Craft writings. But, again, to which Craft writings?

The problem is that the published versions of the Book of Shadows are actually only the versions (and usually rather degenerate ones at that) in specific manuscripts. Some bits and pieces of rituals are included in Gardner's own books, but they don't amount to much. Farrar 1971 (see the Bibliography) contains the full text (except for the "Craft Laws") of the Gardnerian Book of Shadows that Alex Sanders obtained when he was initiated in 1963 by "Medea" (there is a letter in Toronto from Pat Kopanski to Gardner that gives the details of Sanders' initiation). Furthermore, these published versions have surely been tampered with by the publishers' editors; so reliable historical conclusions about what materials Gardner had to start with, and what he added, cannot be based on these published books. Instead, historical accuracy demanded that I work from the original manuscripts themselves. That is, I would have needed access to the "Master" copy of the Book of Shadows, and to whatever books or documents Gardner might have had from the older coven. In 1970, I had no idea whether such things existed. If they did, I thought they would probably be the very private and very secret property of a Gardnerian coven somewhere. Even if I could discover their existence, I would probably not be allowed to see them; so I thought my questions would have to remain unanswered.

However, in 1971 I first saw the document usually called the "Craft Laws"; it appeared in an appendix in June Johns' *King of the Witches: The World of Alex Sanders*. The document fascinated me. Internally it purports to have been written in the mid-18th century, and to include materials dating back to the 16th. My intuition was that the document must somehow be the key to Gardner's historical claims, and this has turned out, in an odd way, to be quite correct.

In 1971 Llewellyn published *Lady Sheba's Book of Shadows*, which was the first time that an almost complete copy of the Gardnerian Book of Shadows had been published and widely distributed. This book also began with a text of the Craft Laws. I had been reading Bruce Metzger's excellent *The Text of the New Testament*, which explains the principles of textual criticism; so it occurred to me to try comparing the two texts of the Craft Laws in Johns and Sheba. Doing so, I discovered that the texts differed in more than 150 places, often in ways for which no immediate explanation was obvious. I wrote up my conclusions in an essay called "Textual Criticism and the Craft Laws." At the time, this exercise led me to suspect there had been an earlier document (or set of documents) from which these two texts had been derived, and I was on the alert for any evidence of its existence.

In 1973 I still did not expect ever to see the kind of original documents that would allow me to satisfy my historical curiosity. To my surprise, all the necessary documents began to fall into my lap in 1974 and 1975. They did so, as it turned out, in approximately the reverse of the order in which they had been written; so I had to work my way back from the most recent material to the oldest. In this Introduction I can explain the actual sequence in which I reached my major conclusions. The history that I begin reconstructing in Chapter 2 is like the history reconstructed from an archaeological dig: it begins with the pieces I found last, and ends with the pieces I found first. (And the only book I know which successfully tells a story in which time flows in both directions is James Michener's *The Source*.)

In March 1974, soon after I had begun my Ph.D. studies at the Graduate Theological Union in Berkeley, my friend Isaac Bonewits was preparing to leave for St. Paul to become Editor of Llewellyn's *Gnostica*. I mentioned to him the essay I had done on the Craft Laws, and he encouraged me to send it to him (it was subsequently published in *Gnostica*, in September 1974). When it arrived in May, he showed it to Carl L. Weschcke, then as now President of Llewellyn Publications, who was thus reminded that he had a file full of Gardnerian materials, which he thought I might like to see. Isaac, upon looking through the file, recognized the importance of the materials, and immediately sent me photocopies of them and of some relevant correspondence from Gardner and others.

When I read through them the evening they arrived, I felt something like Champollion contemplating the Rosetta Stone, the bilingual inscription that made translation of Egyptian hieroglyphics possible, for I could see that these were pages for a Gardnerian Book of Shadows. I was especially delighted that two of the eighteen documents made up the oldest copy I had yet seen of the Craft Laws (and in 1990, they are still the oldest extant text of the Craft Laws, as far as I know). I was also able to deduce immediately, by comparing them with Gardner's letters, that the materials were typed and/or handwritten by Gardner himself; the handwriting matched, and so did the two different typewriter fonts. More importantly, that night I discovered that Gardner was marginally dyslexic. That is, despite his intelligence, which I do not propose to underestimate, and his avid reading and collecting of books, he could not spell or punctuate well enough to meet even minimal standards for being published, and his grasp of grammar was shaky at best. *In other words, Gardner could not by himself have produced the books published in his name*; he could, and almost certainly did, carry out the basic writing, but he must have had much help, almost a collaborator, to carry a book to its final draft. I began to wonder who this helper was.

Further investigation and conversations with Carl revealed that the documents had been sent to him in about 1969 by a man who had been initiated and trained about 1960. The documents are a motley assortment: some originals, but mostly carbon copies; typed variously on white bond, onionskin, and foolscap; of various sizes and conditions, some whole, some torn in half, some wrinkled from many foldings, some clean and never folded at all. Some have staple marks or holes punched in them, and had been fastened together in at least three different binders, no doubt being used in Books of Shadows; others show no marks and no sign of having seen such use. They were certainly not produced all at once, as a "fair copy" intended to be a single Book of Shadows. Instead, they look like, and are, miscellaneous drafts from various stages of the writing process, typed on whatever was handy.

There was no way to be certain what in these 18 documents had come from an older tradition. However, I realized that I could identify most of the quotes or paraphrases of published sources, and set these aside; I could then ask whether what remained made sense as being from anything like the sort of native pagan tradition that Gardner claimed. As I carried out this procedure, I discovered some interesting facts.

First, some of the drafts were different versions of the same basic ritual, and sometimes they incorporated revisions of other pieces of writing. I could therefore establish a relative internal chronology ("A is a revision of B; hence was written after B"). I also had some absolute dates for the bits of ritual and verse that had been published in Gardner's books. I was thus able to establish that the 18 Weschcke documents were written between about 1954 and about 1960, and that most of them had probably been typed up about 1958 or 1959. This allowed me to see that many of the Book of Shadows rituals did not exist in 1954 (when *Witchcraft Today* was published), but instead were still being written.

Second, the major published sources from which the rituals had been constructed included: (a) Mathers' edition of *The Greater Key of Solomon*; (b) Aleister Crowley's *Magick in Theory and Practice*; (c) Leland's *Aradia*; (d) some Masonic rituals akin to those described by Duncan and those of the Hermetic Order of the Golden Dawn (aside from those transmitted by Crowley); and (e) Margaret Murray's *The Witch Cult in Western Europe*. There were also bits and pieces from other works by Leland, Jane E. Harrison, Gilbert Murray, James Frazer, and the other great classicists and mythologists of the 19th century. That accounted for EVERYTHING in the rituals! There was nothing left that differed in any important way from what you can find in those sources—but that is NOT at all what Gardner had claimed.

Still, all that applies only to the *rituals* in the Book of Shadows; and it should therefore not be a startling conclusion, because anyone familiar with western magical traditions can see that the Gardnerian rituals derive from a magical system much like the (essentially Masonic) system of the Hermetic Order of the Golden Dawn, not from any native British religious traditions. Furthermore, the Gardnerians admit that the rituals are exactly where Gardner did the most reconstruction work. Rather, they claim that the pre-1939 stratum is one of concept, customs, traditions, laws, and, in brief, the sorts of things incorporated in the Craft Laws, which is the only piece of writing in the Book of Shadows that claims to be (and at least logically could be) historical.

As I have already said, my hunch was that the Gardnerian claim to historicity must stand or fall on "The Old Laws" ever since I had first seen it, and my analysis of the two typed parts of it among the Weschcke documents simply left the question open. Because it was typed in two parts, which exhibit some curious internal parallels, I thought both parts might have been derived from an older, common source document—and it was that hypothetical older document I hoped to find when I went to Toronto to examine the Ripley's holdings.

I knew there was another possible source of information about Craft history, in the documents and letters acquired by Ripley's International, Ltd., Toronto, when it bought the contents of Gardner's Witchcraft museum on the Isle of Man. In September 1975 I was able to visit their headquarters in Toronto for three days, to look over these books and manuscripts. In Toronto I met Derek Copperthwaite, then Ripley's Vice President for Research and Development, who had arranged the purchase of the museum in 1971 from Gardner's heirs, Monique and Campbell Wilson. For the most part, the story of the museum and their purchase of it belongs in Volume II, and is told there. Here I need mention only a few key facts.

The only item in the museum collection that might have been a Book of Shadows of any sort was a manuscript titled "Ye Bok of ye Art Magical," which Derek had found hidden in the back of a cabinet. It had not begun life as a Book of Shadows, but had become one—in fact, the very first one—during the period 1939 to 1952, when it was retired.

Gardner had saved correspondence from the 1940s or earlier,

but it seemed very odd that there were no mentions of the Craft except in one file of correspondence, dating from 1957 to 1962, which seemed to be complete. Most of these letters were from such well-known Gardnerians as Patricia Crowther, Lois Hemmings, Jack Bracelin, and the Wilsons, as well as from the gentleman who had sent the 18 documents to Carl Weschcke. There was also a very odd letter from "Ameth" to "Dafo"; since I thought "Dafo" had been Doreen Valiente's coven name, I could not imagine who "Ameth" was.

There was a typescript, titled "New Light on Witchcraft," which was the carbon copy of the unedited manuscript of *Witchcraft Today*, in the form in which it went to the publisher. Glancing through it, I discovered it was in excellent shape. But obviously Gardner—who, as I said, was dyslexic—had not produced it by himself; he had had some very competent help, and I guessed at the time that it might have come from his wife. Francis King (p. 180) had asserted that the "reader responsible for its acceptance, himself an occult scholar of distinction, managed to blue-pencil the more rubbishy passages" before it was published. This "reader" was Ross Nichols, a scholarly consultant who made detailed recommendations to Gardner for rewriting the final draft, for which Gardner thanks him in the Foreword, but someone else must have helped Gardner produce this final manuscript.

As I said, I went to Toronto hoping to find some older versions of the "Craft Laws" documents—and so I did, though not in the form I was expecting. In the file of letters about the Craft, I found a document titled "Proposed Rules for the Craft"; it could be dated to June 1957 because a letter of that date from Jack Bracelin, Gardner's supposed biographer, referred to them as "Ned's proposed rules for the Craft." (Ned was obviously well-educated, and wrote with some craftsmanship; so I was very curious about who he was.) These rules greatly overlapped the concerns of the "Craft Laws" document. In fact, I finally realized, many months later, these rules were the first draft of the "Craft Laws." Given that hypothesis, I was able to identify an earlier draft of *every* passage in the "Craft Laws" somewhere else in Gardner's published or unpublished writings. Where later and earlier versions of the same passages have been published, often the later passages have been archaicized by incorporation of obscure words gleaned from the Oxford English Dictionary.

When I returned home, I had found all the facts needed to demonstrate that nothing in the "Craft Laws," or in the entire Book of Shadows, makes sense as part of a tradition received from a pre-1939 coven, although it took me many months to think it all through. When I had finished, I had identified a literary source for every detail. Also, the very ordinary bits of evidence (addresses, letters, diaries, even laundry lists) that we would expect to find for the existence of a pre-1939 coven were nowhere to be found. In nuclear physics, even if a particle has no charge and almost no mass, and is therefore very difficult to detect, its existence must have some detectable effects (if it has no detectable effects at all, there is no reason to suppose that it exists); if those effects cannot be detected after we have made statistically sufficient efforts to detect them, we can be sure the particle does not exist. Similarly, the existence of a pre-1939 coven would have left detectable traces somewhere in the Gardnerian Book of Shadows. Since no effects at all can be found, we have no reason to think that such a coven existed—and so the organizational link with the past is broken: we have no evidence that the Gardnerian movement is in any way a sort of Stone Age religion that was surviving in England in 1939.

Let me emphasize here that I am not arguing from silence. I am NOT saying "There is no evidence to support such claims." I am saying that there is now a great deal of evidence, all of which I have used to reconstruct the history set forth in this volume.

Nor can it be supposed that I overlooked any evidence, because in 1975 and 1976 I still thought Gardner's claims were probably true: I *wanted* the Craft Laws to be based on traditional documents; I *wanted* there to have been some tradition behind Gardner's coven; I *wanted* there to have been an ancient religion of a Mother Goddess. The major reason why it took me months to think through the implications of the evidence I had collected, was that I was being forced step by step to conclude that these things, which I wanted to be true, simply were not historically true. This methodological fact is an important part of my argument. Certainly if I had been an Evangelical going to Toronto to do battle with Satan and all his works, I might easily have overlooked important evidence. But that was not the situation. I was looking for facts that would support the Gardnerian claims, and I wanted to find them; if there had been any in Toronto, I certainly would not have overlooked them. The reason I could not find any, therefore, is that they almost certainly do not exist.

As long as I thought there might be some sort of older tradition behind Gardner, I had been looking back to the 1920s, after Murray's *Witch Cult* came out, wondering why no one had tried to base a coven on Murray's description. If someone had, I thought, there would have to be traces; it is inherently implausible that either the English, with their tolerance for eccentricity, or Americans would keep this sort of flamboyant but harmless religious activity a secret for more than a few months. (I have heard indirectly that the Pentangle Club at Cambridge tried some such experiments in the 1930s; but apparently they had no lasting results.) So it was startling when I finally realized that obviously someone *had* based a coven on Murray's description: that was precisely what Gerald Gardner, Dorothy Clutterbuck, and company did in September 1939. But why did it take that long? Because it actually is *not* obvious what must be done to transform Murray's description into a viable movement. That takes some creative genius; and Gardner and his friends were the first to have it.

I could see this situation because I happened to ask a question—"What can I be sure was added by Gardner?"—that focused my attention on the documents in the 1940s and 1950s. Once I had discovered that I could account for absolutely everything in the documents as being devised by Gardner and his colleagues, there was no longer any reason to suppose there had been any earlier coven or information or sect at all.

I completed a first version of this book in 1976, in the form of a proto-dissertation; it was about 50% footnotes, and was accepted as satisfying one of my comprehensive examination topics at the Graduate Theological Union in 1977. Carl had hoped to publish it— we had even signed a contract—but all those footnotes made it impossible. Once past my comprehensive exams, I naturally began to concentrate on getting my dissertation completed; so rewriting this book was put on a back burner.

Also, for complex personal reasons, I stopped being active in the Craft in 1977, and pursued other paths of spiritual discipline. Here I think I need make only two points. First, I am now accustomed to being in the position of explaining and defending Neopagan Witchcraft to the Christians, and liberal Catholic Christianity to the Neopagans. Second, whereas I stopped being active as a Roman Catholic in 1954 for childish reasons, I stopped being an active Roman Catholic in 1987 for adult reasons, and that was when I became active in the Craft again.

Anyway, in 1979, I was still not satisfied with my conclusions: there were still other missing pieces, which I did not expect to be able to find—until, again, they fell into my lap. For example, in 1979 I received a letter from Margot Adler on the envelope of which she scrawled an excited note that Doreen Valiente had stated (in her *Witchcraft for Tomorrow*, p. 14) that Gardner had initiated her in 1953—and some missing pieces of the puzzle fell into place. She also said in that book (p. 21) that in 1954-1955 she had co-authored the verse that begins "Darksome night and shining moon" and other materials used in the Book of Shadows. Since I knew from independent evidence that someone had been helping Gardner write, I could see no reason not to believe this particular claim. Until then, no one in America had understood the importance of Doreen's work on the Craft; but obviously, if she had begun working with Gardner in 1953, she could have helped get that final manuscript of *Witchcraft Today* into shape. Even more importantly, hers was almost surely the competent hand that I had detected alongside Gardner's helping write the Weschcke documents. I wrote an academic paper setting forth these conclusions in 1980, and it was subsequently republished in at least three periodicals.

Late in 1981, I had the pleasure of a visit from Fred Lamond, who is now generally known in the Craft as Robert, and who was able and willing to answer many questions I had not thought I would ever get answered. He is still a member of Gardner's original coven, into which he was initiated in January 1957 by Gardner and by the Maiden of the coven; Doreen Valiente was at that time, he said, the High Priestess of the coven, but was not there that night. (One reason I knew his statements were accurate is that he knew the names—which I knew from reading the letters in Toronto—of the utterly obscure people who had been members of the coven in 1957. It was a great pleasure to ask him "Who was Ned?" and be told, "Oh, he was someone in the City," which, of course, is British for "rich and well-connected.") At this time Fred explained to me the events of 1957 that I explain in Chapter 4. He also told me that he had thought the "Craft Laws" were the work of Doreen's coven, since they had never been part of the original coven's tradition, and assured me that all the English Gardnerians of his time knew that Doreen had written virtually everything in the Book of Shadows, and that the master copy of that book was still in her possession. Fred said he believed there had been a pre-1939 coven, and said he knew several people who had met "Dafo," who had also been a member of it. However, he admitted, she had never been forthcoming with any data about that coven.

"Wasn't 'Dafo' Doreen's Craft name?", I asked.

Fred said, "No, hers was . . ."

"Ameth," we said, almost together. (And that explained the peculiar letter from Ameth to Dafo I had found.)

"So Dafo was Dorothy Clutterbuck," I said.

"No, Dafo had been the Maiden of the old coven, and after Dorothy died, she became the High Priestess until Doreen took over," Fred said.

I probably should have gotten in touch with Doreen at that point—some things would have been much simpler if I had—but the history of the Craft was not my main concern at that time; survival was, and has remained a major concern ever since. Fortunately, the communications between us have now been straightened out. I received a very helpful and friendly letter from her, just as I was finishing what I thought was the final draft of this manuscript, that cleared up many long-standing puzzles. I sent a copy of the draft to her, and received several more extremely friendly and helpful letters. And then, having been asked to clear up some problems with that draft, I was able to revise this book one last time, and work in the information she had sent me.

The communication problem between us had arisen because, in fact, she hadn't realized that before 1979 no one on this side of the Atlantic knew how central she had been in the Craft, though everyone in England knew; so she did not understand why I was being skeptical about her statements. Actually, I was being skeptical about everybody—the essence of scholarship and all that—and I continue to be impressed by the fact that her story stands up to scrutiny. I have been able to test it against the documentary facts, and she checks out. She deserves credit for having helped transform the Craft from being the hobby of a handful of eccentric Brits into being an international religious movement, and I am glad to see that she has been claiming that credit in her most recent writings.

But I have now set the stage for the history, which I set forth beginning in Chapter 2. In Chapter 1 I give some background on the occult religious movements of modern times that lie behind the

Craft, and on the overall significance of the Craft as a new religion.

I need here to thank some of the people who have made it possible for me to write this book. First and foremost, my friend, colleague, and partner, J. Gordon Melton, whose moral and practical support for me, my work, and my interests during the last decade have kept me going through some extremely thin and discouraging periods. I am especially grateful to him for throwing open the archives of his Institute for the Study of American Religion to me, and allowing me to use first some raw materials that he had been saving for a rainy day or another book.

I wish to thank the staff of Ripley's International, especially Mr. Charles Thielen and Mr. Derek Copperthwaite, for their good opinions of me and for their courtesy that made it possible for me to see the materials in the collection in Toronto that have proved central to my reconstruction of Gardnerian history.

I gladly thank the many other Craft initiates who have helped me in this reconstruction work over the years, especially Margot Adler, Isaac Bonewits, Meredydd Harper, Judith Harrow, Fred Lamond, and Valerie Voigt.

—Aidan A. Kelly, Ph.D.

1. Sources and Significance of the Craft as a New Religion

The Craft was founded, I now believe, as a distinct religion in September 1939, but it did not spring into life fully formed, like Athena from Zeus's head. Like all new religions, it was created from pre-existing raw materials that it combined in new ways and into a new overall structure. That is, its elements are old, but its structure is new. Hence it is not true that the Craft as it now exists is entirely a survival from the past, nor is it true that it is entirely a modern creation. This situation is quite unsatisfactory for persons who cannot tolerate anything but simple answers; but I am merely describing the situation, not creating it.

The Craft movement, by which I mean the overall religion of Neopagan Witchcraft, is based squarely on much of the Western occult tradition that had gone before it, and yet it has transformed the elements from that tradition in new and often surprising ways. In explaining the origins of the Craft movement, I will attempt to explain both the source of its elements in the broader occult movement and the ways in which the Craft does something new with each element.

As J. Gordon Melton has stressed in his monumental *Encyclopedia of American Religions*, the Western occult tradition is, by any objective standards, a religious movement in its own right. Many of its adherents do not like to call what they are doing "religion," because that term, in their vocabulary, means "false"—and so they prefer to call their pursuits "science." Likewise, the Western occult tradition is not organized into a formal church; instead, it manifests as a plethora of small associations and organizations whose lifespan is, on the average, much shorter than that of a healthy human being —but the same is true of a fair number of other religions.

As a genuine religious movement, the Western occult tradition does have a genuine history of its own. However, as is true of most religions, this history is obscured by its foundational myths, which appear, when viewed simplistically, to relate a "false" history, a history contradicted at every point by the facts that can be ascertained from documents, oral history, and the other sources of information that a historian would routinely use. The relationship between myth and history is extremely complex—far too complex to be dealt with adequately in this book, which is going to focus on the history of a single new religion. Nevertheless, I will need to summarize current thought on the topic, in order to explain my viewpoint in this book. Let me begin this task by paraphrasing Wallace Stevens: we must learn to perceive the history that is not there, in order to then perceive the history that is.

In emphasizing that the Craft is a new religion, and not the survival of an old religion, I am not "debunking" it. Rather, I am insisting on its ontological equality with every other religion, because—and this is the current scholarly consensus—all religions begin as new religions, which then survive only because they continue to evolve and adapt themselves to changing circumstances. For Islam and Buddhism, their origin as new religions is obvious. Hinduism as we now have it must be considered a sibling of Buddhism, since it resulted from an acceptance of some, though not all, of the Buddha's reforms. Judaism as the state religion of Judah dates from 621 B.C.E. (I will return to this point); but Christianity and Judaism as we have them are siblings, arising together from the ashes of Jerusalem, which was destroyed in 69 C.E.

There has been a fair amount of media hysteria in recent years, fueled especially by Evangelical Christians, over "cults." People have been running around, saying, "Omigod, people are starting cults. Something must be wrong with our society," and a great deal of energy has been wasted on looking for what's "wrong"—when in fact there's nothing wrong. The members of the Group on New Religious Movements of the American Academy of Religion, and most of the members of the Society for the Scientific Study of Religion (that is, me and Gordon Melton and a whole lot of the folks we talk shop with), have agreed on a definition: "The word 'cult' means 'a religion I don't approve of,'" and so we've agreed to avoid using it. The situation, then, is that people have been starting new religions. Furthermore, when we look at history, we discover that people start new religions all the time, all over the world, whenever they are not forcibly prevented from doing so by an established state church. In other words, *starting new religions is the normal state*; in fact, it appears to be about the second favorite human activity (or maybe third, if you count eating as second).

As a result of our shop talk over the last decade, the current scholarly view is that the creating of new religions is a normal, healthy, and universal activity by which creative people (that is, the educated middle class, not the outcasts) in all societies attempt to meet their own religious needs; and as such, its existence does not need any further explanation. Furthermore, if all religions begin at some time and place as new religions, then the study of new religions is not a luxury; it is not the study of fringe sects, marginal people, epiphenomena, weird hippies, and so on. Rather, it is the study of characteristics central to all religions. (Indeed, having been trained in the techniques of New Testament scholarship, which I have applied to the documents written by Gerald Gardner and Doreen Valiente, I am intrigued and, in fact, rather amused by the light this enterprise has shed for me on the evolution of early Christianity and the formation of the New Testament collection—but those are matters I must report on elsewhere, to another audience.) Let me just emphasize here that, in a free society, people vote with their feet: if their religious needs are not being met by the established churches, then they will set out to create their own religion. Furthermore, since a large bureaucratic organization cannot be all things to all people, there will always be some people whose needs are not being met; and so new religions are being founded all the time.

Let me catalog some of the unmet needs in our society to which the Craft movement is, I believe, a creative response.

First and foremost is the need for a sacramental experiencing of sex. In theory this is possible within Christianity, and I continue to regard myself as a Roman Catholic in some ways because (and only because) of that fact. But in practice such experiencing is not available to ordinary Christians; in practice Christianity continues to be oppressively anti-sexual. At best, it rates sex as harmless—as long as it takes place only under specific circumstances. The modern theologies that value sexuality as a revelation of the divine nature are taught in graduate seminaries—and then are kept more secret from the people than any "secret" in the Craft is. They are certainly never preached about on Sundays, as far as I know. Andrew Greeley is, of course, the outstanding exception to this generalization; he is, I believe, the most important Christian novelist ever. But there is no significant chance that the administration of the Roman Catholic church will pay any attention to him. As my Lady Epona says, "If the Roman Catholic church were actually as Greeley describes it, there would be no need for the Craft." (I don't mean to shortchange those from Protestant, Jewish, and other backgrounds here, however; they too have their reasons for being attracted to the Craft.)

Second, the mainstream churches in America offer ordinary people no practical paths for personal, spiritual development; traditionally, such development was reserved for the cloistered clergy, or for elderly scholars. There was nothing for ordinary people, and that lack has not been repaired. The Western occult tradition has addressed that need, but in many ways has been infected by the viewpoint of the Eastern religions, which are all at least mildly, and often strongly, opposed to the development of psychic or magical abilities, or at least to the use of such abilities for any purpose other than achieving (or helping others achieve) "enlightenment." The Craft rejects such an attitude as dualism, and asserts, in contrast, that the development and use of magical and psychic abilities *is* spiritual development. The Craft as currently practiced in America offers, at least potentially, a balanced and practical approach to development of a person's emotional, spiritual, intuitive, and psychic needs and abilities; I will discuss this in detail in Volume II.

Third, the Craft's organization, based on the principle that every coven is autonomous, gives it a flexibility and viability that huge organizations lack entirely. Like the Jewish synagogue, the coven is inherently democratic; and in many covens, the democracy is kept from degenerating into irresponsibility and anarchy by the presence of a High Priestess whose authority depends upon her magical lineage, which is independent of the coven she leads and serves, just as the Synagogue can employ a Rabbi, but cannot itself ordain a Rabbi. (The analogy breaks down here, since the Craft—aside from the Hasidic Gardnerians—generally recognizes the right of a coven to bootstrap itself into existence and to initiate its own priests and priestesses; but the balancing of responsibility between the Council of Elders and the High Priestess is still a valid structural parallel.) That is, the coven structure empowers its members, giving them control over their own religious practices and development.

The contrast with many of the Eastern religions and with the Roman Catholic church could not be greater. In many Eastern religions, the authority of the teacher is absolute; but Neopagans tend to be extremely anti-authoritarian, and will not submit to arbitrary authority—and in the Craft (at least in most covens) they do not have to. Likewise, despite the rhetoric of the Second Vatican Council, ordinary Roman Catholics have no control whatsoever over their church. Again, trained theologians know that Christianity is inherently democratic, and that Christians have the right to elect their own ministers, priests, bishops, and so on. The founders of what is now Protestant Christianity rediscovered this fact during the Reformation. But no one in the Craft need worry that the Roman Catholic administration will soon relinquish the authority it has usurped over the centuries.

Fourth, the Craft is generally extremely anti-dogmatic in its approach. Although Witches do believe many things, belief is not a requirement for membership or initiation. Rather, the expectation in the Craft is that if a person goes through the training and experiences that the Craft has to offer with an open mind, then personal transformations will in fact happen—and "belief" as such will be unnecessary, since the person will *know* that he or she has been changed. As a result of this attitude, Crafters are not only open to modern science, but positively biased in favor of it—and so are rather well-equipped to live in the increasingly technological civilization of the future. In contrast, most varieties of Christianity, several varieties of Judaism, and many varieties of other "world" religions either try to ignore science or accept its results only if forced to; this sort of spiritual "laziness," as M. Scott Peck would characterize it, merely contributes to their ever-growing obsolescence. History is littered with the carcasses of religions that failed to evolve to meet changing circumstances, and big churches are a lot like dinosaurs—whereas the Craft is much more like the hot-blooded little mammals hiding in the thickets. Similarly, Crafters look with amazement and amusement at how New Agers generally seem devoted to swallowing entire truckloads of metaphysical horse-puckey.

Fifth, the Craft's polytheistic theology suits it for the future much better than the monotheistic or monistic theologies of most other religions. The United States, and the world in general, is becoming more pluralistic: no one could have looked at the amazing sight of the Congress of People's Deputies of the Soviet Union, at the variety of ethnic costumes worn there, and not seen how real their dedication is to ensuring people's right to ethnic diversity. Likewise, given the immigration trends in the USA, our former WASP majority is rapidly losing its numerical and cultural dominance. The model for our future will no longer be the emotionless WASP male; rather, there will be no one model. Male and female, white, brown, or black, Asian or European, and free to feel our own feelings: we will all have the right to be different but equal. No longer will the most socially acceptable theology be, "There is only one God, and the rest of you better shape up, or else!" Nor will it be, "There are many gods, but they are all illusions," as many Eastern religions have taught. Rather, we will recall what the Jews knew when they were writing the Law and the Prophets: that God really is both one and many, both male and female, both father and mother, all things to all people, out of love. The respectable churches have failed to tell the people that for far too long—and so we Witches get to say, "Yes, the Gods are real, and magic is afoot."

Sixth, and last for now, the Craft is a religion dedicated to creativity, because it is a religion that we are creating for ourselves continually. The only way to be a true follower of Gerald Gardner, my friends, is to have the guts to create a religion for yourself that meets your own needs. I think Witches love Tolkien especially because he teaches us that creativity is divine, that the nature of godhead is to be continuously overflowing with creativity like a fountain, and that we participate most completely in the divine nature when we ourselves are being creative. I think it deliciously ironic to know that Tolkien believed all that because he was truly a Roman Catholic theologian—and because his church has disowned him, as it disowns Andrew Greeley, it is up to us Witches to carry on his work and his vision.

Of course, the sort of understanding of religious creativity, of religion as creative, of creativity as religion, that I am proposing here is very recent, and rather sophisticated. It is certainly not held by all the theologians in the professional societies to which I belong; rather, it is the stance of us "young Turks" (in our 40s and 50s) who are trying to penetrate the decisionmaking echelons of these societies, even while wondering if doing so is really worth the bother. It would be unrealistic to expect people in general to think about religion in this way—and, of course, they don't. What generally happens is that the founders of a new religion claim to be instead an old religion, in order to have a counterclaim against the hoary antiquity that the established churches all claim for themselves, in order to speak in terms that ordinary people can make some sense of.

In claiming to be an old religion, a new religion may claim to be a revival of an all-but-defunct religion from the past, or to be a reform of an existing religion that it is revitalizing by reaching back to its true, pure, and pristine roots, or to be a new revelation of ancient truths that had been garbled in all previous transmissions from the Powers That Be Up There, and so on; very often this claim takes the form of a "newly found" copy of a manuscript that had been hidden away long before. The emphasis on elements from the past is the common, universal thread, and this is always an emphasis on something real; but understanding exactly what those elements are, and why they are important, invariably requires a great deal of work.

The confusion arises from the fact that these elements of the past are invariably understood in terms of the new religion's foundational myth, which is the story that states in some way (often quite symbolically or parabolically) the values that are central to this new religion. As Robert Ellwood (1973, p. 32) observed, "In modern cults the functional myth is generally the story of the experience of the founder which establishes his ecstatic (shamanistic) capacity and his access to a new means of ultimate transformation, such as Madame Blavatsky's initiation by the Masters." That is, this foundational myth describes the experience that transmuted the religion's founder from an essentially ordinary person into a living legend, a source of *baraka* (blessedness) worthy to found the movement. For the Craft, the foundational myth is the story about Gerald Gardner's initiation in 1939 into one of the very last surviving witch covens in England, from which he was able to transmit, to the covens that he founded, the elements of the pagan past which that coven had helped to preserve.

The evolution of Western society's understanding of foundational myths is paralleled by the stages of individual religious maturity. The first three of these stages were first identified (as far as I know) by the poet William Blake, who labeled them "Innocence," "Experience," and "Organized Innocence." The first is the stage of childhood, during which the myths of religion, learned from the parents and others, are believed implicitly. The second is the stage of adolescence, during which the critical intellect develops, and the objective facts of ordinary history are taken as the criteria by which to judge the plausibility or possibility of the myths, which are normally rejected as being simply false during this stage, which can last into the late twenties. The third stage is the beginnings of true maturity, in which the person realizes that the facts of ordinary history, being value-free, provide no basis for making decisions about life problems. At this stage the adult can begin to reappropriate the myths, recognizing that they are intended to be primarily statements of value, not statements of fact or of history, and recognizing also that an interpretation of the myths which is much more sophisticated than that of a child must be possible; else these myths would hardly have survived for millennia as the basis for the value systems of world civilizations. One mark of true maturity is therefore the ability to tolerate the ambiguous tension between myth and history. Another is the ability to see that the more-sophisticated understanding of myth is not possible so long as the myth is believed to be mere history.

(There are further stages of religious maturity. One begins with the radical decision in favor of the values asserted by the myths that enables a radical transformation of lifestyle. Another is typified by the ability to dedicate one's talents to the improvement of one's community and society, rather than merely to satisfying one's own wants and needs. These stages appear to be universal, and independent of any specific beliefs.)

Critical analysis of the Craft's foundational myth, and an attempt to reconstruct its ordinary history out of the available documentary and eye-witness data, are therefore tasks identical to those which scholars have carried out for all the major world religions. It is obvious that these religions have not then dried up and blown away—though this is precisely what their most conservative members feared might happen as the process of critical thinking got under way. I do not believe that the Craft will wither away under the impact of critical thought either; and its conservative members (whom I fully expect to misunderstand, resent, and vow vengeance for the work I am doing here), in fearing that it might succumb, thereby reveal that they do not believe deeply enough that the Craft is a religion that can stand up as an equal in comparisons with any other religions.

For clarity, let me set forth the foundational myths and ordinary histories of the two religions that will be most familiar to most readers. Let's begin with Judaism, which, in claiming to be the world's oldest monotheistic religion (which it is not; Zoroastrianism is), is usually the model for similar claims of antiquity.

Myth: Judaism began about 1300 B.C.E., when the one true God revealed himself to Moses, helped Moses rescue the Israelites from Egypt, and revealed the Torah to Moses on Mt. Sinai.

History: Judaism began as the state religion of the kingdom of Judah (whence its name) in 621 B.C.E., when (as set forth in *II Kings* 22-24, and the parallel passage in *Chronicles*) King Josiah persuaded the men of Jerusalem to ratify the "Book of the Law of Moses" that had just been "discovered" (that is, in fact, written) by Hilkiah, high priest of the temple, as the new constitution. After the capture of Judah by Babylon, the Second Isaiah (author of *Isaiah* 40-55) proposed about 550 B.C.E. that Yahweh had allowed this disaster to occur because the Judeans had still not realized that Yahweh was not merely the best God, but was the only God (notice that Xenocrates in Asia Minor was arriving at the concept of monotheism at just about the same time). Accepting this new theology, the Judeans began to think "Now that we know who He is, we can understand what he was doing," and began to rewrite their history in its light, as the story of God's trying to get their attention; the writing continued in Jerusalem, after Cyrus of Persia, the new Emperor, allowed those Judeans who wanted to to go home. The Torah (the first five books) was completed about 400 B.C.E., and the story of its reading to the first synagogue assembly was told in *Nehemiah* 8 (we can even logically suppose that what the people, standing in rows beneath the lectern, heard that day was the story of Moses, standing on the side of Mt. Sinai, above the rows of people, and reading them the Decalogue or other laws; that is, the experience was self-reflexive, as most experiences of sacred time are). The scrolls of the Prophets (the major and minor prophets, and the historical books) were also largely complete by this time, though they were not added to the synagogue liturgy until around 200 B.C.E.

Thus we can see, as Joseph Campbell and other scholars have pointed out, that the experience of captivity and loyalty to Yahweh that became central to the Jewish sense of self-identity did take place, but in Babylon, not Egypt.

Myth: Yahweh himself became a human being, born to the virgin Mary, in the person of Jesus of Nazareth. Jesus began preaching a new revelation to all who would listen at about age 30, but within a year or so was betrayed to the Roman rulers and executed by crucifixion. Three days later he arose from the dead, thus proving that he was God, and after revealing more to many of his followers, he ascended bodily into Heaven, from where he will return in triumph to inaugurate the Kingdom of God on Earth at the end of time.

History: Joshua of Nazareth ("Jesus" is just the Greek form of Joshua) was apparently a young rabbi of the House of Hillel. Nothing in his own teachings (as distinguished from later legend) differs in any significant way from the teachings of the House of Hillel preserved in the Talmud. He apparently attacked the hypocrisy and lack of compassion of the Sadducees, who were the "rich men," and of the House of Shammai, the other major rabbinic house, which was politically dominant in his day. These targets of his irony and sarcasm apparently complained about him to the Romans, who arrested him and executed him summarily as a potential troublemaker. However, some of his friends believed that they had seen him alive (or at least in visions, like Paul) afterward, and began to preach that he had been raised from the dead, that he had received God's special favor, that he was God's anointed (that is, *mashiach* or *christos*) agent, that he had been special all along, and so on. Thinking "Now that we know who he is, we can understand what he was doing and saying," they began to rework his stories and sayings, and stories about him, in the course of their preaching. After the destruction of Jerusalem—which made it obvious that Jerusalem was not going to be the capital city, and Joshua was not going to be right back—some communities began to write these materials down, so that they wouldn't be lost completely, in what became the *Gospels.* (Let us note that only two of the gospels report anything unusual about Joshua's birth to his mother, Miriam; and none of the gospels present his brothers and sisters as being anything but ordinary brothers and sisters.) All Christians had been Jews until about 85 C.E., but in the turmoil after the disaster of the Roman-Jewish war, Judaism shattered into fragments, which became the separate religious communities known as Christianity, Judaism, Gnosticism, and so on. Beliefs about Joshua became the political shibboleth for all of these; so that Joshua, who should have been prominent in the history of the House of Hillel, was instead almost ignored when the Talmud was assembled.

Something similar could be done for all other religions. The foundational myth of Mormonism, for example, focuses on the "finding" of the *Book of Mormon* in Hill Cumorah, at the full moon. Critics and scholars of Mormonism have long since set forth the sources from which it was created. Such claims for rediscovered documents are particularly germane to Craft history, because in recent years many younger and/or more orthodox members of the Craft have come to regard the Book of Shadows in general, and the Craft Laws in particular, as documents preserved from the past by secrecy. As we will see, they are instead a modern creation, as the founding documents of new religions always are. I have no doubt that (the) God(s) could create a book directly if (t)he(y) wanted to, but the evidence throughout history is that (t)he(y) will always have a human being do the actual writing; so everything we know about writing and creativity in general then apply to this situation.

The history of the Western occult tradition could be traced far back into antiquity. Much of it clearly focuses on Alexandria, the great university city (which therefore bears some striking resemblances to Berkeley and other modern university towns). Neopaganism, as the concept of recreating the lost pagan religions of antiquity, appeared early in the Renaissance, and has been one thread in Western occultism ever since. However, it is most practical to begin this part of the story around the year 1800, when Francis Barrett published *The Magus*, the first modern book that attempted to make the arcana of magic accessible to the middle class.

As Galbreath (p. 726) comments, widespread acceptance of the occult had tapered off sharply among the educated by about 1750, but it did not cease altogether, and may have remained more or less constant among peasants. During the next century, the romantic revival of Neoplatonism, Medieval German mysticism, and astrology, the introduction of Asian and especially Indian esotericism, and the sudden enthusiasm for secret societies, Mesmerism, and Swedenborgianism marked the beginnings of the modern recrudescence of the occult, and with varying degrees of popularity, faddishness, and intellectual respectability, it has remained a nearly ubiquitous factor in Western cultural life ever since.

Fascination with the Classics had been a major theme of Romanticism, and the idea of reviving some sort of classical religion gained strength and became programmatic during the late nineteenth century, at which time attention was divided between Greco-Roman and Norse paganism. It was further strengthened as the new discipline of classical archaeology revealed civilizations in the Middle East that had predated the Greeks by millennia, and turned up pagan religious texts that had been baked in clay as palaces burned down around them.

The late 19th century saw the rise of "spiritual occultism," which, as represented by Theosophy, Rudolf Steiner, Gurdjieff, and Ouspensky, and a ritual-magical wing (various Rosicrucian organizations, the Hermetic Order of the Golden Dawn, and its offshoots), denies that it is a religion. According to Galbreath (p. 728), "Spiritual occultists state that it is possible to acquire personal, empirical knowledge of that which can only be taken on faith in religion or demonstrated through deductive reasoning in philosophy. Further, this knowledge, arrived at in full consciousness through the use of spiritual disciplines, is said to reveal man's place in the spiritual plan of the universe and to reconcile the debilitating conflict between science and religion. The goal of occultism, therefore, is the complete spiritualization of man and the cosmos, and the attainment of a condition of unity." It is these "spiritual occultists" who are the immediate progenitors of Wicca.

It is the mindset of spiritual occultism that leads most modern occult organizations to deny that they are religions. However, they exhibit the same ambiguous relation between their foundational myths and their ordinary history that religions in general do. Rosicrucianism has the myths set forth in its major documents—the *Chemical Wedding*, etc.—that claim survival from antiquity, but in fact it appears to have begun as a secret organization among Lutherans, since Luther's family crest was a rose on a cross. Freemasonry in England began as a secret society dedicated to restoration of the monarchy; when Charles II ascended the throne, this society remained intact, but adopted a new purpose.

That is, modern occult organizations typically claim a great antiquity for themselves, but in fact are all quite recent, and are almost all highly interrelated. T. M. Luhrmann has documented the overlapping memberships in magical organizations in the London area in the 1980s; this pattern has, in fact, been typical for the last two centuries. The pattern we see is that of a charismatic leader beginning an organization, which grows well during his or her lifetime, and usually attracts as its most prominent members people who have been or still are members of most of the other extant occult organizations. Upon the leader's demise, the organization usually fractures into two or many factions as the other members struggle to decide who will assume the mantle of the founder, and these factions generally then become independent organizations, which repeat the cycle. Richard Cavendish's *History of Magic* does an excellent job of detailing the complex interrelationships of teachers and students, founders and followers, among occult organizations, especially in France, in the late 19th century; and James Webb does the same for European occultism in general. I see no need to duplicate their work, especially since relatively few of these organizations are direct ancestors of the modern religion of Wicca. Among these few are the Hermetic Order of the Golden Dawn, the Stella Matutina, the Fraternity of the Inner Light, and the Ordo Templi Orientis, which I will therefore discuss in a little more detail.

However, in fairness, we must be aware that not all of the Craft's central concepts can be traced to any known antecedents. Some are *sui generis*, and these are among the best indicators of the specific ways in which the Craft is a unique religion, quite unlike anything else under the sun—or the moon. As an example of this, let us consider the concept of reincarnation. Like New Agers in general, most modern Witches believe strongly in reincarnation, perhaps largely because it provides an alternative to the "traditional" Christian concepts of Heaven and Hell. (However, this is not a dogma, because almost all modern Witches believe even more strongly that Witches must be free to believe whatever they choose.)

The earliest writings of the Greeks—Homer, Hesiod, the pre-Socratic philosophers—assume what has been called a "tripartite anthropology": that human beings consist of body, soul, and spirit. To be more precise, the Greek terms transliterate as *soma, psyche*, and *pneuma*, the recognizable roots of such modern words as psychosomatic and pneumatic. As is evident from its use in the word "psychology," the Greek word *psyche* meant something much more like "mind" or "personality." In order to have something like what we now mean by "soul," we must think of a compound of "mind" plus "spirit," of *psyche*-plus-*pneuma*. In the Greek view, when the body died, the *psyche*-plus-*pneuma* went to the underworld, to stand before the throne of Persephone, who sentenced the person to reward in the Elysian Fields, or to punishment in Tartarus, before he or she was reborn. (Apparently the whole point of being initiated at Eleusis was that you were thus adopted as a child of Demeter; hence when you stood before Demeter's daughter Persephone, she would judge you as a family member, not as a stranger—which made all the difference in Greek society.)

Plato, in the "myths" that conclude many of his dialogues, synthesizes the beliefs of the philosophers who preceded him. He proposes that the natural home of the *psyche*-plus-*pneuma* is the world of pure idea, beyond the realm of the gods as we are able to form some concept of them, and that the *psyche*-plus-*pneuma* is sent down into the body in this imperfect world of decay and corruption as a punishment. He mentions an "Orphic" catchphrase: *soma sema*, "the body is a tomb." Plato suggests that a person may be rewarded for virtue in this life by being born into a better position in society in the next life, but he suggests also that the true reward is to be freed from rebirth entirely, so as to be able to return to the world of pure idea, and that each person has only so many chances (perhaps nine rebirths) to achieve this freedom.

There is no positive evidence that Christians as such ever believed in reincarnation. (Some people who happened to be Christians also happened to believe in a great many things, then as now, but data on popular beliefs do not define the essential doctrines of any religion.) On the other hand, once Christians had adopted the Greek concept of the immortal soul, it also was not clear for some centuries whether they could believe in reincarnation or not. Finally, at the Council of Constantinople in 553 C.E., the theologians voted against reincarnation, largely because they could see no way that a person could be morally responsible for his or her own virtues and vices, and so for the reward or punishment they merited, if after dying and being judged he or she was reborn as another person, and then baptized. It seemed much simpler to the theologians to believe that each soul was created fresh for each person, and had only one lifetime on Earth.

Hence from the sixth century through the 18th century, belief in reincarnation appeared in Western societies only when it was reintroduced from the outside. This happened with the Cathars, who seem to have had historical connections with earlier Manichaean or Gnostic groups in the Middle East. The concept of reincarnation became a belief held in Western society only after Britain and other European nations had been a colonial power in India and in Buddhist countries for several centuries, during which generation after generation of European administrators had been exposed to Eastern beliefs.

Gardner asserts in *Witchcraft Today* that belief in reincarnation was preserved by the witch covens during the middle ages, and this has become part of the foundational myths of the Craft. In fact, belief in reincarnation was reintroduced into the Western world in the 19th century by Spiritualism, and was then taken up by Theosophy. The first wave of belief in reincarnation arose in response to the strange phenomena revealed by Mesmerism, developed by Anton Mesmer in the late eighteenth century. Mesmerism was at first popularly associated more with psychic phenomena than with therapeutic utility. Only when psi became the stock in trade of Spiritualistic mediums did Mesmerism become transformed into hypnosis as a form of medical therapy. The importing of Mesmerism to America was part of what set off the Spiritualist movement, and belief in reincarnation is compatible with Spiritualism, though not necessary for it (one can believe that the soul survives after death, as Christians do, without believing that it has been or will be reborn). It is usually assumed that Spiritualists do not believe in reincarnation, but in fact there have been two camps within Spiritualism, one favoring reincarnation, the other opposing it, since the mid-19th century.

The Theosophical Society was founded in New York City in 1875. Its leading figure, Helena P. Blavatsky, was the person who established "reincarnation" as the standard term for this concept, replacing "metempsychosis," "transmigration," "reimbodiment," and other terms that had been used. It was also she who first linked the concepts of karma and reincarnation firmly in the Western mind. (The two concepts are not interdependent; it is possible to believe in one without the other.) The Theosophical content defined into these terms in the West does not correspond closely with what was believed about these topics in traditional Asian societies, and the concept of reincarnation in the Craft is much closer to that of Theosophy than to those of the ancient world or of Asian religions—which is what we would expect, since the concept of reincarnation in the Craft, as in Western occultism in general, comes from Theosophy.

Nevertheless, Witches do not believe what Theosophists, Buddhists, Hindus, the ancient Greeks, or almost anyone else has believed about reincarnation. In these latter systems, reincarnation is seen as the automatic result of a universal law, and as a punishment for ignorance; the goal of spiritual development is to stop the "wheel of rebirth," to no longer be reincarnated. Witches, in contrast, believe that reincarnation is *not* automatic, that it is controlled by the gods and is the *reward* of the initiates. They believe "that you will be reborn among those you love, and that you will remember them and love them again"; the reward is for being on the side of the gods. I have observed that Witches also tend to believe that there probably are two kinds of souls, both mortal and immortal; that all souls begin as mortal, but can be transformed into immortal souls by certain kinds of initiatory experiences and spiritual growth (specifically, that provided by the training and initiations of the Craft); and that when the uninitiated die, their mortal souls simply cease to exist. (Apparently some of the ancient Greeks had a concept of the soul somewhat similar to this. It has no doubt been wise that Witches have so far said little in public about a belief that non-Witches are "once-born"; it is not something that would help our public image.) That is, the theological concepts of and surrounding reincarnation in the Craft movement cannot be explained in terms of the concepts in the older occult traditions. They are either a new theological creation, or else are part of a secret tradition of whose existence there was never any hint before it was proclaimed by Gerald Gardner.

A second way in which the Craft differs from most other new religions of modern times, and especially from those usually classified as New Age, is in rejecting many typical New Age assumptions about religion. Many New Agers assume, for example, that all religions are ultimately the *same*; that spirituality is best learned by sitting at the feet of a master teacher or guru, preferably from one of the Eastern religions; and that a new world teacher or messiah will appear to usher in the New Age. Neopagans, in contrast, like the Craft specifically because it is so *different* from the Puritanical, world-hating Christianity that many of them were raised in. Most Neopagans believe that they are practicing an ancient folk religion, whether as a survival or a revival; and, being focused on the pagan religions of the past, they are not particularly interested in a New Age in the future. They also generally believe that many religions are radically and irreconcilably different from each other; that the "reformed" religions (especially the monotheistic ones) established by Moses, Jesus, Mohammed, the Buddha, and similar figures were NOT an improvement over the folk religions that they replaced; and that if there were to be a single worldwide religion in the future, it might very well be even more repressive of human freedom than the Roman Catholic Church was in Europe during the "Burning Times." Hence Neopagans are not at all receptive to teachers and teachings from the monotheistic religions nor to any from the East, with the possible exception of Hinduism, which is seen (whether accurately so or not) as an "unreformed" polytheism similar to that of the Greco-Roman world; Neopagans tend to be especially interested in Tantric traditions, since these can easily be seen as a type of magic parallel to that developed in the Western occult tradition. Neopagans also generally tend to be extremely anti-authoritarian (whatever the reasons in personal backgrounds might be), and so are not at all inclined to accept the personal authority of any guru.

Neopagan Witches also operate with an ethic that forbids them to accept money for initiating anyone, or for training anyone in the essential practices of the Craft as a religion. Although this ethic does create some organizational problems, these are minor when compared with the fact that the Craft has so far escaped being exploited by the kinds of entrepreneurs who have created or taken over other new religions, only to use them as vehicles for self-enrichment. Neopagan festivals have grown into national gatherings, often of several thousand people, during the last decade, but they have remained quite inexpensive, since no one is attempting to make a profit from them. As a result of this ethic, Neopagans look upon the "Psychic Fairs" and "New Age Expos" with open contempt, and tend to consider most New Age gurus to be money-hungry frauds who are exploiting the public by charging exorbitant fees for spiritual practices that can be learned for free within a Neopagan coven. This attitude does not, of course, encourage New Agers to look kindly upon Neopagans.

There are, nevertheless, a minority among the Neopagan Witches who do consider themselves to be members of the New Age movement as well. This minority tends to consist of the Witches who understand fairly clearly not only that the Gardnerian Witchcraft movement is a new religion, but also that this newness makes it the potential equal of every other religion in the world. If the Craft is a new religion, then it can be understood as contributing to the spiritual growth in the modern world that is leading up to the New Age, whenever and however that might begin.

The Craft is very specifically a magical religion, but its magic is not anything inherited from a secret tradition of any sort. Rather, the magical system used by the Craft goes back to that of the Hermetic Order of the Golden Dawn (HOGD), which was an offshoot of a Masonic-Rosicrucian organization, the Societas Rosicruciana in Anglia, founded by Robert Wentworth Little in 1865, and supposedly based on old manuscripts found in Freemasons' Hall. The London Lodge of the Theosophical Society was opened in 1883, and members of both these lodges were among the early members of the HOGD, which was founded in 1888 by W. R. Woodman, A. F. A. Woodford, W. Wynn Westcott, and Samuel Liddell Mathers (1854-1918; a relative of Alice Liddell, whose father co-authored the most important Greek dictionary of the 19th century, and whose adventures in Wonderland were chronicled by the Reverend Charles Ludwig Dodgson); all but Woodford had been members of the SRIA, and the first two had died by 1891. Westcott resigned in 1897 to concentrate on the SRIA, of which he was Supreme Magus, leaving Mathers in complete control of the HOGD. The four had claimed to have a charter and a set of rituals from the "secret chiefs" of the Rosicrucian order in Germany, but in fact it was all written by Mathers, who was one of the most brilliant amateur scholars of his generation, who also translated *The Greater Key of Solomon* and several major Kabalistic treatises, and who wrote a major book on the Tarot. The HOGD attracted a stellar cast from among Britain's middle-class intellectuals. Its members included Arthur Machen, Arthur Edward Waite, James M. Barrie, Sir E. A. Wallis Budge, Hugh Schonfield, Florence Farr (at one time a lover of George Bernard Shaw), and Maud Gonne (a lover of Yeats and mother of Sean McBride).

The most famous member of the HOGD was William Butler Yeats, who joined in 1890, and remained a devout member (according to Virginia Moore's masterful biography) until 1900, when a fight over whether Mathers could bring Aleister Crowley rapidly up into the leadership of the organization shattered it into several factions. Most of the members left with Yeats to form the Stella Matutina (Morning Star), which Yeats served from 1901 to 1917 as Grand Master. Mathers and Crowley kept the original name, but their minority organization soon foundered. Crowley, after "channeling" the *Book of the Law* in 1904, founded his own organization, the Astrum Argentinum (Silver Star), in 1907, and began publishing *The Equinox* in 1909. He had also become a member of the Ordo

Templi Orientis (Order of the Eastern Temple) by 1912. According to the painstaking research of J. Gordon Melton, the OTO was actually based largely on the secret sex-magic teachings of P. B. Randolph, founder of a major Rosicrucian society in America. Crowley was recognized as head of the OTO by a majority of its members in 1924-25, but the organization then divided in two over the issue of accepting Crowley's *Book of the Law* as authoritative. (Rudolf Steiner headed an OTO chapter early in this century, before he founded the Anthroposophical league. It is this common background in magic that explains why Steiner's Waldorf schools celebrate the same eight Sabbats as Neopagan Witches.)

Violet Firth was initiated in 1919 into the Alpha et Omega, the HOGD offshoot presided over by Mathers' widow, Moina Bergson Mathers. In 1922 she organized the Fraternity of the Inner Light as an "outer court" for the AEO. She and Mrs. Mathers clashed more and more as Violet matured as a leader; when Mrs. Mathers expelled her in 1927, Firth, now using the name Dion Fortune, took the Fraternity of the Inner Light with her, and it is the parent or ancestor of many other important magical organizations now functioning in England.

The Fraternity of the Inner Light was divided into at least two autonomous inner sections, one of which was avowedly "pagan"—that is, non-Christian. The acting heads of the pagan section from the mid-1930s into the 1940s were Charles R. F. Seymour (1880-1943) and Christine Hartley, who have been ably brought to public notice by Alan Richardson's recent *Dancers to the Gods*. Seymour had written an essay, "The Old Religion—A Study in the Symbolism of the Moon Mysteries," in 1937, but it was not published until 1968, when it appeared in *The New Dimensions Red Book*, edited by Basil Wiltby. On the essay, Alan Richardson comments in *Dancers to the Gods*, "In many ways it is a piece of writing which is years ahead of its time, prefiguring many of the trends in magic today." In another essay, "The Ancient Nature Worship," also written in 1937, Seymour says, "The witch-hunting of the fourteenth to eighteenth centuries was an effort to stamp out an old religion surviving from pre-Christian days. Its sin was that it celebrated with joy and laughter the great nature festivals." In his diary on June 21 (Summer Solstice), 1938, he wrote, "I got the idea of linking the old symbolism of indigenous women's mysteries with the pagan mysteries of England right down to the present day and through the witchcraft period." He had obviously been reading

Margaret Murray.

Christine Hartley, who worked as Seymour's High Priestess, recorded in her diary on June 28, 1938, "Started when I walked over the threshold of the house and felt witchcraft all around me. Went upstairs extremely desirous of being a witch. When we had settled down I kept getting little pictures of Ishtar worship through the ages, the most constant being one of silhouetted witches in pointed hats and ragged skirts dancing round a fire. Then . . . I was aware of the goddess standing before us mistily veiled." As we will see, Seymour and Hartley were certainly in the occult circle surrounding the people who began the New Forest coven in 1939, and their own ideas were obviously pointing in that direction as well.

A separate line of succession connecting earlier occultism with the Craft movement is that of Co-Masonry, an offshoot of Freemasonry which admits both women and men into membership; women are still excluded by the United Grand Lodge of England. Co-Masonry originated in France, and spread to England when its first British Lodge was formed in London in 1902. Annie Besant was initiated in this lodge, and became the national delegate for Britain. When H. P. Blavatsky died, and Annie Besant lost to Bishop Leadbeater in her struggle to succeed Blavatsky as head of the Theosophical Society, she shifted her efforts to organizing Co-Masonry in Britain, and in 1922 Co-Masonry was affiliated to the Grand Orient in France. When Annie Besant died, leadership of Co-Masonry in Britain devolved upon her daughter, Mabel Besant-Scott, who was Gerald Gardner's neighbor in Highcliffe, and a leading member of the Rosicrucian Fellowship of Crotona.

The publication of Margaret Murray's *The Witch-Cult in Western Europe* (Oxford University Press, 1921) set off a new burst of interest in paganism, since Murray proposed that the witch-hunters of medieval and early modern times were actually finding the remnants of the pagan religions of northern Europe. Murray's hypothesis (on p. 12) is that "underlying the Christian religion was a cult practised . . . chiefly . . . by the more ignorant or those in the less thickly inhabited parts of the country. It can be traced back to pre-Christian times, and appears to be the ancient religion of Western Europe." (Let me emphasize that Murray nowhere substantiates this assertion.) The idea of recreating the kind of witch cult described by Murray was discussed by English occultists during the 1920s and 1930s, and (I have heard indirectly from Gavin Frost, who studied at Cambridge) that some work on this may have been done by the Pentangle Club at Cambridge in the 1930s. However, the first successful attempt to recreate Murray's "witch cult" was carried out by Gerald B. Gardner (1884-1964), a retired British civil servant, and his colleagues among the New Forest occultists, under the leadership of one Dorothy Clutterbuck, during World War II. This is the topic of the next chapter.

Before I turn to that story, let me note that there were in fact people around in America (and probably in England, although I have no hard data on that) before 1939 who called themselves witches and practiced witchcraft, and who may have considered their witchcraft to be their religion. Although there were very few of them, their existence is well-documented, and is not a problem in itself. The problems that these pre-Gardnerian traditions raise for Gardnerian history are twofold:

(1) Their beliefs were utterly unlike what Gardner describes for his "cult." The available books on American "witchcraft" before 1939, such as John George Hohman's *Pow-Wows, or The Long-Lost Friend* (1819), or *Zolar's Book of Forbidden Knowledge* (no date), focus on folk-remedies for healing. The vocabulary and concepts in them are strictly Jewish or Christian in background.

(2) Current members of these traditions, despite the contempt they sometimes feel toward the Gardnerians as "Johnny-come-latelies," have for the most part (with the ahistorical eclecticism typical of true pagans) enthusiastically adopted the Gardnerian "reforms" because of their popularity and usefulness, and so have muddied whatever historical traces there might have been.

The most important of the pre-Gardnerian witches is certainly Victor Anderson, founder of the "Fairy" tradition, and, like Sara Cunningham, a major teacher of Starhawk. According to the researches of Valerie Voigt, long-time coordinator of the Pagan, Occult, and Witchcraft Special Interest Group of American Mensa, Victor relates that he was initiated into the Harpy coven in Ashland, Oregon, in 1932; the High Priestess and High Priest were Maybelle and Jerome Warren, and other members included Jim Murdoch and Patricia Fern. The coven was quite eclectic, mixing Huna with varieties of folk magic more common in the continental United States. He says that the emphasis was on practical magic; there was little concern with worship, theology, ethics, or ritual. They did celebrate the

Sabbats by getting together to work magic on them, but the only time they met in a circle, Victor says, was when they were eating—and yet this ordinary-looking meal was for them, he says, part of the celebration of the Sabbat.

Victor agrees that they did not worship a Goddess; rather, the concept of God they dealt with was of a male god opposed to Christianity. He was neither specifically equated with nor specifically distinguished from Satan. Their attitude was apparently much like that described by Richard Cavendish in *The Black Arts*, where he points out that Satan has been made a heroic figure, a rebel against arbitrary authority and injustice, by Western poets and writers since the Reformation; so that modern literature-based Satanism is not at all a worship of evil, but a neo-Gnosticism fighting against systemic injustice in the cosmos—a topic that I cannot get into here, but one that can be pursued by means of Robert Grant's *Gnosticism and Early Christianity*. (I will provide a more detailed history of Anderson and the Fairy tradition in Volume II.)

Another example is the "Gundella" covens in Michigan, which proved to Marcello Truzzi's satisfaction that they had existed pre-Gardner. These Michigan covens had (I am told by J. Gordon Melton) a theology totally unlike that described by Gardner.

The same is true of the immigrant Russian-Jewish coven in Los Angeles that the mother and grandmother of Tanya, David Farren's wife, belonged to, as described in his *The Return of Magic*. Their focus was strictly on working magic; they had no rule against working black magic; and insofar as they were concerned with any concept of a deity, which was very little, it was with a god, not a goddess, and, moreover, a god whom they often did equate with "Satan." Farren says (pp. 27-28), "Tanya's grandmother claims to represent the twelfth generation in the family line to be born a witch," although she is also Jewish and from the Ukraine; "she trained first her daughter and then her granddaughter in a lore which is part Russian and part Anglo-American." Both Natasha, Tanya's grandmother, and her mother "belonged to local covens which . . . reflected the Cabalistic ceremonial magic that was popular in Victorian England . . . Natasha's coven was composed mostly of other European emigrants anxious to keep alive some of the old ways of magic, but . . . any serious apprenticeship in magic was still kept within the family." He notes (p. 52) that Tanya has "recollections of the lore of her grandmother and mother, both of whose commitments to magic have included invocations of the demonic."

J. Gordon Melton's files, in the American Religion collection that his Institute for the Study of American Religion assembled and donated to the library of the University of California at Santa Barbara, contain letters from other traditional witches who know what American witchcraft was like before the influence of Gerald Gardner was felt. One lady, Rhea W., who corresponded with Dr. Melton in the late 1970s and early 1980s, wrote to him, "I will answer what questions I can for you concerning the older groups. There are some answers which I cannot give—such as names. As I am sure you know, then, more so than now, we took an oath of secrecy—and I have not been released from it. As far as I know, two of the members of the group are still alive, and I could never violate the oath I took. However, except for the actual names, there is some information which I would feel free to relate to you." Attempting to write a coherent account of her experience was not possible, given the life problems she was dealing with, but she allowed Dr. Melton to take notes on a conversation with her on June 21, 1980, and mentioned a few other facts in her letters.

Rhea said that "There was a very active group in Louisville, Ky., in 1934 and long before that. They were my first introduction to the Old Religion." As a child in the 1930s in Louisville she was given informal training in meditation, energy uses, visualization, and herbology, by a woman named Hannah in her apartment building. Hannah spoke of "following the Old Ways," and in her apartment a group met weekly. None of the women in the group cut their hair. They believed in a divine duality, in God as mother and father; they drew energy from the sun, and were particular about natural foods and herbs. The children were allowed to hold hands, do rhythmic breathing, and send energy. She never saw an altar or ritual instruments, but there was lighting of candles and calling on the spirits of the four corners.

Rhea said that she was first initiated in 1943 by a group she worked with in New York City from 1942 to 1945. Her initiation required a month of preparation, and involved a three-day fast for purification. The group had been together for quite some time, and she knew of others; they functioned like Communist-Party cells, in that members were recruited by invitation and sworn to secrecy. "Must admit they were a wee bit different than the ones today, but the basic similarity was still there," she said. "However, they did not call themselves 'Pagans' or 'Wicca.' When asked what 'religion' they were, they just replied, 'We follow the Old Ways.' In today's perspective they would be termed eclectic. Rituals were not quite as stylized as they are today. There are similarities and differences. We worked clothed (and/or robed). Sex within the temple or circle was taboo; however, there was a very healthy attitude toward sex." She said that when a Priest and Priestess were "bound together," the sexual act was used, and represented oneness. Most of the members of the group were Lebanese. They said they had brought the "tradition" with them from Lebanon, and that Kahlil Gibran had derived from their tradition there. The group was not called a coven; its numbers fluctuated, but it was tight-knit. It met weekly, and celebrated all eight Sabbats, often at a farm in New Jersey, where many of the members lived. The members worked magic in terms of the phases of the moon, but did not meet specifically at new or full moon; many attended other churches as well. They used the athame, but had no grimoires or written materials aside from personal notebooks for recipes. Basic instructions were oral, and all members of group constituted the priesthood. They believed in reincarnation, and practiced both high and low magic.

They worked in a temple room used only for ritual purposes, and no circle was cast. The altar contained male and female statuettes to represent the Lord and Lady, a sword, a chalice, an incense burner, candles of various colors, and earth. Rituals were in English. They observed the elements and corners, and taught meditation, astral travel, work on the planes, and work with elements.

Rhea's later life involved many frequent moves. As a result, although she had met other folk witches, both groups and individuals, in such places as Gainesville, Nashville, and Jasper, Alabama, as well as in Georgia and California, she had not joined another group. Her impression is that the "Old Way" witches tend to remain underground, and separate from the "new" witches.

There is no way to be absolutely sure that Rhea has not made up some of this information, or that it is totally free of wishful thinking, but I believe that it is probably accurate, for these reasons:

1. Rhea does not seem to have any axe to grind. She is not trying to prove that the pre-Gardnerian witches she knew were totally unlike Gardner's ideas, or that they were identical with them. She sim-

ply says there were both similarities and differences, and that is just what we would expect.

2. Insofar as these "Old Way" witches seem similar to the Gardnerians, that is because they were working from similar materials and concepts, and from just about the same books. The major differences seem to arise from the fact that Margaret Murray was not central to their thinking, and they did not use concepts from Leland's *Aradia* either.

Finally, the other pre-Gardnerian witches we know about are those in the Ozarks. To some extent, the Ozark folk beliefs about witches are like those in Africa: such "witches" are actually demons, spiritual entities that could not be human in real life. However, according to Vance Randolph's data, mixed in with this is an actual society or subculture of witches who are definitely real people. Randolph says (pp. 265-6),

> Although I have known and interviewed 24 persons who were regarded by their neighbors as witches, only three admitted that they had sold themselves to the Devil. These three were quite mad, of course; the point is that their neighbors did not regard them as lunatics, but as witches. The other 21 claim that their efforts are directed *against* the forces of evil, and that their main business is the removal of spells and curses ... These practitioners are variously known as witch masters, white witches, witch doctors, ... and conjure folks, and it is from them that I have obtained much of my information on the subject.
>
> Some hillfolk believe that a woman may become a witch by some comparatively simple hocus-pocus. . . . But most of the genuine old-timers are agreed that to become a witch is a rather complicated matter. Anybody is free to discuss the general principles of witchcraft, but the conjure words and old sayin's must be learned from a member of the opposite sex. . . . the secret doctrines must pass only between blood relatives, or between persons who have been united in sexual intercourse. Thus it is that every witch obtains her unholy wisdom either from a lover or from a male relative.
>
> Not every woman who receives this information becomes a witch. . . . not until someone actually uses the deadly formulae does a genuine witch appear. . . . while a knowledge of witchcraft is admitted to exist in certain families and clans, it sometimes lies dormant for a long time.
>
> A virgin may possess some of the secrets of "bedevilment," . . . but she cannot be a genuine witch . . . A woman can . . . practice the infernal arts in a small way without any ceremony,

but to attain to her full powers she must be formally initiated into the sinister sisterhood.

When a woman decides to become a witch . . . she repairs to the family buryin' ground at midnight, in the dark of the moon. Beginning with a verbal renunciation of the Christian religion, she swears to give herself body and soul to the Devil. She removes every stitch of clothing . . . and delivers her body immediately to . . . the man who is inducting her into the "mystery." The sexual act completed, both parties repeat certain old sayin's . . . This ceremony is supposed to be witnessed by at least two initiates, also nude, and must be repeated on three consecutive nights. . . . the third pledge is final. Henceforth the woman is a witch . . .

I am told, by women who have claimed to experience both, that the witch's initiation is a much more moving spiritual crisis than that which the Christians call conversion [my emphasis]. . . . however, . . . it inevitably results in the death of some person near and dear to the witch. I once attended the funeral of a woman whose death was attributed to her daughter's participation in one of these graveyard ceremonies. The accused girl sat apart from the other members of the family and was ignored . . .

I believe this last paragraph establishes the social reality of the experiences: they are actual practices, not just fantasy. Obviously there are great differences here from the Gardnerian concept of the Craft as a religion, but there are also some striking similarities. I think the similarities must seem less striking when we consider that Randolph's book appeared in 1947, that is, in plenty of time for Gardner to have used it in writing his original Book of Shadows and *Witchcraft Today*, as we will now see.

Source Notes

I have used data from throughout Francis King, but especially from his chapters 4, 5, 11, 13, and 16.

On Seymour and Hartley I have relied on Doreen Valiente's citations of data from Richardson.

2. Beginning of the Gardnerian Movement, 1939-1952

Gerald Brosseau Gardner was born at Great Crosby, near Blundell Sands in Lancashire, on June 13, 1884. His father was a timber merchant and a Justice of the Peace. His education for the most part was in the hands of "Con," a governess to whom the "Bracelin" biography says he was devoted. He did not obtain a university education, but instead went to work for the commercial branch of the British Civil Service in the Far East. In 1927, at age 43, he married Donna Rosedale, a clergyman's daughter. In 1936 he retired from the civil service—he had served as overseer of a rubber plantation in Malaysia, among other posts—and settled in the south of England, in the area of Hampshire known as the New Forest. He had been fascinated by the occult for his entire life, and had accumulated a collection of magical implements and of pamphlets issued by a great variety of new religious movements, which he brought home with him. He had also been initiated into dozens of occult organizations.

Aside from his astonishing self-education on the founding of new religions that is revealed by his pamphlet and manuscript collection, what is most important about Gardner's life for understanding his role in founding the modern Craft movement is the fact that he suffered from a sexual addiction. Specifically, he was addicted to being whipped. To blame him or think ill of him for that would be bigotry, ignorance, or hypocrisy, because he had not chosen to acquire this addiction. Instead, it was forced upon him, as it was upon most Englishmen of his generation, by the English educational system. In this system, as has been ably described by Ian Gibson's *The*

English Vice: Beating, Sex, and Shame in Victorian England and After, normal practice was, until very recently, to beat little boys on their bare buttocks with a cane or birch branch, before witnesses. As a result, their sexual development was distorted and fixated on their buttocks: even as adults, they needed to be beaten on their bare buttocks (or at least to fantasize about that) in order to achieve an erection and so be capable of sexual intercourse. It is eminently clear from Gardner's sexual interests and tastes that this had been his experience, and that fantasizing was not sufficient to meet his needs. Unlike most Englishmen, however, he did not try to hide this fact, or make do by patronizing prostitutes who specialize in what is now called "bondage and domination." No, what Gardner did was far more courageous.

In a sense, Gardner was following in the steps of Algernon Charles Swinburne, the English poet (born in 1840) who recorded his experiences of being beaten at Eton in his verse—although these verses were censored and suppressed from his collected works until very recently. The man who beat Swinburne was his tutor, James Leigh Joynes, who at that time was an Anglican deacon; Joynes was later ordained as a priest. Being beaten in the name of Christianity was a major reason—and, indeed, a sufficient reason—for Swinburne's famous hatred of Christianity:

> "Thou hast conquered, O pale Galilean,
> And the world has gone gray with thy Breath."

Gardner was certainly beaten by Con, but, like Aleister Crowley, he did not settle for passively hating Christianity. Instead, he set out to replace Christianity. Since Christianity condemned his sexuality, distorted in Christ's name, as "perverse," he set out to found a religion that would be based on sex as a sacramental experience, and that could therefore help him meet his needs.

A craft Priestess I know who has worked as a professional "dominatrix" has shared with me some of her insights into Gardner's personality, based on her professional experiences and Gardner's own writings. She says that the instructions in his rituals for exactly how a person is to be bound and scourged show what he himself needed to be done. Furthermore, she says, he was clearly the sort of man called a "SAM, smart-assed masochist," in her trade, because, rather than obeying the orders of the "Mistress," he wanted to tell her exactly what to do to him. That is, like Leopold von Sacher-

Masoch, Gardner's fantasied ideal woman is one who would appear to dominate him, but would in actuality be manipulated by him into meeting his sexual needs. From a Jungian perspective, this pattern also arises from the unconscious search for the lost "ideal mother." We would expect that most Englishmen who had been, as little boys, turned over to a governess or a tutor or a boarding school with the authority and inclination to beat them, would very reasonably feel that they had been abandoned by their mothers, and would mourn that loss for the rest of their lives. Given all that, it seems perfectly reasonable that the archetype of the Goddess would appeal to Gardner far more than the God satirized by William Blake as "Old Nobodaddy."

One may wonder what his wife, Donna, thought of all this. Well, the pattern for the middle-class English wife was apparently to keep her mouth shut and find a way to live with the problem; she might regret that she was not her husband's fantasied ideal woman, but she might also recognize that, as a merely real and imperfect woman, there was in fact no way that she could live up to that fantasy. Some wives would whip their husbands' bare butts in order to have sex. Others would give their husbands permission to meet their needs however they could, and would settle for enjoying the side-effects. Others, to be sure, would give up sex entirely. I am, of course, mostly speculating here, and generalizing from very little data—for there has never been, as far as I know, an objective attempt at a scientific study of this question. But given all this, we can reasonably suppose that after a dozen years of trying to cope with Gerald's sexual problems, Donna might have been glad, or at least relieved, to have him find another path that could meet his needs. All the evidence about her is that, although not involved in the Craft herself, she never interfered with his Craft activity during their last twenty years together.

Before the outbreak of World War II, Gardner had written a letter to the *London Times* suggesting the formation of civilian defense units in the event of war, a letter for which he was denounced in the Nazi press as a warmonger. When the Home Guard was formed—whether or not in part because of his letter—he served as a unit commander during the course of the war. Charles Clifton has written an excellent paper, "Secrecy and Historicity in the Book of Shadows," in which he points out that Gardner's experience during the war, worrying about a possible German invasion, seems to have set the mood for much of his writing about the "Burning Times" in his books and documents. Certainly the British comedy series *Dad's Army*, about a Home Guard unit, seemed to me to shed some light on what Gardner's state of mind might have been during the war.

In the New Forest Gardner became friends with the local occultists, who included Theosophists, Co-Masons, and others. In particular, he met a woman named Dorothy Fordham, who, as Doreen Valiente's research has established, was born on January 19, 1880, and died on January 12, 1951, was the daughter of Thomas St. Quintin Clutterbuck (b. 1839), a British Indian Army Officer, and of Ellen Anne Morgan (b. 1857), and was of a family long resident in the New Forest area. An article from the Bournemouth *Evening Echo* of February 25, 1986, sent to me by Doreen Valiente, describes the finding of Dorothy's wartime diaries, filled with verse and illustrated by a friend, which were on exhibit in London. The article describes her as "the wealthy Mrs. Dorothy Fordham, who owned two magnificent houses near Chewton Glen at Highcliffe: The Mill House and Lattimers." That is, she was precisely the sort of person, slightly above Gardner in social class, with whom he would have wanted to associate. What could not have been guessed (and Ms. Valiente says Mrs. Fordham's old solicitor still does not want to know) is that she was as enthusiastic about witchcraft as Gerald was. Apparently she was the dominant personality in their relationship for as long as she lived. Another woman, whose Craft name would be Dafo, was one of the people who helped found the Rosicrucian Theatre in Christchurch (it opened on June 15, 1938) and who took part in the plays presented there.

In September 1939, probably on the 28th, the evening of the full moon, Gerald Gardner, Dorothy Clutterbuck Fordham, Dafo, and others of their occult circle of friends were, I believe, sitting in Dorothy's living room, discussing England's perilous state, now at war with Germany. Was England in danger of perishing spiritually for want of a truly native British religion they could all believe in? Gardner, at least, had been thinking for years about how to go about creating one. Encouraged by the tension of that moment, they decided to try to recreate the "witch cult of Western Europe" described by Margaret Murray. In the sense that the project of creating their coven was initiated that night, each of them would later feel that his or her own initiation had started that night; this would be the reality behind Gardner's claim that he was initiated in September 1939, and the reason why that particular date appears in his story.

In order to see why this group of friends succeeded (where many others may have failed) in putting together a new religion that was based on Murray and that has survived, we need to look at who they were, and at what resources were available to them. In her recent *The Rebirth of Witchcraft*, Doreen Valiente provides the names of people who were in Gerald and Dorothy's circle of occult friends, and who therefore could have been members of the coven in late 1939 or the early 1940s. Adding a few names from other sources, we arrive at the following list, on which Ms. Valiente commented in recent letters to me.

"Dafo and Old Dorothy, obviously," Ms. Valiente says.

Dolores North (died in 1982), pen-name Madeline Montalban, was known to Gerald "& others as 'The Witch of St Giles' because she lived in St Giles High Street, London." Ms. Valiente says that she "typed out for [Gardner] the manuscript of his book *High Magic's Aid* . . . [and] became well-known as a regular contributor to the popular occult magazine *Prediction*. . . . I believe her family had some connection with the then Lord Louis Mountbatten's estate, Broadlands, in the New Forest area. . . . during the war . . . she had been wearing the uniform of an officer in the WRNS [as] a cover . . . Lord Louis Mountbatten, who knew her because of her family's connection with his estate, had retained her as his personal clairvoyant and psychic advisor. A very curious account of what may be a magical working with Gerald Gardner and Dolores North appears in a book by Kenneth Grant entitled *Nightside of Eden*. . . . this ritual . . . took place in 1949." I think she was clearly a member of the coven from very early on, perhaps from the very first meeting. (Ms. Valiente agrees that she could have been a member of the coven.)

Louis Wilkinson, who wrote novels under the name of Louis Marlow, and contributed to Crowley's *Equinox*, was one of Crowley's literary executors. In 1947 he achieved brief notoriety by reading Crowley's funeral service at the municipal crematorium. (We know about him not from Valiente, but from Francis King's report in *Ritual Magic in England* of a meeting with him in 1953 that I'll come back to shortly. Ms. Valiente agrees that he could have been a member of the coven.)

Next we have George Watson McGregor Reid, Chosen Chief of the Ancient Order of Druids, the group that holds sunrise services at

Stonehenge on Midsummer's Day (several manuscripts of their rituals are among the documents in Toronto), and his son, Robert McGregor Reid, who succeeded his father as Chosen Chief in 1946. (Ms. Valiente thinks it unlikely he could have been a member of the coven; but the evidence of the sword, which we will consider in Chapter 4, must be weighed here.)

J.S.M. Ward, a close friend of Gardner, a leading Freemason and author of several learned books on Freemasonry, a pioneer in rescue and conservation of ancient buildings, was the owner of the "witch's cottage" that Gardner bought and had rebuilt near St. Albans. (He is also discussed by King and in the "Bracelin" biography. Ms. Valiente thinks it very unlikely he could have been a member of the coven, because he was a very sincere, though very unorthodox, Christian bishop, and I must agree. Ward was probably the source of Gardner's own consecration as a bishop, the certificate for which is among the papers in Toronto.)

Charles Richard Foster Seymour and Christine Hartley, whom I discussed in Chapter 1, are, Ms. Valiente agrees, also possibilities. In fact, she wrote to me, "I wish I knew! You see, all the leading people who were seriously interested in the occult in those days tended to know each other; but this does not necessarily mean they were all involved in the same things. And also, because the whole occult scene was so secretive in those times, so furtive almost (witches were, after all, still doing something actually illegal, for which they could have been prosecuted), tracks were very well covered, I can assure you." (The doings of Seymour and Hartley are discussed in great detail in Alan Richardson's *Dancers to the Gods*. They were both active as Co-Masons from 1941 on, and may have met Gardner and Dafo in that context, if they were not already acquainted. I have heard from Alan Richardson that Hartley had said in an interview that she had been in a coven after the war; but this needs to be verified.)

Mrs. Mabel Besant-Scott, daughter of Annie Besant, Gardner's neighbor in Highcliffe, on the edge of the New Forest, and a leading member of the Rosicrucian Fellowship of Crotona. (Ms. Valiente thinks it unlikely that she could have been a member of the coven.)

One last possibility is G. A. Sullivan, whose stage name was Alex Matthews, and who was co-founder and director of the Rosicrucian Theater. He died in 1942, and hence might have been one of the elderly people whom Gardner said had died soon after the cone of power against Hitler at Lammas 1940. He is mentioned by Valiente, in the Farrars 1984, p. 290.

Probably not all of these were actually active members of the coven, but this list surely contains the names of many of the coven's members; there may also have been some very ordinary, non-famous members. If this group began to reconstruct the religion described by Murray, what would their first model have looked like? That is, what information does Murray actually give? Let's see what it looks like when actually pulled together. (Note that in the following I am quoting from *Witch-Cult in Western Europe* except where I specifically cite *God of the Witches*.)

Murray always refers to her subject as "the religion," or "the old religion," or "the cult" (as in the title of the book). She asserts (p. 12) that "underlying the Christian religion was a cult practised . . . chiefly . . . by the more ignorant or those in the less thickly inhabited parts of the country. It can be traced back to pre-Christian times, and appears to be the ancient religion of Western Europe." Hence the group would have felt that any information about pre-Christian religions might be useful for reconstructing the "witch-cult."

Murray's reconstruction focuses almost entirely on the God of the witches, and on the man whom the witches believed to be the living incarnation of that God. He often wore an animal skin or costume, and often dressed entirely in black—and hence was called the Black Man.

> To "the witches themselves . . . [he] was God, manifest and incarnate; they adored him on their knees, they addressed their prayers to him, they offered thanks to him as the giver of food and the necessities of life, they dedicated their children to him, and . . . like many another god, he was sacrificed for the good of his people." Because "the feminine form . . . Diana, is found throughout Western Europe as the name of the female deity or leader of the so-called Witches . . . I have called this . . . the Dianic cult" (pp. 12, 13, 28, 33-43).

Although Murray says that a woman sometimes served as the incarnation of the God, for the most part women took a secondary role. She does not mention the concept of a goddess as the chief deity of the witches except to dismiss it. (In fact, the Craft concept of the Goddess comes primarily from Leland's *Aradia*, and then from the Classical sources that Leland points back to.)

In each district the chief appointed one or more officers, who might be either men or women, whose "duties were to arrange for meetings, to send out notices, to keep the record of work done, to transact the business of the community, and to present new members" for initiation. "At the Esbats the officer appears to have taken command in the absence of the Grand Master; at the Sabbaths the officers were merely heads of their own Covens" (p. 186).

If we are assuming that the New Forest group was basing itself on Murray's concepts, then we must conclude that *the first coven would have kept its focus on the God and on the male High Priest*. We would expect any rituals based on this information to focus on the High Priest, and not on a priestess. Contrary to what Craft members now think, this is precisely the emphasis in the rituals until about 1957, as we will see.

Naturally, the people active in this reconstruction project considered themselves to constitute a coven, about which Murray states:

"There was among the witches a body of elders—the Coven—which managed the local affairs of the cult. . . . The word coven is a derivative of 'convene,' . . . [it means] a 'band' or 'company' . . . composed of men and women . . . set apart for the practice of the rites of the religion and for the performance of magical ceremonies; in short, a kind of priesthood" (pp. 13, 190).

"There were two kinds of assemblies; . . . the Sabbath was the General Meeting of all the members of the religion; the . . . Esbat was only for . . . [those] who carried out the rites and practices of the cult, . . . [and was] primarily for . . . the practice of magic for the benefit of a client or for the harming of an enemy. . . . Very often also the Esbat was for sheer enjoyment only" (pp. 97, 112-3).

"There was no fixed day or hour for the Esbat [though probably] one day in the week was observed . . . The Devil let his followers know the time, either by going to them himself or by sending a message by the officer. . . . The Esbat had less ceremonial, and the religious service was not performed. . . . the witches worked the spells and charms . . . exercised new methods . . . or received instructions [on] how to practise the arts of healing and . . . fertility. . . . The members [of the coven had] . . . to attend the weekly Esbat; . . . The rest of the villagers attended the Esbats when they could [and] attended the Sabbaths as a matter of course. . . . The 'fixed number' among the witches of Great Britain seems to have been thirteen: twelve witches and their officer" (pp. 121, 124, 190-91; and *God of the Witches*, pp. 65, 67).

Notice here that the concept of meeting at the full moon does not come from Murray; instead, it was derived from Leland's *Aradia*. At first the New Forest group probably did meet weekly, as a committee working on the project, and those who showed up regularly for these working sessions would have considered themselves to be the members of the coven. They may have gathered for a party on Halloween in 1939, but it is not likely that they could have had a ritual ready by then. Their first ritual was perhaps worked for Brigid at the beginning of February 1940, and certainly would have been ready to be worked by May Day in 1940. Given the concept that the Sabbats were for all the members of the religion, the New Forest coven would have quietly invited sympathetic friends and acquaintances from the local occult circle to them; and the Rosicrucian Theater would have been a logical place to hold them. And even aside from Murray, May Day and Halloween are the two dates that European custom universally associates with witches.

> "The dates of the two chief festivals, May Eve and November Eve, indicate the use of a calendar which is . . . preagricultural and earlier than the solstitial divisions of the year. . . . The cross-quarter days, February 2 and August 1, . . . also kept as festivals, were probably of later date" (pp. 12-13).

Murray's speculations here are, in fact, completely wrong; but that merely proves that the Gardnerian Book of Shadows, which in 1953 had rituals for only the four Celtic festivals, none for the solstices and equinoxes, was based on Murray, rather than a more accurate source. (In fact, Fred Lamond tells me that even in 1957 only four Sabbats a year were kept, not eight.)

But what might this New Forest coven have done at a Sabbat? The litany of a "Witches' Sabbath" as given by Murray included the following:

(1) worship of the incarnate deity by
    (a) renewing vows,
    (b) kissing,
    (c) turning withershins several times;
(2) the business portion, consisting of
    (a) reports of and instructions on magic,
    (b) admissions to the society, and
    (c) marriages of members;
(3) the religious service, consisting of

(a) a ceremony that varied with the seasons,
(b) fertility rites,
(c) feasting, and
(d) dancing until dawn.

"Though the Chief sometimes gave an address, in which he . . . explained the dogmas of the religion, the main ceremony was the sacred dance. After this came the feast, which was often followed by another dance." "The feasts and dances show that it was a joyous religion" (pp. 15, 124, and *God of the Witches*, p.76).

In the witch-trial records, this feast often appears to be confused with the Christian Eucharist, or is claimed to be a parody of the Eucharist; or else appears to be a simple meal. Neither possibility provides much in the way of a pagan ritual.

Among the dances mentioned are a jumping dance for fertility, the round dance, a follow-the-leader dance, and a processional dance. "As the processional dance was performed by men and women side by side in pairs, or in a long line with the sexes alternately, it was liable to break up into couples who continued dancing together after the procession was ended. . . . [It] could be in itself a complete act of worship, but it was most frequently used to bring the worshippers to the holy place where the round dance or 'Ring' was to be performed" (*God of the Witches*, p. 110).

Aside from mentioning folk-magic procedures and some obvious customs, such as riding a broomstick, lighting candles, boiling a cauldron, and so on, Murray gives no other specific details of what witches might have done. Clearly, then, the New Forest group must have exercised much creativity and ingenuity in attempting to "reconstruct" this religion.

Gardner and his friends were, in fact, faced by a dilemma: the "Old Religion" described by Murray was a religion that focused on the practice of magic; but the only systems for working magic that they could find out about—e.g., the "ceremonial" or "high" magic of the grimoires and secret societies—were inherently Judaeo-Christian in concept and in vocabulary. (If the pagan section of the Fraternity of the Inner Light had evolved a pagan system of magic by 1939, Gardner apparently did not know about it.) Not only was the theory behind these systems derived from certain special branches of Judaeo-Christian theology, but the systems were so complex that the resulting practical details were almost impossible to carry out. In the so-called Abramelin system, for example, any one working would require great expense and months of preparation to carry out, as would the procedures detailed in the *Greater Key of Solomon*. The magical system of the Hermetic Order of the Golden Dawn was somewhat more sophisticated, and its rituals were easier to carry out—if you had a magical lodge whose members could subscribe 100 pounds sterling a year to support it, that is, more that the annual income of the average English home at that time—so these rituals were certainly not suitable for a coven of witches.

The New Forest group was also interested in folk magic, which is always non-denominational, and made as much use of it as they could; but the problem with folk magic is that it is all practice, no theory. To cure a wart, use this herb; to win a girl, recite this charm. From a hundred such workings, no one could deduce a hundred-and-first, since no system lies behind them; they cannot be generalized. Hence such "low magic" did not offer the sort of theological structure that the New Forest people wanted their new "Old Religion" to have. In order to insure the success of their "revival" of the "Old Religion," they needed to have what would in fact be a new system for working magic. To create it, they needed to use some sort of ritual other than that of Kabalistic magic as a framework for it—but since these folks were Rosicrucians, Masons, Co-Masons, and so on, and were also into theater, they had rituals at hand that they could and almost certainly did adapt. Much in the Gardnerian Book of Shadows is Masonic in underlying structure; much that now seems odd in it can be explained in terms of this set of data from Murray that constituted the jumping-off point for the reconstruction.

Gardner had been gathering notes on magical procedures for many years (there are, among the materials in Toronto, half a dozen hand-illuminated manuscript books consisting of material that Gardner had copied from various grimoires and other sources), but he had never written any rituals, because he had never before had a group to write for. Now he had a new agenda: to find out how magic could be worked by a small group. He began gathering his notes on this topic in a notebook labeled "Ye Bok of ye Art Magical." It consists of almost 150 large sheets, which have been folded and sewn into signatures; the resulting pages are somewhat larger than British legal size (8" x 13"). The signatures were then handbound (not very skillfully) into a leather book cover whose previous contents had been removed. On the front cover is inscribed the title (exactly as spelled above), and beneath that appears a triangle above a pentacle, the Gardnerian symbol for a third-degree witch.

Gardner may have at first intended this manuscript book to be a magical workbook, because at first he entered only information about ceremonial magic in it. However, everything copied into "Ye Bok of ye Art Magical" can be carried out by one or a few persons. He searched out and gathered together materials from many sources: Crowley's developments of the HOGD systems; the *Greater Key of Solomon*; Masonic and other fraternal rituals; Murray, Frazer, and the Cambridge classicists—in fact, the sources included the hundreds of books shelved in Derek's office when I made my visit to Toronto.

The activities of the New Forest coven, if they were ever a secret, did not remain secret for long. The English occult novelist Louis Wilkinson told Francis King in 1953 (p. 177) that

> "in the late 'thirties or early 'forties [i.e., exactly at the end of 1939] he had himself become friendly with members of a witch-coven operating in the New Forest. . . . the foundation of the group might have dated from after the [1922] publication of Margaret Murray's *Witch Cult in Western Europe*, [but] he himself was reasonably confident that there had been a fusion of an authentic surviving folk-tradition with a more intellectual middle-class occultism. [He] went on to tell me various interesting details of the practices of these Hampshire witches,"

such as their use of a heavy grease for warmth when working skyclad outdoors, and of fly agaric as a psychedelic drug—practices that, in fact, are rather typical of folk magic. What Wilkinson is saying is that the "intellectual middle-class occultists"—Rosicrucians, Masons, etc.—had joined forces with one or more working-class folk-witches (whose knowledge is always strictly of the "how to" variety, and is not the sort of religious tradition the Gardnerians wish to claim). He is also saying that their intellectual (Masonic) occultism was providing a framework for the spells, charms, and dances of folk magic, precisely what we have already seen is logically necessary in order to "reconstruct" the religion that Murray describes. And notice that he admits without quite admitting it that he knows the coven's practices are based on Murray, a tactic of indirection that Gardner often uses in his writings. Overall, these statements by Wilkinson do not prove there was a coven before 1939; but they are solid evidence for the existence of the coven at the end of

1939. However, Wilkinson is almost certainly not an independent witness here. He describes himself as a member of the occult circle of friends around the New Forest coven, and so was probably a member of the coven himself (how else would he know the details of its practices?)

The group apparently did dance a spell to keep Hitler from invading. Francis King writes,

> "On at least one occasion the Hampshire witches indulged in human sacrifice—but done in such a way that there could not possibly be any legal unpleasantness. This was done in May 1940, when Hitler's invasion was felt to be imminent. The witches felt that it was essential that he be deterred from invasion plans by a powerful ritual, the central point of which was to be the death of a (volunteer) sacrificial victim. The oldest and frailest member volunteered for sacrifice and left off his protective grease so that he might die of the effects of exposure. Unfortunately enough, it was the coldest May night for many years, and not only the volunteer but two other members of the coven died from pneumonia within the next fortnight."

This information about the grease is not in any other published source—but the only way Wilkinson could have known about it is if he had been there himself; that is, again, he appears to have been a member of the coven.

Gardner's own description of this event (in the "Bracelin" biography) reads,

> "We were taken at night to a place in the Forest, where the Great Circle was erected; and that was done which may not be done except in great emergency. And the great Cone of Power was raised and slowly directed in the general direction of Hitler. The command was given: 'You cannot cross the Sea. You cannot cross the Sea. YOU CANNOT COME. YOU CANNOT COME.' . . . Now to do this means using one's life-force; and many of us died a few days after we did this. My asthma, which I had never had since I first went out East, came back badly. We repeated the ritual four times; and the Elders said: 'We feel we have stopped him. We must not kill too many of our people. Keep them until we need them.'"

Gardner also described this ritual to Doreen Valiente, as follows:

> A very large circle was marked out with brushwood, and people stationed to whip up the dancers [a detail based on Murray]. The fire, not too large because of wartime blackout restric-

tions, was lit in what was roughly the direction that the invasion was thought likely to come from, probably the southeast. Then all danced round until they felt they had raised enough power. Since the rite was to banish, they started deosil and finished widdershins, so many rounds of each. Then they formed a line with linked hands and rushed toward the fire, shouting the thing they wanted, in this case, "Can't cross the sea! Not able to come!" They kept it up till they were exhausted or until someone fell in a faint, when they were said to have taken the spell to its destination.

Valiente argues that if the cone of power against Hitler was repeated four times, it was probably carried out first on May Eve 1940 (Wilkinson's date), at the full moon on June 19, at the full moon on July 17, and at Lammas 1940, which is the date given by Cecil Williamson (in an article, "Witchcraft in Britain," *Illustrated*, September 27, 1952). Williamson mentions that there were 17 people at the Lammas working.

Let us return to Murray, who (p. 14) states that most ceremonies were for securing fertility:

> "If the women believed that sexual intercourse with the priests would increase fertility, how much more would they believe in the efficacy of such intercourse with the incarnate God of fertility himself. They would insist upon it as their right" (p. 178).

Given this emphasis in Murray, we can presume that sex was present in the Craft, and in Craft initiation, from the start. Sex was, and is, a major reason why people become interested in the Craft. The great emphasis on sexuality in the rituals, as we will see, is neither hedonistic nor exploitative, but genuinely sacramental, since it arises out of a search for communion and for community. As we saw in considering the pre-Gardnerian witches in America, the one element of a Craft initiation that seems to be universal is that it involves sexual intercourse. Insofar as the Craft is conceived of as a rebellion against Christianity, that rebellion would obviously focus on and emphasize the aspect of human nature to which Christianity seems most opposed.

Murray states (*God of the Witches*, p. 63) that there were apparently three different "admission ceremonies," one in public, one for consecration as a priestess, and one for being made an officer of the coven. These could take place at either Sabbath or Esbat, and were the same for either sex; they could involve being rebaptized, being given a new name, being given a mark or tattoo, and signing one's name in a book (pp. 74-6). As Murray comments, "the renunciation of previous errors of faith and the vows of fidelity to the new belief are part of the ceremony of admission of any convert to a new religion" (p. 77), but, as she also points out (p. 15), such a ritual would be invented only after the arrival of Christianity and in reaction to it; it would not be part of an earlier religion existing in isolation.

The New Forest coven must therefore have begun creating initiation rituals for their own use. Whether or not they did some sort of initiation at the Sabbats, they certainly must have begun creating initiation rituals for use within the coven almost immediately. No identified copy of those rituals has survived, as far as I know, but fortunately, I think we have probably been given the New Forest coven's original rituals, or at least rituals very similar to them, in Rhiannon Ryall's *West Country Wicca*. Let me emphasize this point: Ms. Ryall's coven was clearly derived from the New Forest coven. However, it was in fact pre-Gardnerian, in this sense: *Ryall gives us the New Forest coven's rituals as they were worked before Gardner rewrote them to better meet his own sexual needs.*

Ryall says that she worked in a coven in the West Country of England (specifically, along the Devon/Somerset border) in the 1940s, and that it was pre-Gardnerian. On the latter point she was misinformed, because her basic theological concepts, the overall structure of the coven's rituals, and all the details of its circle-casting procedure are strictly Gardnerian. They are, to be sure, quite different from (in fact, a logical subset of) current Gardnerian practices, but they are identical with the procedures of the early 1940s recorded in Gardner's "Ye Bok of ye Art Magical" manuscript, which we will look at in Chapter 3 (and of whose existence Ms. Ryall had no way to know). They had no "Book of Shadows," she says, and that is reasonable, since apparently Gardner had not created that book, nor devised the name for it, until the late 1940s. Likewise, she had not been familiar with the Charge or the legend of the Descent of the Goddess; and again the evidence is that Gardner did not write these until late in the 1940s. Clearly her coven must represent a hiving off from the New Forest coven some time before the end of World War II. (Since we now know that Dorothy Clutterbuck wrote excellent verse, it is possible that the ritual verses that Ryall gives were actually written by Old Dorothy, *if* they go back that far.)

The initiation rituals she gives are quite different from Gardner's. They are based much more directly on Murray, and incorporate many elements from folklore and fairy tales; and the second (and final) initiation consists of sexual intercourse, carried out on the altar, between the candidate and a masked High Priest or High Priestess from another coven. This logically looks like a transition stage between the one initiation of folk-magic witchcraft and the three initiations of Gardner's system. However—and this is a major clue to help unravel the puzzle—Ryall never mentions any scourging at all; in fact, she says specifically that no sword, scourge, or cords were on the altar. Gardner certainly had his own sexual agenda all along, but he did not impose it on the other members of the original New Forest coven.

Ryall's story, plus other stray remarks I have run across, indicates that the personnel of the original New Forest group had become widely scattered by the end of the war. Some of them continued practicing the Craft, and in Ryall's home area apparently allied immediately with the local folk-witches. Reduced to working with a small core group, Gardner began about the end of the war to rewrite the rituals, and create new rituals, in order to meet his own needs more directly; and in Chapter 3 we will look in detail at what Gardner wrote, during the period 1946 to 1952.

In Gardner's system there were three initiations, just as Murray says, and they incorporate elements from Murray within a framework taken from the three-degree system of the Masonic Blue Lodges; they also incorporate a great deal of "binding and scourging," all of which was Gardner's own addition to the earlier raw materials. About a hundred pages into "Ye Bok of ye Art Magical" the First-Degree Initiation begins, and the rest of the initiations are scattered throughout the rest of the book, along with about a dozen other entries relevant to the Craft as currently practiced. Obviously, Gardner chose "Ye Bok of ye Art Magical" to be his first working Book of Shadows because it looks right—at least from a few feet away—so where better to write out the initiation rituals in a form that could actually be used?

The initiation rituals (unlike all the other entries) in "Ye Bok of ye Art Magical" are written large and clear, in calligraphy careful enough to be read from three or four feet away. These initiation rituals are designed to be worked by one person for one other person at a time. Although this would indicate that his coven was very small,

Gardner was not working in isolation as he created the rituals in the "Ye Bok of ye Art Magical" manuscript, which is clearly intended for liturgical use in the circle. Rather, like all liturgy, they resulted from a lengthy group process. We now know that he remained in touch with Dafo, Dolores North, and probably others all along, and that they did work together when they had a reason to.

I also doubt that Gardner alone created the vision of a medieval pagan religion in the novel *High Magic's Aid*, which Gardner says he wrote around 1946, and which was published in 1949; rather, it seems to me to be the product of a group process. In fact, as we will see, Gardner was working on the novel and on rewriting the rituals simultaneously, around 1946. This is much too late for the rituals in "Ye Bok of ye Art Magical" to have been the original initiation rituals of the New Forest coven; they would not have waited even a year, let alone seven, to begin initiating themselves.

The novel *High Magic's Aid* is a fanciful and rather detailed description of the beliefs and practices of an English witch cult in about the 15th century. It reveals that Gardner (and whoever else helped him write it) had already given much thought to what a medieval, magical, pagan religion might have been like, and to how it might be now "reconstructed." (Louis Wilkinson is exactly the sort of person who might have helped write *High Magic's Aid*.) It also reveals how thoroughly familiar Gardner and his people were with Murray; dozens of elements from *The Witch-Cult in Western Europe* are incorporated in *High Magic's Aid*, and that is one of the major clues that allowed me to realize they had begun from her data. The book includes step-by-step descriptions of the First- and Second-Degree rituals, following the text of "Ye Bok of ye Art Magical" rather closely, and explains that these "witch" initiations have to be worked within a magical circle cast by a ceremonial magician! This is quite antithetical to current Craft practice—but it is how the Gardnerian circles had been worked, and would continue to be worked, until about 1957.

Valiente has suggested quite plausibly that Gardner may have gotten the term "Book of Shadows" from an article about an ancient Sanskrit manuscript that appeared in 1949 in *The Occult Observer*, a journal edited by Michael Houghton, the publisher of *High Magic's Aid*. Similarly, she suggests (in *Witchcraft for Tomorrow*, p. 78) that he may have gotten the term "athame" from "The Master of the Crabs" by Clark Ashton Smith in a 1947 issue of *Weird Tales*; Smith introduced it as a tool of magic, and spelled the name "arthame."

An article in the *Sunday Pictorial* for July 29, 1951, carried an article by Allen Andrews captioned "Calling All Covens." It announced the forthcoming opening of the Folklore Centre of Superstition and Witchcraft, founded by Cecil H. Williamson at the Witches Mill, Castletown, Isle of Man. The opening ceremony was to be performed by the "resident witch, Dr. Gerald B. Gardner." Williamson had put up a memorial to the estimated nine million people killed during the witch persecutions in Europe, for which Gardner later claimed credit.

In 1952 Gardner bought the museum from Williamson, and used it to display the magical and occult curiosities he had been accumulating all his life. (And in his customarily devious manner, he never mentions Williamson in any of his own writings, and gives the impression that he had himself founded the museum.) In 1951 the very last antiwitchcraft law—which had been enacted in 1736—was repealed because of lobbying by the Spiritualist churches, and this, Gardner later implied, made it possible for him to admit the existence of the religion.

I doubt that the members of the original New Forest coven intended to claim that they were a survival from the middle ages. Gardner's statements that the coven insisted on secrecy, and would only allow him to publish a description of their beliefs in the form of a novel, may reflect more than a desire for privacy. Dorothy Clutterbuck may not have allowed Gardner to claim a continuity with the past which she knew was not true. In any event, it was only after she had died in 1951 that Gardner, freed of her domination, began thinking about how to write *Witchcraft Today* in such a way that it would present a plausible claim to such continuity. That is, it was Dorothy's death in 1951, not the repeal of the 1736 Witchcraft Act, that removed Gardner's constraints.

Source Notes
Some data here has been taken from Valiente, *Rebirth of Witchcraft*, pp. 14, 30-32, 38, 40, 42, 44-45, 49-50, 56, 288-93.

3. The Book of Shadows in 1949 and 1953

In this chapter we will see what Gardner wrote in his Book of Shadows during the period between roughly 1945 and 1953. I have established the text of the Book of Shadows as it stood in about 1949 from "Ye Bok of ye Art Magical" and *High Magic's Aid*. I have established its content in 1953 from *Witchcraft Today*, "Ye Bok of ye Art Magical," *High Magic's Aid*, the Weschcke manuscripts, and the data in the Farrars 1984. The entries in Gardner's working books are not in any logical or chronological order. Also, there is really no such thing as *the* text of the Book of Shadows, because Gardner never bothered to word things the same way twice; whenever he copied something, he simultaneously rewrote it. But this, of course, is the way that an author treats his own original material; it is not how anyone treats authoritative texts preserved from an earlier generation.

Doreen Valiente does own the Books of Shadows that Gardner was using when he and Dafo initiated her in 1953. The older of them (which Stewart Farrar labeled Text A) is more or less the Book of Shadows as it stood in 1949; Gardner led her to believe that he had copied it from Dorothy Clutterbuck's Book of Shadows, but the extant evidence is that Dorothy never had any such book. The second book (which Farrar labeled Text B) is much fuller, and is essentially the Book of Shadows as it stood in 1953. The inventory of their contents has provided another control on my reconstruction.

As I observed, and as Doreen Valiente also comments, Gardner habitually copied rituals into his books piecemeal, on widely separated pages, often onto pages containing other material as well. What his reasons were for doing this one can only guess, but it did provide some protection for the "secrets," since a person not already familiar with the Craft, upon picking up such a book, would not be able to make head nor tail out of it. For these reasons, I am here placing materials in an arbitrary order in order to simplify my discussion of them. Please note that I use square brackets [these things] to indicate my own numbering, comments, and so on. I use *italics* within the text of the documents to flag passages that are word-for-word quotes from known sources.

A. The Book of Shadows in 1949.

3.1. Casting the Circle

To begin, let us note that the procedure in use before 1953 for casting the circle is described in general terms in *Witchcraft Today* on p. 28. This passage says, "It is most convenient to mark [the circle] with chalk, paint or otherwise, to show where it is; but marks on the carpet may be utilized. Furniture may be placed to indicate the bounds. The only circle that matters is the one drawn before every ceremony with either a duly consecrated Magic Sword or . . . [an] Athame. . . . The circle is usually nine feet in diameter, unless made for some very special purpose. There are two outer circles, each six inches apart, so the third circle has a diameter of eleven feet." This triple circle is derived from the procedures in *The Greater Key of Solomon*, and so we can be sure that the procedure for casting the ceremonial magician's circle given in *High Magic's Aid* is also the basic procedure for casting the witches' circle. The fact that there was originally a *triple* circle is the reason why the circle is cast, censed, or otherwise circumambulated three times at various points in these instructions.

[Page 65 of "Ye Bok of ye Art Magical" reads as follows.]

[1] *Having chosen a place* proper, *take the sickle or scimitar of Art* or a Witch's Athame, if thou mayest obtain it, *and stick it into the center, then take a cord*, and 'twere well to use the Cable Tow for this, and loop it over the Instrument, four and one half feet, and so *trace out the circumference of the circle, which* must *be* traced *either with the Sword, or the knife with the black hilt*, or it be of little avail, but ever *leave open a* door *towards the North*. Make in all 3 circles, one within the other, and write names of power between these.

[This follows the instructions in *The Greater Key of Solomon* (p. 103) exactly; the italics indicate identical wording. Next, page 46 of "Ye Bok of ye Art Magical" gives the procedures for charging the circle, as we would now call it. These are terse and cryptic, and refer to data from *The Greater Key of Solomon* that Gardner had copied onto yet other pages. Written out in full, they read as follows.]

[Text]	[Comments]
[2] First draw circle with Magic Sword or Athame.	[as in paragraph 1]
[3] Consecrate Salt and Water: Touch water with Athame, saying, "*I exorcise thee, O creature of Water, that thou cast out from Thee all the impurities and uncleannesses of the Spirits of the World of Phantasm, so they may harm me not, through the virtue of God almighty who liveth and reigneth unto the Ages of the Ages. Amen.*"	[These formulas are from *The Greater Key of Solomon*, pp. 93 and 94; the italics indicate identical wording. They are actually formulas for preparing the bathwater, and are given as such in *High Magic's Aid* (pp. 144, 265f). Doreen Valiente says (in the Farrars 1984, pp. 41-42) that some of the "names of power" are also written in Text A; Gardner included them by mistake, since *The Greater Key of Solomon* says that they are to be recited while disrobing or in the bath.]
[4] Touching Salt with Athame, say, "*The Blessing of the Father Almighty be upon this creature of Salt, and let all malignity and hindrance be cast forth hencefrom, and let all good enter herein, for without Thee man cannot live, wherefore I bless thee and invoke thee, that thou mayest aid me.*"	
[5] Then put the Salt into the water.	
[6] Sprinkle with exorcised water.	
[7] Light candles / say, "*I exorcise thee, O Creature of Fire, by Him through Whom all things have been made, so that every kind of Phantasm may retire from thee, and be unable to harm or deceive in any way, through the invocation of the Most High Creator of all. Amen.*"	[From *The Greater Key of Solomon*, p. 106.]

[8] Caution initiate (if any); warn companions; enter circle and close doors with 3 pentagrams / saying "Agla / Azoth / Adonai."

[This refers to the instructions in *The Greater Key of Solomon*, pp. 103-104, immediately after the passage that paragraph [1] is based on.]

[9] Ritual of pentacle (p. 44).

[10] Proclaim object of working.

[11] Circumambulate 3 times or more before commencing work.

[The reference here is to a "pentacle consecration" of the kind given by Crowley, *Magick*, pp. 379-382, or by Regardie, *Golden Dawn* (I, 106f, and III, 9-19).]

[12] Summon: "I summon, stir, and Call thee up, thou Mighty Ones of the East, South, West, and North" saluting and [diagram of pentacle to be drawn in the air with the magic tool, with an arrow indicating the first stroke to be from top down to left].

[A longer version of this summoning is given in *High Magic's Aid* (pp. 269f) as part of a ceremonial-magic ritual; it is based loosely on the conjurations given in *The Greater Key of Solomon*, pp. 18-35. The rule that "witches start in the East when forming the circle" (*Witchcraft Today*, p. 25) also derives from magical practice, since the sequence E, S, W, N is prescribed in *The Greater Key of Solomon* (e.g., on p. 97), by the HOGD (Regardie, *Golden Dawn*: e.g., I, 106ff), and by Crowley, *Magick*, pp. 282, 328.]

Commentary on 3.1.

The procedures here are those of Judaeo-Christian (i.e., Kabalistic) ceremonial magic, not of what is now thought of as Neopagan Witchcraft. The specific procedure given here for casting a circle to work in could come from *The Greater Key of Solomon* (e.g., pp. 14f, 96f, 103) or from almost any grimoire. The overall sequence follows closely that of *The Greater Key of Solomon*, pp. 15-17. That is, we have here precisely the situation described in *High Magic's Aid*, in which the male magician must form the circle before the female witch can work her initiation rituals.

There is no indication here of who is to carry out these procedures. Presumably the circle will be cast and charged by whoever is doing the initiating, which appears to be the sole reason for casting the circle at first. Hence the circle would be cast and charged by the Magus when he is initiating a new Witch. However, as we will see, a later draft of the casting procedure from about 1957 specifies that the Magus is to cast the circle; so we may suppose that such a rule also applied in 1949.

I have added paragraphs [3] to [5] in order to include the procedures for "exorcising" the water that are written out elsewhere in "Ye Bok of ye Art Magical"; the text on p. 46 actually leaps from [2] to [6], but logically the water must be "exorcised" before it can be sprinkled.

It could not be more obvious that Gardner has adapted the casting procedure here from *The Greater Key of Solomon*. As the Farrars (1981, p. 37 n.1) sagely comment, "That these were Gardner's own borrowings, rather than part of the traditional material he obtained from the New Forest coven which initiated him, is suggested by the fact that their English corresponds to that of Mathers, instead of deriving independently from the original Latin."

In the casting procedure in paragraph [1], the reference to the Cable Tow, which is a Masonic term for a cord used to partially tie and lead an initiate in a ritual, is Gardner's own insertion, replacing the *Greater Key of Solomon* reference to a simple piece of string used as a compass. Gardner uses the Cable Tow in his initiation rituals quite differently from the way it is used in Masonic ritual (as we will see later); and the reference to it is inserted here in order to integrate the binding and scourging that characterize his initiations more firmly into the overall ritual.

The casting procedure in "Ye Bok of ye Art Magical" shows us in miniature the origin of the Craft movement: we do not have an originally pagan ritual that has been disguised by Christian trappings; rather, Gardner began with a Judaeo-Christian ritual that he later "paganized" by removing the obviously Judaeo-Christian terms, and replacing them with terms that appear more neutral. This is also an analog for the fact that the Craft movement arises from dissatisfaction with Christianity.

Gardner obviously feels that a ritual has to be worked in a "magic circle," but the only procedures he knows for casting such a circle are from books on ceremonial magic, as is described in *High Magic's Aid*. Doreen Valiente comments (in the Farrars 1984, p. 42) that *High Magic's Aid* "was published in Old Dorothy's lifetime; so I think she and Gerald probably used the *Key of Solomon* wording for these consecration rituals." If he had learned any "traditional" procedures for casting a circle from an earlier coven, he would have used them instead of borrowing procedures, formulas, and Judaeo-Christian terminology alike from the *Greater Key of Solomon*. That is, if there had been a pre-1939 coven into which Gardner was initiated, its members either did not cast a circle to work in or else simply used the procedures of ceremonial magic. Either alternative flatly contradicts Gardner's claim in *Witchcraft Today* (p. 28) that whereas

> "the magician . . . draws a circle . . . and summons . . . demons to do his bidding, the circle being to prevent them from doing him harm, and he dare not leave it . . . the Witches' Circle . . . is to keep in the power which . . . they can raise from their own bodies [so that] they can mould it to their own will. They can and do step in and out if they wish to, but this involves some loss of power, so they avoid doing so as much as possible."

We therefore see in both "Ye Bok of ye Art Magical" and *High Magic's Aid* a situation in which Judaeo-Christian magic—which at least has a coherent theology, if its underlying assumptions are granted—provides a framework, a circle, within which non-Christian folk magic can be worked. The trend that we can see beginning with these early documents, and that is still continuing, was to find concepts that could both "explain" folk magic and be used to replace the obviously Judaeo-Christian concepts that came from the tradition of ceremonial magic.

Looking at how Neopagan Witchcraft actually functions these days, we can see that the purpose of the circle is not to keep anything in or out, but (using Eliade's concepts) to define a "sacred space" within which "worship"—something other than ordinary, workaday activities—can take place. The Craft term for this, already stated in *Witchcraft Today*, is that "the circle is between the worlds." The Craft circle is a far more portable "sacred space" than a church building.

3.2. Drawing Down the Moon

[The invocation of the Goddess appears in "Ye Bok of ye Art Magical" only buried within one of the Sabbat rituals, and in very terse form. Spelled out, it would read as follows.]

High Priestess stands in front of Altar, assumes Goddess position (arms crossed).

Magus, kneeling in front of her, draws pentacle on her body with Phallus-headed Wand, invokes,

> "I Invoke and beseech Thee, O mighty Mother of all life and fertility. *'By seed and root, by stem and bud, by leaf and flower and fruit, by Life and Love, do I invoke Thee'* to descend into the body of thy servant and High Priestess [name]."

The Moon having been drawn down, i.e., link established, Magus and other men give Fivefold Kiss:

> (kissing feet) "Blessed be thy feet, that have brought thee in these ways";
> (kissing knees) "Blessed be thy knees, that shall kneel at the sacred altar";
> (kissing womb) "Blessed be thy womb, without which we would not be";
> (kissing breasts) "Blessed be thy breasts, formed in beauty and in strength";
> (kissing lips) "Blessed be thy lips, that shall speak the sacred names."

Women all bow.

[This would then be followed by some instruction such as the following.]

If there be an initiation, then at this time the High Priestess in Goddess position (Arms Crossed) says the Charge while the Initiate stands outside the circle, or else the Magus reads it if the Initiate be a girl.

3.3. "Lift Up the Veil" [*The Charge*]

[The following gives Gardner's original wording of the Charge, from pp. 263-68 of "Ye Bok of ye Art Magical." This is the text that

Doreen Valiente rewrote into verse, then later into a new prose version.]

Listen to the words of the Great mother, who of old was also called among men Artemis, Astarte, Dione, Melusine, Aphrodite, Cerridwen, Diana, Arianrhod, Bride, and by many other names.

"At mine Altars the youth of Lacedaemon in Sparta made due sacrifice.

"*Whenever ye have need of anything, once in the month, and better it be when the moon is full, ye shall assemble in some secret place and adore the spirit of Me who am Queen of all Witcheries and magics.*

"*There ye shall assemble, ye who are fain to learn all sorcery, yet have not won its deepest secrets. To these will I teach things that are yet unknown.*

"*And ye shall be free from slavery, and as a sign that ye be really free, ye shall be naked in your rites, both men and women, and ye shall dance, sing, feast, make music, and love, all in my praise.*

"There is a Secret Door that I have made to establish the way to taste even on earth the elixir of immortality. Say 'Let ecstasy be mine, and joy on earth even to me, To Me,' For I am a gracious Goddess. *I give unimaginable joys on earth, certainty, not faith, while in life! And upon death, peace unutterable, rest, and ecstasy, nor do I demand aught in sacrifice.*"

Hear ye the words of the Star Goddess.

"*I love you: I yearn for you: pale or purple, veiled or voluptuous.*

"*I who am all pleasure, and purple and drunkenness of the innermost senses, desire you, put on the wings, arouse the coiled splendor within you, 'Come unto me.'*

"*For I am the flame that burns in the heart of every man, and the core of every Star.*

"Let it be your inmost divine self who art lost in the constant rapture of infinite joy.

"*Let the rituals be rightly performed with joy and beauty.* Remember that all acts of love and pleasure are my rituals. So let there be beauty and strength, leaping laughter, force and fire by within you.

"And if thou sayest, I have journeyed unto thee, and it availed me not, Rather shalt thou say, 'I called upon thee, and I waited patiently, and Lo, Thou wast with me from the beginning,' For they that ever desired me, shall ever attain me, even to the end of all desire."

[This would be followed by a short paragraph of instruction such as the following.]

This much of the rites must ever be performed to prepare for any initiation, whether of one degree or of all three.

Commentary on 3.2 and 3.3.

It seems simplest to comment on 3.2 and 3.3 together, since they normally fall together in a ritual. In 3.3 we have the original draft of the liturgical element usually called the "Charge of the Goddess." Since it is in careful calligraphy in "Ye Bok of ye Art Magical," it is probably an early entry. It was probably written about the same time as the initiation ritual (which it follows, and which we will look at next), that is, before 1948, and it was certainly written before 1953, when Gardner read it during Doreen Valiente's initiation.

What about content? The quotation in 3.2 is from Crowley's "Gnostic Mass" in *Magick in Theory and Practice.* The first long quotation in 3.3 is from Leland's *Aradia,* and the rest are from Crowley: first a sentence from the *Book of the Law,* no. 58, then the rest from the "Gnostic Mass." If Gardner had received anything comparable to this material from an older coven, why would he need to lift material wholesale from published sources? Notice that the line about Lacedaemon and Sparta is Gardner's own insertion, not a quotation from anything. He adds it as an attempt to claim a classical precedent for the scourging in the ritual: the allusion is to the whipping of youths before the altar of "Upright" Artemis—which was not done for "ecstasy"! All the rest of the material is a homily validating the Great Rite; hence the Charge does not make a great deal of sense if it is recited when the Great Rite (or something equally powerful) is not going to be worked. That is, the Charge was written in order to create a framework for the binding and scourging in the initiation that would—for Gardner—lead to sexual intercourse.

3.4. The Initiation

[The earliest known text of the Craft initiation rituals appears in "Ye Bok of ye Art Magical," on pp. 46-47, 91, 94-99, 101-106, 108-112, and 225-27. I have augmented the text for the first two degrees from the full script in *High Magic's Aid,* pp. 290-303.]

[*First Degree*]

Magus leaves circle by the doorway, goes to Postulant, and says, "Since there is no other brother here, I must be thy sponsor, as well as priest. I am about to give you a warning. If you are still of the same mind, answer it with these words: 'Perfect Love and Perfect Trust.'"

Placing the point of the sword to the Postulant's breast, he says, "O thou who standeth on the threshold between the pleasant world of men and the domains of the Dread Lords of the Outer Spaces, hast thou the courage to make the Assay? For I tell thee verily, it were better to rush on my weapon and perish miserably than to make the attempt with fear in thy heart."

Postulant: "I have two Passwords: Perfect Love and Perfect Trust."

Magus drops the sword point, saying, "All who approach with perfect love and perfect trust are doubly welcome."

Going around behind her, he blindfolds her, then putting his left arm around her waist and his right arm around her neck, he pulls her head back, says, "I give you the 3rd password, a Kiss to pass through this dread Door," and pushes her forward with his body, through the doorway and into the circle. Once inside, he releases her saying, "This is the way all are first brought into the circle."

Magus closes the doorway by drawing the point of the sword across it three times, joining all three circles, saying, "Agla, Azoth, Adonai," then drawing three pentacles to seal it.

Magus guides Postulant to south of altar, and whispers, "Now there is the Ordeal." Taking a short piece of cord from the altar, he ties it around her right ankle, saying, "Feet neither bound nor free." Taking a longer cord, he ties her hands together behind her back, then pulls them up, so that the arms form a triangle, and ties the cord around her neck, leaving the end dangling down in front as a Cable Tow.

With the Cable Tow in his left hand and the sword in his right hand, the Magus leads her sunwise around the circle to the east, where he salutes with the sword and proclaims, "Take heed, O Lords of the Watch towers of the East, (name), properly prepared, will be made a Priestess and a Witch."

Magus leads her similarly to the south, west, and north, making the proclamation at each quarter.

Next, clasping Postulant around the waist with his left arm, and holding the sword erect in his right hand, he makes her circumambulate three times around the circle with a half-running, half-dancing step.

He halts her at the south of the altar, and strikes eleven knells on the bell. He then kneels at her feet, saying, "In other religions the postulant kneels, as the Priests claim supreme power, but in the Art Magical, we are taught to be humble, so we kneel to welcome them and say:

"Blessed be thy feet that have brought thee in these ways." (He kisses her feet.)

"Blessed be thy knees that shall kneel at the sacred altar." (He kisses her knees.)

"Blessed be thy womb, without which we would not be." (He kisses her Organ of Generation.)

"Blessed by thy breasts, formed in beauty and in strength." (He kisses her breasts.)

"Blessed be thy lips, which shall utter the sacred names." (He kisses her lips.)

Take measure.

Magus says, "Be pleased to kneel," and helps her kneel before the altar. He ties the end of the Cable Tow to a ring in the altar, so that the postulant is bent sharply forward, with her head almost touching the floor. He also ties her feet together with the short cord.

Magus strikes three knells on the bell and says, "Art ready to swear that thou wilt always be true to the Art?"

Witch: "I am."

Magus strikes seven knells on the bell and says, "Before ye are sworn, art willing to pass the ordeal and be purified?"

Witch: "I am."

Magus strikes eleven knells on the bell, takes the scourge from the altar, and gives a series of three, seven, nine, and 21 strokes with the scourge across the postulant's buttocks.

Magus says, "Ye have bravely passed the test. Art always ready to help, protect, and defend thy Brothers and Sisters of the Art?"

Witch: "I am."

Magus: "Art armed?"

Witch: "With a knife in my hair."

Magus: "Then on that knife wilt thou swear absolute secrecy?"

Witch: "I will."

Magus: "Then say after me. 'I, (name), in the presence of the Mighty Ones, do of my own will and accord, most solemnly swear that I will ever keep secret and never reveal the secrets of the Art, except it be to a proper person, properly prepared, within a circle such as I am now in. All this I swear by my hopes of a future life, mindful that my measure has been taken, and may my weapons turn against me if I break this my solemn oath.' "

Magus now unbinds her feet, unties the Cable Tow from the altar, removes the blindfold, and helps her up to her feet.

Magus says, "I hereby sign thee with the triple sign.

"I consecrate thee with oil." (He anoints her with oil on the womb, the right breast, the left breast, and the womb again.)

"I consecrate thee with wine." (He anoints her with wine in the same pattern.)

"I consecrate thee with my lips" (he kisses her in the same pattern), "Priestess and Witch."

Magus now unbinds her hands and removes the last cord, saying, "Now I Present to thee the Working Tools of a Witch.

"First the Magic Sword. With this, as with the Athame, thou canst form all Magic Circles, dominate, subdue, and punish all rebellious Spirits and Demons, and even persuade the Angels and Geniuses. With this in your hand you are the ruler of the Circle. [Here "kiss" means that the initiate kisses the tool, and the Magus then kisses the Witch being initiated.]

"Next I present the Athame. This is the true Witch's weapon and has all the powers of the Magic Sword [kiss].

"Next I present the White-Handled Knife. Its use is to form all instruments used in the Art. It can only be properly used within a Magic Circle [kiss].

"Next I present the Wand. Its use is to call up and control certain Angels and geniuses, to whom it would not be mete to use the Magic Sword [kiss].

"Next I present the pentacles. These are for the purpose of calling up appropriate Spirits [kiss].

"Next I present the Censer of Incense. This is used to encourage and welcome Good Spirits and to banish Evil Spirits [kiss].

"Next I present the scourge. This is a sign of power and domination. It is also to cause suffering and purification, for it is written, to learn you must suffer and be purified. Art willing to suffer to learn?"

Witch: "I am."[kiss]

Magus: "Next, and lastly I present the Cords. They are of use to bind the sigils in the Art, the material basis, and to enforce thy will. Also they are necessary in the oath. I Salute thee in the name of Aradia and Cernunnos, newly made Priestess and Witch."

Magus strikes seven knells on the bell and kisses Witch again, then circumambulates with her, proclaiming to the four quarters, "Hear, ye Mighty Ones, (name) hath been consecrated Priestess and Witch of the Gods."

(Note, if ceremony ends here, close circle with "I thank ye for attending, and I dismiss ye to your pleasant abodes. Hail and farewell." If not, go to next degree.)

[*Second Degree*]

Magus binds Witch as before, but does not blindfold her, and circumambulates with her, proclaims to the four quarters, "Hear, ye Mighty Ones, (name), a duly consecrated Priestess and Witch, is now properly prepared to be made a High Priestess and Witch Queen."

Magus now leads her thrice around the circle with the half-running, half-dancing step, halts south of the altar, has the Witch kneel, and ties her down to the altar as before.

Magus: "To attain this sublime degree, it is necessary to suffer and be purified. Art ready to suffer to learn?"

Priestess Witch: "I am."

Magus: "I prepare thee to take the great oath."

He strikes three knells on the bell, and again gives the series of three, seven, nine, and 21 strokes with the scourge as before.

Magus: "I now give thee a new name: _____. [kiss]

Magus: "Repeat thy new name after me, <saying> I, (name), swear upon my mother's womb and by mine Honor among men and among my brothers and sisters of the Art, that I will never reveal to any at all any of the secrets of the Art, except it be to a worthy person, properly prepared, in the center of a Magic Circle, such as I am now in. This I swear by my hopes of Salvation, my past lives, and my hopes of future ones to come, and I devote myself to utter destruction if I break this my solemn oath."

Magus kneels, placing left hand under her knees and right

hand on her head, thus forming magic link.

Magus: "I hereby will all my power into you." Wills.

Magus now unties her feet, unties the Cable Tow from the altar, and helps the Witch to her feet.

Magus: "I hereby sign and consecrate you with the great Magic Sign. Remember how it is formed and you will always recognize it.

"I consecrate thee with oil." (He anoints her with oil on her womb, right breast, left hip, right hip, left breast, and womb again, thus tracing a point-down pentacle.)

"I consecrate thee with wine." (He anoints her with wine in the same pattern.)

"I consecrate thee with my lips" (he kisses her in the same pattern), "High Priestess and Witch Queen."

Magus now unbinds Witch's hands and removes the cord, saying, "Newly made High Priestess and Witch Queen" [kiss] "you will now use the working tools in turn. First, the Magic Sword; with it you will scribe the Magic Circle [kiss]

"Secondly, the Athame" [The initiate uses the Athame and the next four tools to complete the casting and charging of the circle, as described in *High Magic's Aid*, p. 302.] (Form Circle) [kiss]

"Thirdly, the White Handled Knife" (use) [kiss]

"Fourthly, the Wand" (Wave to 4 Quarters) [kiss]

"Fifthly, the Pentacle" (Show to 4 Quarters) kiss]

"Sixthly, the Censer of Incense" (Circle, cense) [kiss]

"Seventhly, the cords; bind me as I bound you."

Witch binds Magus and ties him to Altar.

Magus: "Learn, in Witchcraft, thou must ever return triple. As I scourged thee, so thou must scourge me, but triple. So where you received 3, return 9; where you received 7, return 21; where you received 9, return 27; where you received 21, return 63."

Witch scourges Magus as instructed, 120 strokes total.

Magus: "Thou hast obeyed the Law. But mark well, when thou receivest good, so equally art bound to return good threefold."

Witch now unbinds Magus and helps him to his feet.

Magus, taking the new Initiate by the hand and holding the Athame in the other, passes once round the Circle, proclaiming at the Four Quarters, "Hear, Ye Mighty Ones, (name) hath been duly consecrated High Priestess and Witch Queen."

(Note, if ceremony ends here, close circle with "Hail and farewell." If not go to next degree.)

[*Third Degree*]

Magus: "Ere we proceed with this sublime degree, I must beg purification at thy hands."

High Priestess binds Magus and ties him down to the altar. She circumambulates three times, and scourges Magus with three, seven, nine, and 21 strokes. She then unbinds him and helps him to his feet.

Magus now binds the High Priestess and ties her down to the altar. He circumambulates, proclaiming to the four quarters, "Hear, ye mighty Ones, the twice consecrate and Holy (name), High Priestess and Witch Queen, is properly prepared and will now proceed to erect the Sacred Altar."

Magus scourges High Priestess with three, seven, nine, and 21 strokes.

Cakes and wine may now be taken [see section 3.5].

Magus: "Now I must reveal to you a great Mystery." [kiss]

Note: if High Priestess has performed this rite before, omit these words.

High Priestess assumes Osiris position. [To the right of this line appears a set of illuminated concentric triangles, point down. These probably represent the female genitalia.]

Magus: "Assist me to erect the Ancient Altar, at which in days past all worshipped, the Great Altar of all things. For in the old times a woman was the Altar. Thus was the altar made and so placed [Priestess lies down in such a way that her vagina is approximately at the center of the circle], and the sacred place was the point within the center of the circle, as we of old times have been taught, that the point within the center is the origin of all things. Therefore should we adore it." [kiss]

"*Therefore, whom we adore, we also invoke, by the power of the lifted lance.*" Invokes.

"*O circle of stars* [kiss], *whereof our Father is but the younger brother* [kiss],

"*Marvel beyond imagination, soul of infinite space, before whom time is ashamed, the mind bewildered and understanding dark, not unto thee may we attain unless thine image be of love* [kiss].

"*Therefore, by seed and root, and stem and bud and leaf and flower and fruit do we invoke thee, O, Queen of space, O dew of light, O continuous one of the Heavens* [kiss].

"Let it be ever thus, that men speak not of Thee as one, but as none, and let them not speak of thee at all, since thou art continuous, for thou art the point within the circle [kiss], which we adore [kiss], the fount of life without which we would not be [kiss].

"And in this way truly are erected the Holy Twin Pillars Boaz and Jachin [kisses breasts]. In beauty and strength were they erected, to the wonder and glory of all men." (Eightfold Kiss: 3 points, Lips, 2 Breasts and back to lips; 5 points)

"O Secrets of secrets that art hidden in the being of all lives. Not thee do we adore, for that which adoreth is also thou. Thou art that and That am I [kiss].

"I am the flame that burns in every man, and in the core of every star [kiss].

"I am Life and the giver of Life, yet therefore is the knowledge of me the Knowledge of Death [kiss].

"I am alone, the *Lord within ourselves whose name is Mystery of Mysteries* [kiss].

"Make open the path of intelligence between us. For these truly are the 5 points of fellowship [on the right appears an illuminated diagram of the point-up triangle above the pentacle, the symbol for the third degree], feet to feet, knee to knee, groin to groin, breast to breast, arms around back, lips to lips, by the Great and Holy Names Abracadabra, Aradia, and Cernunnos."

Magus and High Priestess: *"Encourage our hearts, Let thy Light crystallize itself in our blood, fulfilling us of Resurrection. For there is no part of us that is not of the Gods."*

(Exchange Names.)

Closing the Circle

High Priestess circumambulates, proclaiming, "The twice consecrate High Priestess greets ye Mighty Ones, and dismisseth ye to your pleasant abodes. Hail and Farewell." She draws the banishing pentacle at each quarter.

Commentary on 3.4.

The First-Degree Initiation is now the most widely published of all the Gardnerian rituals, having been described in more or less complete detail by Glass, Johns, Holzer, Huson, the Farrars (1971 and 1984), and *The Grimoire of Lady Sheba*. Its first full publication, however, was in *High Magic's Aid* (pp. 290-296) in 1949; so 1948 is the latest date at which it could have been written.

The text in "Ye Bok of ye Art Magical" is actually the draft on which the expanded and cleaned-up version in *High Magic's Aid* is based. Many revisions made in a narrow point in "Ye Bok of ye Art Magical" were also made in the version in *High Magic's Aid*; and passages marked "not used" (or some such) in "Ye Bok of ye Art Magical" are not reflected in *High Magic's Aid*. On the other hand, some changes in "Ye Bok of ye Art Magical"—for example, those about taking the measure—were not made in *High Magic's Aid* at all, and yet they appear in later versions of the ritual; so they must have been entered in "Ye Bok of ye Art Magical" after *High Magic's Aid* had gone to the printer in about 1948. And since this initiation ritual is apparently the earliest of the "Craft" entries in "Ye Bok of ye Art Magical", it follows that the rest of the "Craft" entries in "Ye Bok of ye Art Magical" must postdate 1948. Given a book with no dates in it at all, this is a good beginning for a chronology for the Gardnerian rituals.

Next, let's consider whether anything here probably comes from a native British non-Christian religious tradition (or something like that). Much light can be shed on this question by considering a ritual with a similar purpose, the Neophyte ritual of the Hermetic Order of the Golden Dawn, as given by Regardie, *Golden Dawn* (II, 12-43). For the most part, the Golden Dawn rituals seem quite unlike current Craft rituals, since they consisted mainly of long set speeches full of metaphysical moral uplift. However, the Neophyte ritual contains so many similarities to the Gardnerian first-degree initiation that we must suppose Gardner used something like it as a source (indeed, at this time we can suppose that he specifically used rituals from the Society of the Inner Light). Let us list these similarities, in order.

1. An Officer purifies by sprinkling the temple, East, South, West, North.
2. Another Officer censes the temple, in the same pattern.
3. All the Officers circumambulate the temple three times.
4. The candidate (C) is led in, blindfolded, and with a threefold Cord about his waist.
5. C is given a new name.

6. C is purified by being sprinkled, consecrated by being censed.

7. C is made to kneel and repeat an oath of secrecy, from which we can pick out phrases: "I, . . . in the presence of . . . do of my own free will . . . most solemnly promise to keep secret . . . Furthermore, if I break this, my Magical Obligation, I submit myself . . . " and there are some relevant phrases in later oaths: "never to reveal the secrets . . . save in" (p. 165) and "if I fail . . . may . . . my power in Magic cease" (p. 215).

8. C is led sunwise around the circle 1.5 times from North to South, where he is stopped, challenged, and sprinkled and censed again. He is then led sunwise 1.25 circuits to the West, where he is stopped, is threatened with a sword, and has to give a password, which his guide supplies for him. He is then led 1.25 times around to the North, and 1.25 times around to the East, where the two procedures are repeated, but in the East the threat is made with a scepter. He is then led to the altar at the center.

9. All including C kneel, and the Hierophant invokes the "Mighty One."

10. C is raised to his feet, has the blindfold removed, and is formally accepted into membership.

11. C is then shown various secrets.

12. C is sprinkled and censed again, has the Threefold Cord removed, and is given the badge of his degree.

13. C is proclaimed a new initiate to all present.

14. The temple is then "closed" by a withershins circumambulation.

We can also find some exact correspondences with Masonic rituals as described by Duncan, pp. 29-34:

"the Senior Deacon . . . presents one point of the compasses to the candidate's naked left breast. . . . The Deacon . . . puts a rope, called a cable-tow, once round his neck, letting it drag behind. . . . Senior Deacon asks if candidate is "duly and truly prepared, and properly vouched for." . . . The candidate, having been brought in, is conducted once around the Lodge, in the order east, south, west (and presumably ending in the north). . . . The candidate takes an oath containing the words, "I . . . of my own free will . . . in the presence of [God and saints] most solemnly . . . swear that I will always . . . conceal, and never reveal, any of the arts . . . of the hidden mysteries . . . except to a true and lawful brother . . . in a regularly constituted Lodge . . . All this I most solemnly . . . swear . . . without any mental reservation . . . binding myself under no less penalty that of [gruesome details] . . . should I ever knowingly violate this my . . . obligation."

Page 41 of Duncan says: "it is necessary that you should have the working tools of an Entered Apprentice." The ruler and hammer are then shown and explained to the new Apprentice. The homilies on the "emblems" are even more similar to what follows here. Almost all the Masonic symbols are referred to as "working tools." Furthermore, the third degree in the Blue Lodges is referred to repeatedly as a "sublime degree."

To reinforce all this, let us notice two passages from Dewar's article on "Masonic Ceremony": "The drama of the third initiation ceremony is the most powerful of the craft degrees" (p. 101); in the "third-degree working," a death and rebirth are enacted, then "the candidate is read a charge," and is asked to "demonstrate the secret signs of their degrees" (p. 103).

Now, it cannot be claimed that these similarities are fortuitous, that all initiations into secret societies will be more or less similar in general. The similarities here are both specific and numerous, occur in the same order, and include the almost identical phrases in the oaths. The only element actually needed for a "mystery initiation," after all, is an oath of secrecy. Many of the other elements here—the blindfold, the new name, the censing and sprinkling, challenge with a sword and password given by guide, the showing of "secrets," the formal proclamation—are perfectly obvious as possible elements for such a ritual. But that all should happen to occur, and in the same order, in the two rituals is quite outside the bounds of probability. Hence Gardner must have used some such Masonic ritual as his major source for this initiation ritual. If he had been initiated into an earlier coven by means of some other sort of ritual, why would he not have used that ritual here?

Now that we have identified the Masonic and Golden Dawn elements in this ritual, let us consider Gardner's own additions.

1. The triangle binding of the arms behind the back is Gardner's own addition. It is simply the way he liked to be bound while being

scourged.

2. The scourging of forty strokes is Gardner's addition. There is no reference to scourging in any Masonic or magical ritual that I have yet seen.

3. The integrating of the scourging into the oath-taking is Gardner's addition.

4. The presenting of the scourge and the cords as magical tools is Gardner's addition. The presenting itself is Masonic, and all the other tools come from *The Greater Key of Solomon*, but not the scourge or cords.

5. In the second-degree ritual, Gardner would have given the woman initiate forty strokes, but she would then give him 120.

6. In the third-degree ritual, after having some cakes and wine, Gardner and the new High Priestess again give each other forty strokes, and this leads to sexual intercourse, at the words "groin to groin."

Hear a plain truth: the reason Gardner included all this scourging is that he could not "work the Great Rite" without it. As Gibson says (p. 269), "the whole point of the exercise is to overcome impotence and, having been whipped to erection, the 'victims' are as a rule only too happy to effect penetration of the nearest complacent vagina." Furthermore, the reason Gardner created a type of "witchcraft" that usually proceeds by "working a script" is that this is the situation demanded by his sexual needs. Gibson goes on to say, "The beatings . . . are, invariably, ritualistic in character. Nothing unforeseen is ever allowed to happen, and the ceremony, carried out with great solemnity, proceeds according to a set plan, any variation in which would result in a loss of meaning, power, and effectiveness: the spell would be broken, the magic dispersed. Spontaneity is totally absent from these performances." Gibson is here describing a prostitute beating a client—but any "orthodox" Gardnerian will immediately recognize this description as being typical of Gardnerian circles as well.

Now hear another: anyone who can have sex without being scourged has no reason to include scourging in the ritual.

Leaving the scourging aside, we can see that in this third-degree ritual we are dealing with a genuinely sacramental attitude toward sexuality, not an exploitative one. This heightening of significance, from "mere sex" to sacrament, is the reason for all the quotes (indicated by italics) from Crowley's "Gnostic Mass" in the third section of the initiation. Gardner does not include this third-degree ritual in *High Magic's Aid*, but he does hint at it when he has Morven say (p. 300), "after that, there is what is called a degree. There is no oath, and all who have taken the second degree are qualified to work it, but 'tis the quintessence of Magic, and 'tis not to be used lightly, and then only with one whom you love and are loved by, may it be done, all else were sin."

Unlike all the Masonic ritual, the concept of sexual intercourse as initiation actually might come from a genuinely pagan tradition. Sex magic has long been used to promote fertility of crops and flocks (and I beg off from providing references on this point). Fertility magic and initiation overlap in the concept of the "sacred marriage," where the King (embodying the people) and the Queen (embodying the homeland) consummate their marriage for the benefit of the cosmos. We find this concept reflected in the Irish coronation ritual, in the Akitu Festival of Babylon (as described by Gaster), and, of course, in the vision of the Marriage of the Lamb and the New Jerusalem in the Apocalypse of John, which is the particular source of the marriage imagery in the Liturgy of the Eucharist.

In fact, where sexual intercourse occurs as part of a "pagan" or non-Christian religious initiation, it is always used during the first initiation that the person undergoes (as among the Ozark witches), not the second or third; hence the procedure here, in which the new witch is taken through all three stages at once, is actually much closer to what is known of pagan or witch initiations in general than the later pattern (of initiations separated by a year and a day) would be. However, the historical probability is that Gardner had the concept from Crowley, who in turn had it from P. B. Randolph.

The final procedure, for closing the circle, is based on the "license to depart" of ceremonial magic (e.g., on pp. 38 and 52 of *The Greater Key of Solomon*). A different version of this formula appears on p. 296 of *High Magic's Aid*.

3.5. Cakes and Wine

[This consists of p. 28 of "Ye Bok of ye Art Magical." To the left of the title "Of the Wine" appear the letters O.T.O., as Doreen Valiente interpreted them to me.]

Magus kneels, fills Cup, offers to Witch [she is seated on the altar, holding her athame, and the Priest kneels before her, holding up the cup].

Witch, holding Athame between palms, places point in cup.

Magus: "As the Athame is the Male, so the Cup is the female; so, conjoined, they bring blessedness."

Witch lays aside Athame, takes Cup in both hands, drinks and gives drink.

Magus holds paten to Witch, who blesses with Athame, then eats and gives to eat.

Commentary on 3.5.

Clearly the sources of this consecration are Judaeo-Christian. The action of placing the athame in the cup no doubt comes from Crowley's "Gnostic Mass" in *Magick in Theory and Practice*, pp. 356f, 359f (though ultimately it comes from the Grail legends), but whereas Crowley's concern was to attack the orthodox Catholic Mass, the concern here is the positive one of emphasizing the similar and inherent goodness of wine, cake, and sex. Again we find, in the Magus' speech, sex glorified as the greatest sacrament. In fact, the phrase in the Sabbat rituals about "the Great rite . . . in token" refers to this consecration, as is now common knowledge in the Craft.

3.6. The Sabbat Rituals

[On pp. 271-288 of "Ye Bok of ye Art Magical" are outlines of rituals for the four cross-quarter days. The outlines are terse and cryptic, but they do not differ in any essential way from the later texts of the Sabbat rituals. They can be fleshed out as follows.]

November Eve

Walk or slow dance, Magus leading High Priestess, both carrying Phallic wand or broom, people with torches or candles. Witch chant or song:

> "Eko, eko, Azarak
> Eko, eko,
> Bazabi lacha bachabe
> Lamac cahi achababe
> Karrellyos
>
> Lamac lamac Bachalyas

Cabahagy sabalyos
Baryolos

Lagoz atha cabyolas
Samahac atha famolas
Hurrahya!"

Form circle.

High Priestess assumes Goddess position.

High Priest gives her Fivefold Kiss and is scourged.

All are purified [that is, bound and scourged with forty strokes, as in the initiation rituals].

Magus assumes God position.

High Priestess invokes with Athame: "Dread Lord of the shadows, god of *'life and the giver of life. Yet is the knowledge of thee the knowledge of death.'* Open wide, I pray thee, thy gates through which all must pass. Let our dear ones who have gone before, return this night to make merry with us. And when our time comes, as it must, O thou the comforter, the consoler, the giver of peace and rest, we will enter thy realms gladly and unafraid, for we know that when rested and refreshed among our dear ones, we shall be born again by thy grace and the grace of the Great Mother. Let it be in the same place and the same time as our beloved ones, and may we meet and know, and love them again. Descend, we pray thee, upon thy servant and Priest (name)."

High Priestess gives Fivefold Kiss to High Priest.

Initiations if any; all others are purified.

(Note: Couples may purify each other if they will.)

Cakes and wine.

The Great Rite if possible, either in token or truly.

Dismiss [the guardians, and close down the magic circle; the people then stay to] feast and dance.

February Eve

After usual opening, all are doubly purified [that is, with eighty strokes].

Dance round outside circle, High Priestess with sword girded on and drawn, Phallic wand in left hand.

Enter circle.

High Priest assumes God position.

High Priestess gives Fivefold Kiss, invokes: "Dread Lord of

death and Resurrection, *life and the giver of life, Lord within ourselves, whose name is Mystery of Mysteries, encourage our hearts. Let the light crystalize in our blood, fulfilling us of resurrection, for there is no part of us that is not of the gods.* Descend we pray thee upon this thy servant and Priest (name)."

All should be purified in sacrifice before him. He then purifies the High Priestess with his own hands, and others if he will.

Cakes and wine.

Great Rite if possible, in token or real.

Games·and dance as the people will.

Dismiss [the guardians, and close down the magic circle; the people then stay to] feast and dance.

May Eve

If possible ride poles, brooms etc. High Priestess leading, quick dance step, singing

> "O do not tell the priests of our arts.
>   For they would call it sin,
> For we will be in the woods all night
>   A conjuring summer in.
> And we bring you good news by word of mouth
>   For women, cattle, and corn:
> The sun is coming up from the south,
>   With oak and ash, and thorn."

Meeting dance if possible.

Form circle as usual, and purify.

High Priestess assumes Goddess position; officers all give her the Fivefold Kiss.

She purifies all.

High Priestess again assumes Goddess position.

Magus invokes, draws down moon, "I invoke thee and call upon thee, O mighty Mother of us all, bringer of all fruitfulness, *'By seed and root, by stem and bud, by leaf and flower and fruit, by life and love, do we invoke thee,'* to descend upon the body of the servant and Priestess here."

High Priest gives Fivefold Kiss to High Priestess.

All should be purified in sacrifice before her, and she should purify Magus and some others with her own hands.

Cakes and wine.

Games.

Great Rite if possible, in token or truly.

Dismiss [the guardians, and close down the magic circle; the people then stay to] feast and dance.

August Eve

If possible, ride poles, broomsticks, etc.

Meeting Dance if possible.

Form circle.

Purify.

High Priestess stands in pentacle position.

Magus invokes her: "O mighty Mother of us all, Mother of all fruitfulness, give us fruit and grain, flocks and herds and children to the tribe that we be mighty, by thy rosy love, do thou descend upon thy servant and Priestess (name) here."

High Priest gives Fivefold Kiss to High Priestess.

Candle game: Seated, the men form a circle, passing a lighted candle from hand to hand "deosil." The women form circle outside, trying to blow it out over their shoulders. Whoever's hand it is in when it is blown out is 3 times purified by whoever blew it out, giving Fivefold Kiss in return. This game may go on as long as the people like.

Cakes and wine, and any other games you like.

Dismiss [the guardians, and close down the magic circle; the people then stay to] feast and dance.

Commentary on 3.6.

The four rituals in "Ye Bok of ye Art Magical" are virtually identical in content with those included in the Weschcke documents, even though they are separated by ten years; obviously there was little rewriting of them. These Sabbat rituals mostly incorporate the basic procedures for all rituals, with some rather minor variations. The invocations are compounded of quotations from Crowley (from the "Gnostic Mass" in *Magick in Theory and Practice*, pp. 351-360, exactly the same passages used in the Charge, which immediately precedes these Sabbat rituals in "Ye Bok of ye Art Magical") and of bits of liturgy already used in the initiation rituals. The verse for May Eve is from Kipling, of course (though perhaps relatively few Americans can recognize Kipling, or any other poetry, these days). There is nothing new here, nothing that might come from pagan celebrations of the seasons.

The calligraphy here is plain, but very neat; by this criterion, these pages might have been written fairly early, about 1949 or so. However, the rituals are rather sketchy, as if "Ye Bok of ye Art Magical" were being used merely as a notebook, and seem to be addressing a situation in which perhaps a dozen people (at least, more than two or three) are meeting, though perhaps this is still wishful thinking. These indications point toward a date when the group had been growing for a few years, that is, around 1952.

However, "Ye Bok of ye Art Magical" does not contain any rituals for the Lesser Sabbats at the solstices and equinoxes, whereas *Witchcraft Today* contains a Yule ritual. If "Ye Bok of ye Art Magical" had been in use by a coven when that ritual was being written in 1953, then very likely the ritual would have been copied into it. Since it was not, we must deduce that "Ye Bok" was not being used by a coven in late 1953, when *Witchcraft Today* was being written, and was already or soon to be retired from service.

The "meeting dance" at the beginning of the Lammas ritual is probably the double-spiral dance described in *Witchcraft Today* (p. 167). Many have failed to notice its significance (Farrar 1971 did not describe it at all) or have confused it with a whirling dance given by Crowley (*Magick*, p. 80); it is discussed by the Farrars (1984). It is actually a British folk dance, often called "Troytown." In the NROOGD, we combined it with the "Thout, tout a tout tout, throughout and about" words of the Somersetshire witches (*Witch-Cult in Western Europe*), set to a simple tune; and it quickly became, and remains, one of NROOGD's biggest crowd pleasers.

If Gardner had received any information about traditional ways to celebrate these Celtic festivals from the coven he claimed initiation into, why did he not use it for these rituals? And if that coven did not celebrate the Sabbats, then what in the world did it celebrate? Obviously, if Gardner had known any traditional rituals for the Sabbats, he would have used them, instead of piecing these rituals together from bits of folklore, quotes from Crowley, and parts of the workings intended to be used at almost any meeting. It will not do to argue that "pagans" would have gone for the "Great Rite" (by another name), feasting, and dancing, and would not have bothered with drawing magic circles. The human need for meaningful, periodic rituals seems to be as deep and as ancient as any other need, and all religious ritual sets apart some sort of "sacred time" and "sacred space" to distinguish it from ordinary time and space. Hence a pre-1939 coven would have had some way of doing that.

If we ask just what structural principle underlies these rituals, the answer becomes fairly obvious: they are focused on scourging, and on meeting Gardner's sexual needs. In fact, they generally reproduce the pattern of the initiations exactly, as follows.

November Eve: the High Priest is scourged with forty strokes; then all are bound and scourged with forty strokes; then follows either initiations or purifications of all with forty strokes; then cakes and wine; then the Great Rite "if possible."

February Eve: all are purified with eighty strokes; then all are purified before the High Priest with forty strokes; then he purifies others with forty strokes; then comes cakes and wine; and then the Great Rite "if possible."

May Eve: all are purified with forty strokes; then the High Priestess purifies all with forty strokes; then all are purified before her with forty strokes; she purifies the High Priest and others with her own hands (rather than the scourge?); then come cakes and wine; then the Great Rite "if possible."

August Eve: Here the pattern is reversed; there is only the purification at the beginning, and the Great Rite is not called for—because without all the scourgings it was not possible.

Most current members of the Craft, not being obsessed with scourging, find these rituals to be quite uninteresting, as well as unsuitable for the large public gatherings at the Sabbats that have become fairly common since the late 1960s. As a result, they have been replaced by much more elaborate and much more carefully researched reconstructions of what various sorts of European pagan festivals might have been like.

3.7. Consecrating Tools

["Ye Bok of ye Art Magical" contains, on pp. 22-25, 30-33, the following procedures from *The Greater Key of Solomon* for consecrating tools; these have been incorporated into later drafts of the Book of Shadows.]

In order to carry out the greatest and most important Operations of the Art, various Instruments are necessary, [such] as a Knife with a white hilt, another with a black hilt, [etc.] . . . With this Knife [with the white hilt] thou mayest perform all the necessary operations of the Art, except the Circles. . . . the Knife with the black hilt [is] for making the Circle.

Swords are also frequently necessary for use in Magical Arts. Thou shalt therefore take a new sword which thou shalt clean and polish . . . ; sprinkle and cense it, and repeat over it the following conjuration: "I conjure thee, O Sword, by these names . . . that thou servest me for a strength and a defence in all Magical Operations, against all mine enemies, visible and invisible. . . . I conjure thee anew . . . O Sword, that thou servest me for a protection in all adversities. . . . I conjure thee, O Instrument of Steel, by God the Father Almighty, . . . that thou receive such virtue that thou mayest obtain without deceit the end which I desire in all things where I shall use thee." [pp. 98, 101, 118]

[The symbols to be inscribed on the various tools are shown in two plates, reproduced here as Figures 3.1 and 3.2.]

It was the material in these first seven sections, plus some other materials from *The Greater Key of Solomon*, that Gardner copied about 1952 into the first Book of Shadows as such, the one now owned by Doreen Valiente that the Farrars (1984, p. 3) label "Text A." In 1976 I had already deduced from the internal evidence in "Ye Bok of ye Art Magical" that these materials had been copied into a new book about 1952. Hence it was a pleasure to find from the discussion of "Text A" in Chapters 1-4 of the Farrars' 1984 book that its contents exactly matched what I had deduced. But this also proves that Text A, "Gerald Gardner's own Book of Shadows," was in fact copied from "Ye Bok of ye Art Magical," not from any hypothetical book ever owned by Dorothy Clutterbuck.

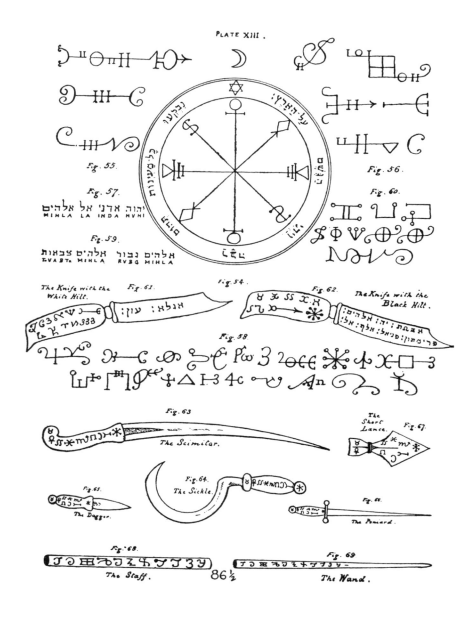

Figure 3.1.

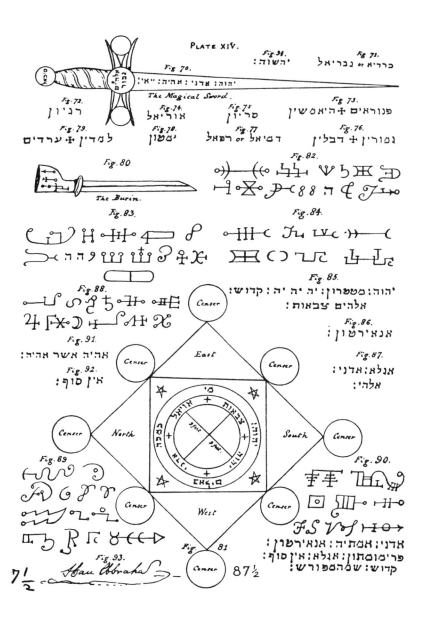

Figure 3.2.

B. The Book of Shadows in 1953.

I reconstruct the text of the Book of Shadows in 1953 from the sources listed at the beginning of this chapter. This is very close to Text B, the second Book of Shadows owned by Doreen Valiente, and the one that Gardner was actually using when he and Dafo initiated Doreen in 1953. However, Gardner continued using Text B for the next year or two, so that some of its contents were not made final until about 1955 or 1956.

3.8. On Chants

[This entry consists of the first paragraph on p. 151 of "Ye Bok of ye Art Magical." The writing is fairly careful and fairly legible: not as neat as in the Charge, much neater than in the rest of the entries we will consider. The words within the curly brackets {these things} were written in the Theban script, a magical alphabet published in Francis Barrett's *The Magus* in 1801.]

Of old there were many chants and songs used especially in the Dances. Many of these have been forgotten by us here, but we know that they used cries of {IAU} which seems muchly like the cries {EIO} or {EAUIE} of the ancients. Much dependeth on the pronunciation if this be so. In my youth, when I heard {IAU} it seemed to be {AEIOU}, or rather, {AAA.EE.I.OOOO.UU}. This may be but the natural way to prolong it to make it fit for a call, but it suggesteth that these be possibly the {INITIALS} of an invocation as {AGLA] is said to be, and of sooth 'tis said that the whole {HEBREW ALPHABET} is said to be such, and for this reason is recited as a most powerful charm, but at least this is certain, these cries during the dances do have profound effect, as I myself have seen.

Commentary on 3.8.

The entries in "Ye Bok of ye Art Magical" that I deal with here in Sections 3.8 to 3.12 are all written from much the same viewpoint as *Witchcraft Today*. We find use of archaizing language, a "present time" that seems to waver between the eighteenth and twentieth centuries, and a great concern with making it seem plausible that there could have been a "secret history" of witchcraft unknown to occultists, historians, and persecutors alike. As we will see, much of the material in these five sections was used directly or rewritten in *Witchcraft Today* or in later documents in the Book of Shadows.

There is a certain amount of experimenting going on here, attempting to find just the right tone to use in *Witchcraft Today*. Consider the opening lines: "Of old there were . . . Many of these have been forgotten by us here . . . In my youth, when I heard . . . These cries . . . have profound effect, as I myself have seen." Who is speaking here? Gardner? Apparently. But the implicit claim here to have been in the circle as a youth contradicts his published claim to have been initiated in 1939. This first paragraph, which is based on Graves' speculations about ancient mystical vowel sounds (see *The White Goddess*, particularly Chapter 16), seems to be a precursor of the comments about chants in *Witchcraft Today* on p. 167.

This paragraph was copied into Text B, where a second, similar paragraph, discussing various chants given by Murray, was added to it. Valiente (Farrars 1984, p. 56) argues that this passage, since it cannot be true of Gardner, must be from Dorothy Clutterbuck's Book of Shadows. But the real explanation, I am sure, is that Gardner had simply not yet decided on all the details of what his public claims would be. More examples of writing from about 1952 in exactly the same tone as these documents also appear in Text B (see the Farrars 1984, pp. 53-57, 61-62).

3.9. To Help the Sick

[This consists of the rest of the material on pp. 151-54 of "Ye Bok of ye Art Magical."]

[1] Ever remember the promise of the goddess, "For ecstasy is mine and joy on earth" so let there ever be joy in your heart. Greet people with joy, be glad to see them. If times be hard, think, "It might have been worse. I at least have known the joys of the Sabbath, and I will know them again." Think of the grandeur, beauty, and Poetry of the rites, of the loved ones you meet through them. If you dwell on this inner joy, your health will be better. You must try to banish all fear, for it will really touch you. It may hurt your body, but your soul is beyond it all.

[2] And ever remember, that if you help others it makes you for-

get your own woes. And if another be in pain, do what you may to distract his attention from it. Do not say "You have no pain," but if you may, administer the drugs which sooth as well as those that cure. But ever strive to make them believe they are getting better. Install into them happy thoughts. If you can only get this into his inner mind so that it be always [believed?].

[3] To this end it is not wrong to let people think that we of the cult have more power than we have. For the truth is that if they believe we have more power than we really possess, we do really possess these powers, insomuch we can do good to them.

[4] You must try to find out about people. If you tell a slightly sick man, "You are looking better. You will soon be well," he will feel better, but if he is really ill, or in pain, his Knowledge that he is in pain will cause him to doubt your words in future. But if you give him one of the drugs and then say, "The pain is growing less. Soon it will be gone," because the pain goes, the next time you say, "The pain is going," he will believe you and the pain will really get less. But you must ever say so with conviction, and this conviction must come from your believing it yourself, because you yourself know that if you can fix his mind so that he believes you, it is true.

[5] 'Tis often better to look exactly between their eyes, looking as if your eyes pierced their heads, opening your eyes as wide as you may and never blink. This continued gazing oft causes the patient to grow sleepy. If they show signs of this, say "You are growing sleepy. You will sleep, you are tired. Sleep. Your eyes grow tired. Sleep." If they close their eyes, say "Your eyes close, you are tired, you cannot open your eyes." If they cannot, say "Your arms are tired, you cannot raise them." If they cannot, say "I am master of your mind. You must ever believe what I tell you. When I look like this into your eyes you will sleep and be subject to my will," then tell them they will sleep and wake up refreshed, feeling better. Continue this with soothing and healing drugs, and try to infuse into them the feeling of ecstasy that you feel at the Sabbath. They cannot feel it in full, but you can command them to feel what is in your own mind, and try to concentrate on this ecstasy. If you may safely tell that you are of the Cult, your task may be easier. And it were well to command them to know it only with their sleeping mind, and forget it, or to be at least unable to tell anyone about it when awake. A good way is to command them that if they are ever questioned about Witchcraft or Witches, to immediately fall asleep.

[6] Ever remember if tempted to admit or boast of belonging to the Cult you be endangering your brothers, for though now the fires of persecution may have died down, <but> who knows when they [may] be revived? Many priests have knowledge of our secrets, and they well know that, though much religious bigotry has calmed down, <that> many people would wish to join our Cult. And if the truth were known of its joys, the Churches would lose power, so if we take many recruits, we may loose the fires of persecution against us again. So ever keep the secrets.

[7] Think joy, think love, try to help others and bring joy into their lives. Children are naturally easier to influence than grown people. Ever strive to work through people's existing beliefs. For instance, more than half of the world believes in amulets. An ordinary stone is not an amulet but if it hath a natural hole in it, it must be something unusual, so if the patient hath this belief give him one. But first carry it next your skin for a few days, forcing your will into it, to cure pain, to feel safe, or against their particular fear, and this amulet may keep imposing your will when you are absent. The masters of talismans knew this full well when they said they must be made in a circle, to avoid distraction, by someone whose mind is on the subject of the work.

[8] But keep your own mind happy. Remember the Words of the Goddess "I give unimaginable joys on Earth, certainty not faith while in life, and upon death peace unutterable, rest, and ecstasy, and the promise that you will return again." In the old days many of us went to the flames laughing and singing, and so we may again. We may have joy in life and beauty, and peace and Death and the promise of return.

[9] The Bible speaks sooth, "A merry heart doeth good like a medicine but a broken spirit breaketh the bones." But you may not have a merry heart. Perchance you were born under an evil star. I think that the effects of the stars are overestimated, but you cannot make a merry heart to order, you say. But you can, in the Cult; there be secret processes by which your will and imagination may be influenced. This process also affects the body, and brings it to joy. Your body is happy, so your mind is happy. You are well because you are happy, and you are happy because you are well.

[10] Prayer may be used with good result if the patient believes it can and will work. Many believe it can, but do not believe their God or saint will help. Prayers to the Goddess help, especially the

Amalthean Horn Prayer, as it causes stimulation to the body as well as to the mind.

Commentary on 3.9.

This document as such Gardner apparently decided was not totally suitable for inclusion in the Book of Shadows, but it also is not a first draft, a jotting down of ideas by free association. Rather, it is a careful weaving together of three different themes: altered states of consciousness (produced by chants, dancing, drugs, hypnotism, scourging, etc.); techniques for faith healing; and the need for dissimulation and secrecy. Try reading paragraphs [1], [6], [8] by themselves—this sequence is very close in tone and content to the "Preface" or "Warning" in Section 3.13, which was later incorporated into the Craft Laws. Paragraph [6] was copied into Text B, but not the rest of this, which Gardner instead kept in reserve, raiding it for raw materials to be used in the Craft Laws. The mention of the Amalthean Horn prayer in [10] shows that scourging is, as always, uppermost in Gardner's mind.

Is there anything here that might be traditional? No, despite the obvious attempt to claim traditional knowledge about chants, hypnotism, drugs, etc., there is nothing that can be recognized as part of a pagan religious tradition. Furthermore, the quotes from Crowley render it impossible for this all to be traditional. There is much more innuendo than information here, and the information could all too easily have come from books.

3.10. The Scourge and the Kiss.

[This appears on p. 29 of "Ye Bok of ye Art Magical," and is so carelessly scrawled that it is very difficult to read, as is also true for Sections 3.11 and 3.12. Presumably these are first drafts, using "Ye Bok of ye Art Magical" as a notebook, of material Gardner then entered in Text B in about 1952. To paragraph [1] I have added Gardner's comments on this spell that were included in the Weschcke documents.]

[1] *Invocation*

(Feet, knees, and wrists should be tightly bound to retard

blood.) Scourge 40 or more, to make skin tingle, then say, invoking Goddess,

> Hail, Aradia, from the Amalthean horn
>> Pour forth thy store of Love. I lowly bend
> Before Thee! I invoke thee at the end
>> When other Gods are fallen and put to scorn.
> Thy foot is to my lips! My sighs inborn
>> Rise, touch, curl about thy heart. Then spend,
>> Pitiful Love, loveliest Pity, descend
> And bring me luck who am lonely and forlorn.

Ask the Goddess to help you to obtain your desires, then Scourge again to bind the spell. This be powerful in ill luck and for sickness. It must be said in a Circle, and you must be properly prepared and well purified, both before and after saying, to bind the spell.

Before starting you must make a very clear picture in your mind of what you wish. Make yourself see the wish obtained. Be sure in your own mind exactly what it is and how it is to be fulfilled. This spell is the one that was taught to me long ago and I have found it works, but I don't think there is any special virtue in these words. Any others can be substituted provided they ask the goddess's (or gods') help, and say clearly what you wish and you form the clear mental image; and if it doesn't work at first, keep on trying till it works. Your helper, who wields the scourge, must know what you wish, and also form the mental image. And at first at any rate, it will be better for you to work the spell, then for the girl to take your place and work it also; you scourge her. Don't try anything difficult at first, and do it at least once a week till it works. You have to get into sympathy with each other, before anything happens, and regular working helps this.

Of spells, the exact words matter little if the intent be clear and you raise the true power, and sufficient thereof. Always in rhyme they are. There is something queer about rhyme. I have tried, and the same seem to lose their power if you miss the rhyme. Also in rhyme, the words seem to say themselves. You do not have to pause and think: "What comes next?" Doing this takes away much of your intent.

[2] Order and discipline must be kept. A High Priest or Priestess may and should punish all faults to this end, and all of the Cult [must accept] such corrections willingly. Each fault should be cor-

rected separately. The Priest or Priestess must be properly prepared and call the culprit to trial. They must be prepared [as for] initiation and [kneel, be] told their fault and sentence pronounced. Punishment should be the scourge, followed by a [forfeit] such as several fivefold kisses or something of this nature. The culprit must acknowledge the justice of the punishment by kissing hands and scourge on receiving sentence and again when thanking for punishment received.

[3] The scourgings are 3, 7, 9 (thrice three), and 21 (thrice seven) 40 in all. It is not meet to make offerings [scourgings] of less than two score to the Goddess, for here be a mystery. The fortunate numbers be: 3 and 5. For three added to two (the Perfect Couple) be five. And three and five be eight; eight and five be thirteen; thirteen and eight be twenty-one.

The Fivefold Kiss is called 5, but there are 8 kisses, for there be 2 feet and 2 knees and genitals and 2 breasts and the lips. And 5 times 8 be two score. Also, fortunate numbers be 3, 7, 9, and 21, which total 40, or two score. For each man and woman hath ten fingers and ten toes, so each totals a score. And a perfect couple be two score.

So a lesser number would not be perfect prayer. If more are required make it a perfect number, as four score or six score.

Also there be Eight Elemental Weapons.

[4] To make the anointing ointment, take some glazed pans filled half full with grease or olive oil. Put in one sweet mint, marjoram in another, ground thyme in a 3rd, and if you may have it, patchouli, dried leaves pounded. Place pans in hot water bath. Stir and cook for several hours, then pour into linen bags, and squeeze grease through into pans again, and fill up with fresh leaves. After doing this several times, the grease will be highly perfumed. Then mix all together and store in a well-corked jar.

Anoint behind ears, throat, armpits, breasts, and womb. Also, for all ceremonies where the feet are kissed, they should also be anointed.

Commentary on 3.10.

Like the preceding entry, this one has been constructed with more subtlety than is at first apparent, and was also rewritten into several other documents. Notice that paragraph [1] presents the charm used to accompany scourging as a means for working magic separately from initiation. The Farrars (1981, p. 41) say that it is a poem by Aleister Crowley, originally addressed to Tyche. (However, the Crowley mavens I know beg to differ, and I have not been able to find it in *The Equinox* or several other of Crowley's books I have skimmed through.) Gardner's chatty comments present the same sort of casual claim to historicity for the material, while disclaiming any specific knowledge of the details of that history, that we can see over and over again in *Witchcraft Today*.

Paragraph [2], which Gardner appended to the Craft Laws in the 1960s, then deals with scourging as a means for enforcing discipline within the coven; it seems to be addressing a situation in which perhaps a dozen, rather than just two or three, people are meeting regularly as a coven. This, together with the carelessness of the handwriting, would point toward a date of around 1952 for this entry.

I happened to run across this passage in Schad-Somers, *Sadomasochism* (p. 39): "A mother who is uncomfortable with her own animalistic impulses . . . will persecute these same impulses in her own child, a process . . . [whose] goal is not teaching but *humiliation*. In the extreme, that form of persecution may entail that the child smiles after a severe punishment and—in one case I know of—that the child should first kiss the punishing parent and then kiss the very rod with which the beating has been administered."

Paragraph [3], rewritten into a passage in Chap. 10 of *Witchcraft Today*, and copied into Text B as an appendage to "The Eightfold Way" (see Farrars 1984, p. 52), deals with the number symbolism of the scourging, then with that of the Fivefold Kiss. "It is not meet . . ." means that Gardner needed at least forty strokes to become sexually aroused.

Paragraph [4], which underlies a passage toward the end of Chap. 4 of *Witchcraft Today*, and was also copied into Text B separately (see Farrars 1984, p. 62), then discusses anointing because of its connection with the Fivefold Kiss.

That is, what we have here is not mere free association, but a careful attempt to build up a complex set of associations with scourging, kissing, and anointing, that is, to create a rich sacramental system focused on sexuality in general, and on scourging in particular.

3.11. The Priestess and the Sword

[This material appears on p. 125 of "Ye Bok of ye Art Magical."]

It is said, "When a woman takes the main part in worship of the Male God, she must be girt with a sword."

Note. This hath been explained as meaning that a man should be Magus representing the God, but if no one of sufficient rank and knowledge be present, a woman armed as a man may take his place. The sheath should be worn in a belt. She should carry the sword in hand, but if she has to use her hands, she should sheath the sword. Any other woman in the circle while this worship is performed shall be sword in hand. Those outside the circle only have the athame.

Commentary on 3.11.

Here "Ye Bok of ye Art Magical" is again being used as a notebook to work on a draft of a passage in *Witchcraft Today*, at the end of Chap. 3:

> My great trouble in discovering what their beliefs were is that they have forgotten practically all about their god; all I can get is from the rites and prayers addressed to him. . . . there are certain rites where a man must by the leader, but if a man of requisite rank is not available, a chief priestess belts a sword on and is thought of as a man for the occasion. But although woman can on occasion take man's place, man can never take woman's place.

We can observe not only similar wording, but the use of the third person plural, which Gardner uses throughout *Witchcraft Today* in order to sound like an outside observer, an anthropologist, commenting on the mores of a folk culture he is observing. We can certainly date this entry to the period when *Witchcraft Today* was being written. And why are quotation marks used in the first line? For the same reason that archaicizing language ("hath" and "it be" and suchlike) is used: it is an attempt to find a combination of technical tricks, viewpoint, tone, and attitude that will lend verisimilitude to the claims for a secret history of witchcraft.

3.12. The Warning

[This is scrawled on p. 7 of "Ye Bok of ye Art Magical," in hand-writing so bad that it is almost illegible.]

Keep this book in your own hand of write. Let brothers and sisters copy what they will, but never let this book out of your hands, and never keep the writings of another, for if it be found in their hand of write, they may well be taken and tortured. Each should guard his own writings and destroy them whenever danger threatens. Learn as much as you may by heart, and when the danger is past, rewrite your book if it be safe. For this reason, if any die, destroy their book if they have not been able to, for, an it be found, 'tis clear proof against them, and "Ye may not be a Witch alone." So all their friends be in danger of the Question, so destroy everything not necessary.

If your book be found on you, 'tis clear proof against you alone. You may be tortured. Keep all thought of the cult from your mind. Say you have had bad dreams, that a Devil caused you to write this without your knowledge. Think to yourself, "I Know Nothing. I Remember nothing. I have forgotten All." Drive this into your mind. If the torture be too great to bear, say, "I will confess. I cannot bear this torment. What do you want me to say? Tell me and I will say it." If they try to make you talk of the brotherhood, do not, but if they try to make you speak of impossibilities, such as flying through the air, consorting with the Devil, sacrificing children, or eating men's flesh, to obtain relief from torture, Say, "I had an evil dream. I was not myself. I was crazed." Not all Magistrates are bad. If there be an excuse, they may show you mercy. If you have confessed aught, deny it afterwards. Say you babbled under the torture; you knew not what you did or said. If you be condemned, fear not. The Brotherhood is powerful. They may help you to escape if you are steadfast. If you betray aught, there is no hope for you, in this life, or in that which is to come. But, 'tis sure, that if steadfast you go to the pyre, drugs will reach you. You will feel naught, and you go but to Death and what lies beyond, the ecstasy of the Goddess.

The same with the working Tools. Let them be but as ordinary things that anyone may have in their homes. The Pentacles shall be of wax that they may be melted or broken at once. Have no sword unless your rank allows you one. Have no names or signs on anything. Write them on in ink before consecrating them and wash it off at once when finished.

Commentary on 3.12.

In introducing this passage in *Witchcraft Today* (p. 57), Gardner says, "In all witch writings, there is this warning, usually on the first page," and the passage follows. Now, this statement is certainly true of "Ye Bok of ye Art Magical"; the passage is on the first page after the list of contents. Hence we can be sure that he considered "Ye Bok of ye Art Magical" to be a "witch writing," that is, a Book of Shadows. Had he seen this passage in any other "witch writings?" There is no evidence that he had.

What this passage says is, "Copy this book—including this page—in your own handwriting, and here's why." That is, Gardner was thinking about having initiates write out their own copies of the Book of Shadows. But much in "Ye Bok of ye Art Magical" is unsuitable for a Book of Shadows; it would be simpler to copy only the suitable material into a new book. Gardner did just that about 1952. All of this "warning" (with Gardner's usual variations in wording) was also copied into "Text B" (Farrars 1984, pp. 50-51), but there it includes the last two sentences given in *Witchcraft Today*, which did not appear in "Ye Bok of ye Art Magical." Hence we can see that some of the content of Text B does postdate the writing of *Witchcraft Today*.

Have we any reason to think the content here traditional? Is it the sort of document that might have been written in a time of persecution? No, it is not. We have many examples of what people write to encourage their colleagues in the face of death, and this is nothing like them. Now, in fairness, I need to quote here what Elliot Rose says of this material in *Witchcraft Today*. He begins his comments about this document by acknowledging that Gardner

> recognizes that this cannot have genuinely referred to English conditions at any time; and I am bound to recognize that . . . it does indeed refer to the innocuous goddess-cult he describes. His view is that it is an uneducated translation from a continental source in the times of fierce persecution; and this is *prima facie* reasonable. However, he points out (and the text itself emphasizes) that witches do not keep old documents, but as a matter of policy copy what they require for their own use and destroy all dispensable relics. Thus, if he is right, we have to ex-

pect an extreme degree of textual corruption [as errors made by generations of copyists accumulate]; he does not claim to have seen manuscripts of any age . . . But I doubt if the text is genuine at all. It enjoins the frequent destruction of books, yet has itself survived after the tortures it speaks of have ceased to be feared, and in a country where they were never employed. . . . it still contains fancy archaisms that would have presumably dropped out if it had in fact been constantly recopied from memory: "ye" and "aught" and "'tis" and so forth. It makes . . . [a] feeble attempt at seventeenth-century grammar . . . and seems to disprove the accusations made against witches with a suspicious neatness. It seems designed to create an impression of injured innocence, and I suspect that someone has been supplying the cult in its modern form with retrospective historical evidence.

Rose is quite right about this. In fact, his last sentence is a wonderful example of a trained historical intuition at work.

Look at the third paragraph. What does "Same" refer to? It must refer back to "Destroy everything not necessary" in the first paragraph. That is, the text originally jumped from "everything not necessary" to "The same with the working tools." This earlier draft was thus concocted specifically to explain why no old witch books or tools exist; it was written as part of an overall strategy of making the "secret history" of witchcraft seem plausible. All the business about secrecy in the face of persecution was therefore inserted later, in order to create a plausible setting. That is, the reason for this entry is to "explain" why there is no evidence for the existence of a witch-cult so totally unlike what professional historians think might have existed. Such a problem is of no interest to persons facing persecution, but it is of great interest to persons who are inventing a new religion that they wish to claim is old. The fact is that for the last 250 years, anyone in England who could read and write was perfectly safe in owning any sort of weird literature or magical implements (although Doreen Valiente has pointed out to me that this was true only for the upper classes, not the working class); and given that safety, educated people would have stopped destroying old magical books by late in the eighteenth century. A book even 100 years old would seem antique enough to most current seekers after ancient wisdom. If Gardner had had something that old to offer, he would have said so. But he does not, because he has no such thing.

3.13. *Of the Ordeal of the Art Magical*

[This appears on pp. 71-73 of "Ye Bok of ye Art Magical."]

Learn of the spirit that goeth with burdens that have not honour, for 'tis the spirit that stoopeth the shoulders and not the weight. Armour is heavy, yet it is a proud burden and a man standeth upright in it. Limiting and constraining any of the senses serves to increase the concentration of another. Shutting the eyes aids the hearing. So the binding of the initiate's hands increases the mental perception, while the scourge increaseth the inner vision. So the initiate goeth through it proudly, like a princess, knowing it but serves to increase her glory.

But this can only be done by the aid of another intelligence and in a circle, to prevent the power thus generated being lost. Priests attempt to do the same with their scourgings and mortifications of the flesh. But lacking the aid of bonds and their attention being distracted by their scourging themselves and what little power they do produce being dissipated, as they do not usually work within a circle, it is little wonder that they oft fail. Monks and hermits do better, as they are apt to work in tiny cells and coves, which in some way act as circles. The Knights of the Temple, who used mutually to scourge each other in an octagon, did better still; but they apparently did not know the virtue of bonds and did evil, man to man.

But perhaps some did know? What of the Church's charge that they wore girdles or cords?

Commentary on 3.13.

This material is more theologizing about scourging, attempting to justify its use in a magical context. As I have already said, there is certainly no mention of scourging in *The Greater Key of Solomon*, nor of the scourge as a magical tool. The tone and viewpoint are similar to those in various other entries here, in looking for ways to make the "secret history" plausible. Notice Gardner's standing assumption, which runs throughout the earliest entries, that the initiate will be a woman. Note also his homophobia, which was for a long time a source of political problems in the Craft movement in America. Aside from English bigotry in general, homophobia was particularly characteristic of flagellants, Gibson (p. 276) points out, the line of thought being something like, "Well, even if I am addicted to being beaten and humiliated by prostitutes, at *least* I'm not a faggot!"—as if homosexuality were somehow even worse.

3.14. The Eightfold Way.

[This document was included among the Weschcke documents.]

EIGHTFOLD PATH OR WAYS TO THE CENTRE

1 Meditation or Concentration. This in practice means forming a mental image of what is desired, and forcing yourself to see that it is fulfilled, with the fierce belief and knowledge that it can and will be fulfilled, and that you will go on willing till you force it to be fulfilled. Called for short, "Intent."

2 Trance, projection of the Astral.

3 Rites, Chants, Spells, Runes, Charms, etc.

4 Incense, Drugs, Wine, etc., whatever is used to release the Spirit. (Note: One must be very careful about this. Incense is usually harmless, but you must be careful. If it has bad aftereffects, reduce the amount used, or the duration of the time it is inhaled. Drugs are very dangerous if taken to excess, but it must be remembered that there are drugs that are absolutely harmless, though people talk of them with bated breath, but hemp is especially dangerous, because it unlocks the inner eye swiftly and easily, so one is tempted to use it more and more. If it is used at all, it must be with the strictest precautions, to see that the person who uses it has no control over the supply. This should be doled out by some responsible person, and the supply strictly limited.)

5 The Dance, and kindred practices.

6 Blood control (the Cords), Breath Control, and kindred practices.

7 The Scourge.

8 The Great Rite.

---

9 These are all the ways. You may combine many of them into the one experiment, the more the better. The most important is "Intention": you must know that you can and will succeed; it is essential

in every operation.

10 Preparation. (You must be properly prepared according to the rules of the Art; otherwise you will never succeed.)

11 The Circle must be properly formed and purified.

12 You all must be properly purified, several times if necessary, and this purification should be repeated several times during the rite.

13 You must have properly consecrated tools.

These five essentials and Eight Paths or Ways cannot all be combined in one rite. Meditation and dancing do not combine well, but forming the mental image and the dance may be well combined with Chants. Spells, etc., combined with scourging and No. 6, followed by No. 8, form a splendid combination. Meditation, following scourging, combined with Nos. 3 and 4 and 5, are also very good. For short cuts concentration, Nos. 5, 6, 7, and 8 are excellent. Nos 9, 10, 11, 12, and 13 are essential in all experiments.

Commentary on 3.14.

Did Gardner learn these techniques from an older coven? It is clear from his long note after entry 4 that he was personally not familiar with the use of drugs as part of a magical training process—whereas this is one of the few things we could expect of almost any sort of native shamanism—and so was not trained in such use by an earlier coven; instead, he has learned the concept from reading. It also follows that his organizing of these methods into an "Eightfold Path" was his own idea, not part of what he might have learned from an earlier coven. Only the first two or three of these eight "ways" make sense as part of the techniques of a magical lodge. Where did Gardner get the rest of them? The use of a Buddhist term here points toward the simplest, most probable conclusion: that Gardner had learned about all these "mind-altering" techniques by reading about Tantric systems, but almost certainly at second hand, via Randolph, whose *Eulis* was in his library, or Crowley (see Melton, "The Origins of Modern Sex Magick," 1985). His listing of binding and scourging among these magical techniques is his own contribution; and notice that #12 emphasizes the use of several scourgings during every working. Notice that his recommended sequences of 3, 7, 6, 8, and 5,

6, 7, 8, both reproduce the typical sexual pattern for a flagellant.

Rules 10 to 13 seem to be a rewriting of passages in *The Greater Key of Solomon*, p. 14: "If thou wishest to succeed, it is necessary to make the following Experiments . . . with the requisite solemnities and ceremonies . . . which can in no way be brought to perfection without the Circle; and in order to accomplish this perfectly it is necessary to take note of all the preparations which the Master of the Art and his Disciples must undertake before constructing the circle." Gardner's use of "experiment" is good evidence that he had this passage before him. Also, his use of "Art" throughout these documents derives from *The Greater Key of Solomon*; "Craft" came to be used only in the late 1950s. The concept in Rule 13 comes from *The Greater Key of Solomon*, e.g. (p.98), "In order to properly carry out the greatest . . . Operations of the Art, various instruments are necessary." Notice "operations," another term that Gardner uses.

The page in Text B titled "The Ways of Making Magic" is a rewriting of this material, which therefore must date to 1953 or before.

3.15. To Gain the Sight

[This was included among the Weschcke documents.]

[1] This cometh to different people in diverse ways. 'Tis seldom it cometh naturally, but it can be induced in many ways. Deep and prolonged meditation may do it, but only if you be a natural, and usually prolonged fasting was also necessary. Of old monks and nuns obtained visions by long vigils, combined with fasting, flagellation till the blood came, and other mortifications of the flesh, and so undoubtedly had visions. In the East it is tried with various tortures, at the same time sitting in cramped postures, which retard the flow of blood, and these torments, long and continued, give good results. But in the Art we are taught an easier way to intensify the imagination, at the same time controlling the blood supply, and this may best be done by using the ritual.

[2] Incense is also good to propitiate the Spirits, but also to induce relaxation and to help to build up the atmosphere which is necessary to suggestibility. For our human eyes are so blind to what really is, that it is often necessary to suggest that it is there, before we may see it, as we may point out to another something at a distance before they may see it themselves. Gum mastic, aromatic rush roots,

cinnamon bark, musk, juniper, sandalwood, and ambergris in combination are all good, but patchouli is best of all. And if you may have hemp, 'tis better still, but be very careful of this.

[3] The circle being formed, all properly prepared, and the Rites done, and all purified, the aspirant should warlock and take his tutor round the circle, saluting the Mighty Ones, and invoke them to aid the operation. Then both dance round till giddy, invoking or using chants. Scourge. Then the Tutor should warlock very tightly, but not so to cause discomfort, but enough to retard the blood slightly. Again they should dance round, chanting, then scourge with light, steady, monotonous, slow strokes. It is very good that the pupil may see them coming (this may be arranged from position, or if a big mirror is available, this can be used with excellent effect) as this has the effect of passes, and helps greatly to stimulate the imagination, and it is important that they be not hard, the object being not to do more than draw the blood to that part and so away from the brain. This with the tight warlocking, which should be warricked, slows down the circulation of the blood, and the passes soon induce a drowsiness and a stupor. The tutor should watch for this. As soon as the aspirant sleeps, the scourging should cease. The tutor should also watch that the pupil become not cold, and if they struggle or become distressed, they should be at once awakened. (Note: if it cannot be arranged for the pupil to see, the wand may be used, for a time, then return to scourging.)

[4] Do not be discouraged if no results come after two or three attempts. It will come, when both are in the right state. When you get some result, then results will come more quickly. Soon some of the ritual may be shortened, but never neglect to invoke the Goddess, and the Mighty Ones, or to form the Circle and do everything rightly. And for good and clear results, it is ever better to do too much ritual than too little.

[5] It hath been found that this practice doth often cause a fondness between aspirant and tutor, and 'tis a cause of better results if this be so. If for any reason it is undesirable that there be any great fondness between aspirant and tutor, this may be easily avoided, by both parties from the onset firmly resolving in their minds that if any doth ensue, it shall be that of brother and sister or parent and child. And it is for this reason that a man may only be taught by a woman and a woman by a man, and that man and man, and woman and woman, should never attempt these practices together. And may all

the Curses of the Mighty Ones be on any who make the attempt.

[6] Remember, the Circle, properly constructed, is ever necessary to prevent the power released from being dissipated. It is also a barrier against any disturbances of mischievous forces, for to obtain good results you must be free from all disturbances. Remember that darkness, points of light gleaming amid the surrounding dark, incense, and the steady passes by a white arm are not stage effects. They are the mechanical implements which start the suggestions, which later unlocks the knowledge that it is possible to obtain the divine ecstasy, and so attain knowledge and communion with the Divine Goddess. When once you have attained this, Ritual is not needed, as you may attain the state of ecstasy at will, but till then, or if you having attained this yourself, and wish to bring a companion to this state of joy, ritual is best.

Commentary on 3.15.

There are two rough drafts of this document in Gardner's notebooks in Toronto; these date from somewhere in the early 1950s. Likewise, since a rewriting of this document is included in "Text B" (see the Farrars 1984, p. 58) we can date it to 1953 or later. Let us look at how it is constructed.

First, notice from the language, especially the verb tenses in [1], that this is strictly a modern document, despite the use of archaicizing verbiage. Second, notice that [2] rewrites the ideas in the long note to no. 4 in 3.14; [3] explains in detail the procedure used with the Amalthean Horn prayer described in 3.10; [4], and all but the first two sentences of [6], expand the ideas in the chatty commentary appended to the Amalthean Horn verse; and the third sentence in [4], and the first two sentences of [6], expand the ideas in items 9 to 13 in "The Eightfold Way." Consider, finally, the formal tone and rather flowery language of the whole. Obviously, what we have here is a rewriting of earlier notes, jottings, and comments—some of which we happen to have—into a formal document suitable for inclusion in a Book of Shadows.

Now consider paragraph [5]. Its content is referred to several times in *Witchcraft Today*, which also helps to date it. Notice that it formalizes what is implicit in the commentary on the Amalthean Horn prayer, that a man and a "girl" should work together, just as the surrounding paragraphs, [4] and [6], formalize other matters touched on in that commentary. Since we even have early drafts of it in the notebooks, we can be quite certain that this document was written all in one piece, and does not show any evidence of including quotations from earlier, traditional documents. That is, we have here a paragraph, [5], later claimed to be part of Craft Law, in its original context, and analysis of the document gives us no reason to suppose this paragraph is being quoted from any other source.

The procedures described in this document, and all the comments about them—except for those in [5]—seem perfectly sensible as part of a basic shamanistic technique. But we need not suppose that Gardner had such information from any source other than books. Rather, we have here yet another example of his theologizing about scourging.

Conclusions

Judging from the details of Gardner's rituals as they existed between 1945 and 1953, I don't think there were ever more than half a dozen people active in the coven at any one time during this period, although there may have continued to be an informal "Outer Court" consisting of people in occult circles who were privileged to know of the coven's existence, and who were invited to any larger Sabbat rituals that were held. However, after 1951, freed from Dorothy's domination, Gardner began building the "cult" up, and rituals for larger groups of people (up to a dozen) begin to appear. By 1953, Gardner had started a new coven in London, and the new religion that he and his friends had founded—for that is what they did—had evolved far from Murray's concepts. For that matter, it is still evolving, since it seems typical of healthy religions to evolve (and to claim that they are not evolving at all). However, their system for working magic had not progressed much beyond the situation described in *High Magic's Aid*; there was still the uneasy amalgam of the male ceremonial magician and the female folk-magic witch.

Furthermore, there really wasn't very much in the Book of Shadows by 1953. Gardner was not prolific at creating rituals himself. This is surely why Gardner was so delighted to be able to initiate a bright, hard-working young writer, who in 1953 began revising and augmenting the Book of Shadows, turning it into the type of liturgical manual still used by Gardnerians today. This writer was Doreen Valiente.

4. The Reign of Doreen Valiente, 1953-1957

Late in 1952 came what has turned out to be the turning point in the evolution of the Craft as a new religion: Gardner and Dafo met, and later initiated, Doreen Valiente (who was born in 1922). This talented young woman promptly threw herself into work on the new religion, rewriting the existing rituals and creating new ones, and some of this work was reflected in the final draft of *Witchcraft Today*.

In the September 27, 1952, issue of the English popular magazine *Illustrated* appeared an article entitled "Witchcraft in Britain" by Allen Andrews. The article quoted at length the remarks of Cecil Williamson, who had opened a witchcraft museum on the Isle of Man in 1951. Williamson described various practices of the "Old Religion of the witches," mentioned the New Forest as being the meetingplace of the "Southern Coven of British Witches," and "revealed how, on the night of 1 August 1940, the Sabbat of Lammas, seventeen men and women had gathered in a clearing in the New Forest to raise a 'cone of power' to prevent Hitler from crossing the Channel and invading Britain." He had invited members of the Southern Coven of English Witches to be present at the formal opening of his museum. Gerald Gardner had accepted the invitation, and also talked to the reporter about the "Old Religion."

Doreen Valiente, who says that she had walked out of her convent school at age 15 and flatly refused to return, relates that she read this article in 1952, when she was living in Bournemouth (which is fairly near the New Forest), with great excitement. She had been reading everything on magic that she could get her hands on for years, but this was her first indication that witches might still exist. She wrote to Williamson, detailing her occult studies until then, and asking if he could put her in touch with the witch cult. Williamson passed her letter along to Gardner, and after a few more letters were exchanged, Gardner invited Doreen to meet him and a lady known as Dafo at her house near Christchurch. This she did late in 1952, and she liked both Gerald and Dafo from the start. At that time Dafo, since she was a teacher of music and elocution, since her daughter had married a dentist, and since her health was poor, was no longer active in the Craft. As Doreen left that day, Gerald gave her a copy of *High Magic's Aid* to read, saying that it would tell her a great deal about "the witch cult as it really was."

It was not until the summer of 1953 that Doreen was actually initiated. Gardner came down to Dafo's house from his home on the Isle of Man in order to attend the Druid's Midsummer ritual at Stonehenge, bringing with him the sword which the Druid Order used in their ceremony, and which had belonged to Dorothy Clutterbuck. In his brochure about the Witches' Mill, Gardner says, "She had a very fine ritual sword, which for many years was lent to the Druid Order which holds the annual Midsummer ceremony at Stonehenge, because it fitted exactly into the cleft in the Hele Stone." Gardner had been a friend of both the current Chosen Chief of the Druid Order, Robert McGregor Reid, and his father, George Watson McGregor Reid, whom he had succeeded as Chosen Chief in 1946; and certainly Dorothy must also have been a friend of the latter. (The overlapping use of magical tools is almost certain proof of overlapping membership.)

At her initiation, Doreen says, the ritual was virtually identical to that in *High Magic's Aid*, except that it also contained a section called "The Charge" that Gerald read to her. She recognized passages in it as being from Leland's *Aradia*, and from Crowley's *Book of the Law* and "Gnostic Mass" in *Magick in Theory and Practice*, and says that when she later mentioned this to Gerald, he "seemed none too pleased at my recognition of its sources."

The next day Doreen went to the Stonehenge ritual with Gerald and Dafo. It felt very appropriate to her that her initiation should be sealed by her first visit to "one of the great spiritual centers of Britain." Later in the year Gerald invited her up to his London flat to meet the rest of his coven. There were about eight or ten of them, most being members also of the nudist society that Gardner belonged to, some claiming to have already been witches.

About the time that Doreen was initiated, Gardner was using two different Books of Shadows, as I have already mentioned. The first and shorter one (Text A) consisted only of the ritual documents that Gardner had copied out of "Ye Bok of ye Art Magical": the procedure for casting the circle, the initiation ritual, the "Lift the Veil" version of the Charge, the short "Cakes and Wine" ritual, and the four Sabbats for the cross-quarter days. The second Book (Text B) consisted of these rituals and/or revisions of them, plus other, newer materials; and this was the book that Gardner actually used during Doreen's initiation.

Gardner was already being far less than forthright in his dealings with Doreen. He never told her about the existence of "Ye Bok of ye Art Magical" (which is why, according to her 1985 letter to *Iron Mountain*, she was unaware of its existence until 1982, when she read a copy of my *Inventing Witchcraft* manuscript; she wrote to me, "No, Gerald never told me anything about 'Ye Booke of ye Art Magical.' But I had had those typewritten scraps [e.g., of the first-degree initiation] in the old book he gave me [that is, Text A], and never knew what they were until I saw your typescript"). Gardner kept "Ye Bok of ye Art Magical" at his museum, and used it as a notebook. Not only did Gardner not tell Doreen about the existence of "Ye Bok of ye Art Magical," but, she has written to me, "Gerald certainly led me to assume that the text of the Book of Shadows had been copied originally from 'Old Dorothy's' book." As I have said, there is no evidence at all that Dorothy ever had any such book. Rather, "Ye Bok of ye Art Magical" itself, since it was obviously intended for liturgical use in the circle, was probably the only book that the original coven used.

Gardner used "Ye Bok of ye Art Magical" as a notebook for drafts of passages that would later appear in *Witchcraft Today*, as well as for drafts of new rituals that he copied into "Text B." The emphasis in these entries (as we have seen in Chapter 3) was on finding a stance that would lend plausibility to the historical claims: that there was an earlier coven; that there was a pagan religion; that a pagan religion could have the characteristics described in *Witchcraft Today*. Hence, although "Ye Bok of ye Art Magical" was not intended to be read, it was clearly written with an audience always in mind. But if it were what the "Warning" proclaims it to be, a "witch's book," whether an individual's notebook or a group's liturgical manual, it would focus on the content of the religious tradition. It would not be ultimately concerned with manipulating audience reaction. The fact "Ye Bok of ye Art Magical" is focused on audience reaction demonstrates that Gardner was thinking deliberately and primarily about how to found a new religious movement. Once "Ye Bok of ye Art Magical" was full, and no longer useful even as a notebook, Gardner hid it in the back of a cabinet in the museum, where it was found by the team from Ripley's in 1971; the Wilsons, who arrived after it had been retired, probably didn't even know it existed; thus it was preserved, to provide the clues to unravel the puzzle.

The Farrars (1981, p. 148 n3) report that the Yule Sabbat ritual in *Witchcraft Today*, Chapter 1, was "written by Doreen Valiente, with words suggested by a Christmas carol in *Carmina Gadelica*, I, 133, . . . 'It was the first chant or invocation I ever wrote for Gerald,' Doreen tells us —at Yule 1953, she thinks. He gave her the task of writing words for the evening ritual without warning, after lunch, 'deliberately throwing me in at the deep end to see what I would do.' " Let us look at what is said about it in *Witchcraft Today*.

> I have seen one very interesting ceremony: the Cauldron of Regeneration and the Dance of the Wheel, or Yule, to cause the sun to be reborn, or summer to return. This in theory should be on December 22, but nowadays it is held on the nearest day . . . that is convenient for the members. The ceremony starts in the usual way. The circle is cast and purified, the celebrants also being purified in the usual manner, and the ordinary business of the cult is done. Then the small ceremony is performed (sometimes called 'Drawing down the Moon') so that the High Priestess is regarded as the incarnation of the goddess. The Cakes and Wine ceremony follows. Then a cauldron (or something to represent one) is placed in the middle of the circle, spirit is put in and ignited. Various leaves, etc., are cast in. Then the Priestess stands by it in the pentacle (goddess) position. The High Priest stands on the opposite side of the cauldron, leading the chant. The others stand round in a circle with torches. They are lighted at the burning cauldron and they dance round in the 'sunwise' direction, i.e. clockwise. The chant I heard was as follows, but others are sometimes used:
>
> > 'Queen of the Moon, Queen of the Sun,
> > Queen of the Heavens, Queen of the Stars,
> > Queen of the Waters, Queen of the Earth
> > Bring to us the Child of Promise!

It is the great mother who giveth birth to him,
It is the Lord of Life who is born again.
Darkness and tears are set aside
When the Sun shall come up early.

Golden Sun of the Mountains,
Illumine the Land, Light up the World,
Illumine the Seas and the Rivers,
Sorrows be laid, Joy to the World.

Blessed be the Great Goddess,
Without beginning, without end,
Everlasting to eternity.
I.O.EVO.HE Blessed Be.'

They dance round furiously, crying:

'I.O.EVO.HE
Blessed Be I.O.EVO.HE Blessed Be.'

Sometimes couples join hands and jump over the blazing cauldron, as I have seen for myself. When the fire had burnt itself out the Priestess led the usual dances. This was followed by a feast.

The concept of this dance is from Murray (*Witch-Cult in Western Europe*, p. 13), who says, "To February 2, Candlemas Day, probably belongs the sun-charm of the burning wheel, formed by the whirling dancers, each carrying a blazing torch." To this Valiente added her own verse, based on that in the *Carmina Gadelica*. I believe her about all this because: (a) someone wrote the verse; (b) Gardner could not write verse at all; and (c) Valiente writes very competent verse. (This ritual must have been inserted into the manuscript of *Witchcraft Today*, which was published in 1954, at almost the last minute.)

Given that, we can see how very devious Gardner is being in what he says about this ritual: "I have seen," "I have heard," and so on. That is quite true—but he does not admit that this is a ritual he himself had commissioned. We therefore must be aware that he is equally devious about everything he describes. Notice that this Sabbat is now held on the nearest day to December 22 that is convenient for the members, because so Gardner and Valiente and their coven decided. What is implied, but not said, is that it used to be held some other way—but there is no independent evidence that this sort of Sabbat ritual had ever been held for the winter solstice.

"Io Evohe" is based on the cry of the Bacchantes in Euripides' *The Bacchae*. Actually, I believe it is a multilingual pun based on "yod he vau he," the Tetragrammeton of the Kabala, since the Greek would other wise transliterate more exactly as yo eh-oo-hoy. If the parting phrase of the Somersetshire witches, "A boy! Merry meet, merry part!" actually began with "Evohe!" (*Witch-Cult in Western Europe*, p. 167), we must presume that their coven had been taken over by a renegade Elizabethan classicist, and that they are therefore not a trustworthy source for information about native English paganism.

Someone other than Gardner, who could not write even a line of verse, must have written the poems "The Witch Remembers her Last Incarnation" and "Twilight is over" in *Witchcraft Today*; it now appears that Dorothy Clutterbuck Fordham might have written them. In addition, "The Myth of the Goddess" (which is yet another theologizing of the scourging) and the portion of the Charge that appear in its Chapter 3 are so different in literary style from (and so much better than) the rest of Gardner's writing, that I believe someone else must have written them. I had thought this person was Doreen Valiente, but she says not—and since she admits what she did write, there is no reason not to believe her. It may also be that Ross Nichols, whom Ms. Valiente says was a schoolteacher, author, and member of the Druid Order headed by the Reids (Nichols became Chosen Chief of it in 1965), did do a thorough copyediting and rewriting of *Witchcraft Today*, not just a critical review. Certainly someone other than Gardner typed the clean and correctly spelled final manuscript of "New Light on Witchcraft" that went in to the publisher, who renamed it *Witchcraft Today*. Doreen Valiente tells me that it was not her who retyped it, and she does not know who else did—though it might have been Dolores North again. Or Gardner might just have hired some professional help.

In 1954 *Witchcraft Today* was published. In it Gardner claimed that Margaret Murray had been right: that the "witchcraft" of the Middle Ages had been a surviving pagan religion. He knew this, he said, because that religion had survived in secret down into this century; having stumbled upon one of the last surviving covens in England, he had been initiated into it, and was now free to write a description of its actual beliefs and practices, which went back to Elizabethan times and ultimately to the stone-age religions of Europe. Gardner may have actually told Margaret Murray that his group had begun by trying to reconstruct the religion she described. This may be why she fails to notice, in her enthusiastic Introduction, what

Elliot Rose points out: that the religion Gardner describes in *Witchcraft Today* is utterly unlike what Murray had described 20 and 30 years earlier. Many current members of the Craft movement fail to see that the "Great Goddess" is NOT one of the concepts in *Witchcraft Today*, which instead presents a domesticated sort of classical polytheism.

As time went on, Doreen says, she became in practice Gerald's High Priestess, and became more vocal about her dissatisfaction with the Book of Shadows as it stood when she was initiated. Many of the rituals whose existence was asserted in *Witchcraft Today* were then only in the planning stages. If a "Gardnerian" coven is defined as one that works the basic Gardnerian rituals—and this is one of the basic rules by which Gardnerians judge the authenticity of any coven that claims to be Gardnerian—then *no Gardnerian coven could have existed before 1955, because the basic Gardnerian rituals had not yet been written.* In fact, none of the circle rituals in use in 1953 were based on a "pagan" theology; instead, they were all adapted from the Kabalistic procedures of *The Greater Key of Solomon*, and contained great swatches of quotation from Crowley, as we saw in the preceding chapter. Doreen says that other witches were quoted in the 1952 *Illustrated* article as saying that their rituals were based on "instructions handed down from the elders, eked out with the *Clavicules of Solomon*," and argues that therefore "Gerald Gardner did not introduce this practice of blending witchcraft with ceremonial magic." However, all the witches known to Williamson seem to have been members of the one and only coven that we know was then in existence, the Southern Coven, and their description of the rituals exactly fits those in Gardner's Book of Shadows at that time; so there is no independent evidence here.

After Gardner had gotten over his discomfiture at realizing that Doreen had been able to spot all the Crowley quotations in his rituals, he defended their presence by telling her that the rituals he had received from the old coven were very fragmentary, and that in order to make them workable, he had to supplement them with other material. He had felt that Crowley's writings "breathed the very spirit of paganism" and were expressed in what he felt was "splendid" poetry (which provides an adequate measure of just how bad Gardner's literary taste was).

The publication of *Witchcraft Today* had brought Gardner some measure of fame, and more and more people were contacting him, asking for initiation into the "witch cult." He began to realize that he had a real chance to popularize his "Old Religion," but Doreen told him flatly that he would never do so as long as Crowley's influence was so obvious in the rituals, for the simple reason that Crowley's name and reputation stank to the heavens.

"Gerald's reaction was, 'Well, if you think you can do any better, go ahead.'" Doreen accepted the challenge and set out to rewrite the Book of Shadows, cutting out the Crowleyanity as much as she could and trying to bring it back to what she felt was a more genuinely pagan wording. She felt that the words from *Aradia* qualified in this respect, so she retained them as the basis for her new version of "The Charge," which she originally wrote in verse quatrains. However, people seemed to have some difficulty using this verse in rituals, and it was also rather short; so she later wrote what has come to be the much better-known prose version of "The Charge." She, or she and Gardner jointly, continued to work on rewriting the rituals in his Book of Shadows, ending up with the version that the Farrars labeled Text C. She notes in *Witchcraft for Tomorrow* (p. 21) that she and Gerald wrote the poem "Darksome night and shining moon" in 1954 or 1955.

For some time Gerald and she had been collaborating on a new book to follow *Witchcraft Today*. They proposed to call it *The Meaning of Witchcraft*. During 1956 she worked hard on the research and writing for it. The book did eventually appear under that title, in 1959, but by that time, she and Gerald had ceased working together. Her work was not a loss, though; much of it, transmogrified, made its way into her *Where Witchcraft Lives* in 1962, and her later books.

During 1956, two factions developed in the coven: a pro-publicity faction, consisting of Gerald and mostly newcomers; and an anti-publicity faction, consisting of Doreen and most of the other old-timers. Gerald's inability to be discreet with or even reasonably skeptical about reporters had been a long-standing problem, because the raunchiest of the tabloids sold by the check-out stands in American supermarkets are staid and scholarly in comparison with the exploitative journalism allowed in Britain; Doreen says that this was actually Dafo's major reason for ceasing to work with Gardner. These two subgroups also had somewhat different theories about how to run a coven; so in February 1957 (I was told by Fred Lamond), they divided the original coven in half, or Doreen hived a new coven off, depending on how you look at it, taking Ned and five or so others with her. At this time she also took with her all the correspondence, and all the operative Books of Shadows. (She has written to me that, as far as she can remember, this chronology seems to be about right.)

Fred also told me that the remaining members of the original coven soon thereafter decided to use the circle-dance-and-drop technique as their major way to raise power, rather than the bound scourging that had always been Gardner's favorite technique. As a result, Fred said, Gardner soon "wandered off" to initiate new priestesses and found new covens that would be more to his liking. The original coven has continued to exist; it was the coven studied by Tanya Luhrmann in her exceedingly scholarly and monumentally boring *Persuasions of the Witches' Craft.* We will consider Gardner's activities during the last seven years of his life in Chapters 6 and 8.

At first the hiving off of the new coven had been a peaceful process, and the two covens continued to cooperate with one another, and to meet jointly on occasion. However, because of Gardner's publicity-seeking, tensions continued to rise; the old-timers feared the worst. As a last resort, Ned, Doreen's High Priest, drew up a set of proposals, entitled "Proposed Rules for the Craft," hoping that Gerald would agree to abide by them. Doreen typed them up, and sent them to Gerald in about June 1957. The text of these rules (which I discovered in Toronto) read as follows.

1. No member of the Craft will initiate any person unless that person has been interviewed by at least two Elders and accepted as suitable.

2. No affairs of the Craft will be discussed by members in the presence of uninitiated persons, or in places where conversation is likely to be overheard.

3. No copies of any papers relating to the Craft will be made or retained without the Elders' permission. Such papers as are permissible will be kept in a secure place.

4. As it is essential for the successful working of ritual by a group that here should be unity of purpose and an harmonious psychic atmosphere, members who create dissension and discord within the Craft will be asked to resign. Should they fail or refuse to do so they will be informed in writing by the Elders that they have been expelled.

5. No member of the Craft will give any information or interview about the Craft to any journalist or writer, or cause any such information to be published in any way, without the approval of the Elders, nor will any of the Elders do so with out the approval of the rest of the Elders.

6. If any member of the Craft feels that he or she has reason to complain of the conduct of any other member in matters affecting the Craft, or of any misdemeanour towards any member whilst on Craft premises, he or she will bring the said complaint to the notice of the elders as soon as possible. The Elders, after considering all available evidence, will, if they find the complaint justified, take appropriate action.

7. No member will be present at any meeting where the working is that of a higher Grade than he or she has attained, except by invitation of the Elders. These invitations will only be extended on very rare occasions where special circumstances exist.

8. No member will disclose the name and address or telephone number of any other member to any person whatsoever, without the said other member's previous permission.

9. Members will meet upon the traditional occasions, or as near to them as possible, and such meetings will be arranged by the Elders, or such Officers as the Elders authorize to do so. If the Elders be not present at such meetings, they will receive a report of them. Members may arrange other meetings for their private working if they so desire, but if more than two members be present at such a meeting the elders will receive a report of it. This report will take the form of a short letter to the Elders giving place and date of the meeting, names of members attending, and details of ceremonies carried out. Where convenient, verbal reports will be accepted.

10. Members will endeavor to acquaint themselves with the traditions of the Craft, and will not introduce innovations into the workings without the Elders' approval. Nor will the Elders give approval to any important innovation without first asking the approval of the rest of the Craft.

11. In the event of any member resigning from the Craft, he or she will honourably observe the Oath of Secrecy taken at initiation, and will also return to the Elders any written matter relating to the Craft which may be in his or her possession.

12. All members will receive a copy of these rules, and all new members will be given a copy of these rules upon initiation. New

members, prior to initiation, will read these rules and declare upon their honor that they will abide by them in letter and in spirit. This declaration will be made to the Elders in writing, and signed.

13. It will be understood by all members that these rules are equally binding upon all Grades of the Craft, including the Elders, and that serious and/or persistent breach of these rules will be grounds for expulsion.

Notice that here the term "Craft" must actually mean something like "coven" (in rules 4, 6, 10, and by implication, 9); that is, it is the affairs of a group not much larger than a single coven that are being dealt with here. In 1957 there was, for the first time, not a single small group, which could run by unwritten rules, but an organization, the "Craft," with at least two covens, which therefore needed written rules that all could agree on. Obviously, there were not so many members in all that the group consultations required by rules 5 and 10 would have been clumsy to carry out.

We can also suppose that some (if not all) of the things forbidden by these new rules had been happening; else why have a rule against them? That is, we can suppose that Gardner (or someone) had in fact been: initiating newcomers without having them screened; talking to the uninitiated, including reporters, about Craft business; passing out copies of the rituals; fighting with others in the circle; giving out personal information; holding secret or unauthorized rituals; introducing innovations without discussing them; refusing to abide by group decisions; and so on. In these circumstances, the Elders felt they had to insist on their authority to maintain order in the organization. It is obvious that the Elders wanted to have veto power over whom Gardner decided to initiate—which is what Rule 1 says—and that he had no intention of granting them that power.

Although Gardner did not like the Proposed Rules as such, the idea of having some sort of rules in the Book of Shadows apparently caught Gardner's fancy, and he began to work on the project. Certainly he would have felt that the new document had to be in the sort of flowery, formal, and often archaic-sounding language in which most of the other documents had been written. He would also have wanted it to look and sound traditional in itself. Furthermore, he would have wanted it to have some theological content—to be concerned with how a coven is to work magic—not be just a set of organizational rules. In order to have raw materials for writing it, he combed through his earlier writings, both the published books and various Book of Shadows documents, gathered together passages that had some connection with the concept of a traditional collection of laws that defined and governed the "Craft," and rewrote them.

Doreen writes that, after Gardner had received the "Proposed Rules," he prevaricated as long as possible, and then astonished them: from his museum in the Isle of Man he sent them a long document, with a message saying that there was no need for the proposed rules, because these "Laws of the Craft" already existed. The document, Doreen says, "was couched in mock-archaic language and ornamented with awesome threats of 'So be it ardane' (meaning 'ordained') and invocations of 'the Curse of the Goddess' upon anyone who dared to transgress them"; so it clearly must be the same as the "Old Laws" included among the Weschcke documents. (However, it consisted, I believe, of only a first draft of the first of the two documents that make up the "Old Laws," ending with #88, and leaving out #82 and #83, as numbered in *The Grimoire of Lady Sheba*.)

Doreen says that they were apparently supposed to be overawed. Their actual reaction was to be extremely skeptical. None of them had ever set eyes on these alleged "Laws" before, though they noticed that they incorporated the "Warning" from the Book of Shadows (see Section 3.12), which had always before been a complete document in its own right. They asked why, if these Laws were so ancient and authoritative, Gerald had never mentioned them before. The issue had become one of confidence in Gardner, and the more they examined the alleged "Laws," the less confidence they felt. Doreen specifically rejected the passages (about "a man loveth a woman by mastering her" and retiring in favor of a younger woman) that she believed were sexist. Doreen believes that Ned wrote back to Gerald and told him that they regarded the alleged "Laws" as "an *ad hoc* invention of your own."

(I had realized in 1975 that if the "Craft Laws" had been in existence in July 1957, at least half of the "Proposed Rules" would not have been needed, and that the "Proposed Rules" therefore probably occasioned the writing of the "Craft Laws" sometime after mid-1957. I then carried out a technical analysis of the Craft Laws, and discovered that they had originally emphasized the authority of the Elders, just as the "Proposed Rules" did, and that the emphasis on the High Priestess had been introduced in a secondary reworking. Hence I was certain that the "Craft Laws" were based on the "Proposed Rules," and not vice versa. In her 1985 letter to *Iron Mountain*, Doreen denied that the "Proposed Rules" had anything to do with the Craft Laws, because she had not grasped that Gerald was being so devious that he had taken her and Ned's proposal, rewritten it into archaic language, and sent it back to them. I am glad that she has now confirmed my reasoning.)

Later, after Gerald was caught in a lie about yet more publicity seeking, and refused to admit he was lying, even in the face of independent proof, Doreen says that she and the rest of those who felt as she did went their own ways. Actually, during 1957 and 1958, Doreen and Ned were running their own coven independently of Gardner; it was not until some time later that she resigned from the Gardnerian Craft. In 1964 she began her period of working with Robert Cochrane, who claimed (falsely) to belong to a type of "traditional" witchcraft that had existed before 1939.

Doreen was predisposed to believe Cochrane's claims because she still wanted to believe Gardner's basic claim, which serves as the Craft's foundational myth, that there had been an older coven before September 1939 that had survived from the past. She says that when she broke off from Gardner, "We had had enough of the Gospel according to St. Gerald; but we still believed that the real traditional witchcraft lived . . . that when Gerald said he had found an old coven surviving in southern England, he was telling the truth." She has repeatedly mentioned the testimony of Louis Wilkinson, and her own confirmation of the real existence of Dorothy Clutterbuck, as supporting her belief; but as we have already seen, the facts that Wilkinson knew the coven intimately in early 1940, and that Dorothy Clutterbuck really was a member of it, do not prove the existence of anything before September 1939. Doreen Valiente continues to believe in the existence of traditional witchcraft before 1939 because that, for her, is an article of faith, and there is no evidence to disprove it. However, like the resurrection of Jesus of Nazareth, it does not qualify as historical fact.

Source Notes

The material quoted and paraphrased herein from Valiente, *Rebirth of Witchcraft*, can be found on its pages 14, 36-40, 47, 57, 60-62, 66-72.

5. The Book of Shadows in 1957

The major changes recorded here resulted from the writing and rewriting done by Doreen Valiente between 1953 and 1957, but Gardner also began rewriting the rituals in 1957. Text has been reconstructed from *Witch*, the Weschcke documents, data in *Witchcraft Today* and *Meaning of Witchcraft*, and the data given by the Farrars 1984.

5.1. A Revision of the Casting Procedure

[This was included among the Weschcke documents.]

ALL ARE PURIFIED

[1] Magus consecrates salt and water.

[2] High Priestess kneels at Altar, takes up Sword, says, "*I conjure thee, O Sword* of Steel, to serve me as a *defense in all Magical Operations*. Guard me at all times *against mine enemies*, both *visible and invisible*. Grant that I may obtain what *I desire in all things wherein I* may use *Thee*, Wherefore do I bless Thee and invoke Thee in the names of Aradia and Cernunnos." Gives Sword to Magus.

[3] Magus kneeling hands her vessel of consecrated Water and Aspergillum. He Casts the Circle, three circles, on the lines marked out, starting at the East and returning to the East. High Priestess follows, Asperging Circle (sprinkling it to purify it) and all present and finally herself. Then she goes round again censing it. (Everyone in

the circle must be sprinkled and censed.) She returns vessel, etc., to Magus, who places them on altar, or convenient place, *and hands her Sword* [handwritten].

[4] She walks slowly round Circle, saying, "I conjure Thee, O Circle of Space, that thou be a Boundary and a Protection and a meeting place between the world of Men and that of the Dread Lords of the OUTER SPACES, that Thou be cleansed, Purified, and strengthened to be a Guardian and a Protection that shall preserve and contain THAT POWER which we so earnestly desire to raise within thy bounds this night, *wherefore do I bless thee and entreat thee to aid me in the endeavor* in the names of Aradia and Cernunnos." *Hands sword to Magus* [handwritten].

[5] Magus then summons the Mighty Ones as usual.

[6] High Priestess stands in front of Altar (which may be pushed back for this). High Priestess assumes Goddess position (arms crossed). Magus kneeling in front of her, draws pentacle on her body with Phallus-headed Wand, Invokes (Drawing Down the Moon), "I Invoke and beseech Thee, O mighty MOTHER of all life and fertility. *'By seed and root, by stem and bud, by leaf and flower and fruit, by Life and Love, do I invoke Thee'* to descend into the body of thy servant and High Priestess (name)." (The Moon having been drawn down, i.e., link established, Magus and all male officers give fivefold kiss; all others bow.)

~~<Assembly form a semicircle at north of Altar (which should be replaced if it has been moved). High Priestess in south, inserts point of Sword or Athame in decorated bundle of 13 candles, saying>~~

[7] High Priestess in Goddess position says (Arms crossed)

"I the Mother, Darksome and Divine,
    Mine the Scourge and Mine the Kiss,
    The Five Point Star of Love and Bliss;
Here I charge ye in this Sign.
       (Opens out Arms to pentacle position)

Bow before my Spirit bright   (All bow)
    Aphrodite, Arianrhod,
    Lover of the Horned God,
Queen of Witchery and Night.

Commentary on 5.1.

This innocent-looking document—a working draft from the process of writing what would become the standard Gardnerian procedure for beginning a Craft ritual—is the most important of all the documents I have seen, except for "Ye Bok of ye Art Magical" itself, for reconstructing the history of the Gardnerian movement.

This is certainly not a first draft; the consecration of salt and water in [1] and the summoning of the Mighty Ones in [5] are already "standard operating procedures." On the other hand, one does not type over two sentences with m's when copying or writing down an established procedure; that is what I have indicated by use of strikeout type. The sources of formula [2] are *The Greater Key of Solomon*, pp. 98, 101, 118; it has been rewritten from the form that Doreen Valiente says (in the Farrars 1984, p. 44) was used in 1954-1956; therefore this document was written sometime in or after 1957.

The censing in [3] agrees with the HOGD Neophyte ritual and with the procedures of *The Greater Key of Solomon*, pp. 96-97. The formula in [4] is patterned after those in *The Greater Key of Solomon*, although only the part in italics is a close paraphrase of a line in *The Greater Key of Solomon*, p. 94.

Let see what becomes of the various elements here. The "Conjuration of the Sword" is soon dropped from the basic ritual (see 7.3), but becomes part of the special procedure used for charging tools, in 5.10. The "Conjuration of the Circle" in [4] and the formula for "Drawing Down the Moon" are still used in 7.3, but have been slightly rewritten; the wording in 7.3 is exactly that of the Alexandrian Book of Shadows (Farrar 1971, pp. 54, 64), and so the version here must be earlier.

There are handwritten corrections in [3] and [4], because Gardner, looking the manuscript over after it was typed, realized that he had asked the Priestess to walk around the circle with no tool in her hands; so he added the instructions that give her the sword. But this caused the circle to be cast first by the Magus in [3], then again by the Priestess in [4]. The casting procedure had to be greatly simplified to remove this redundancy, which still appears in 5.6 and 7.3, but has been eliminated in 7.4.

Who is dominant here, the Magus or the Priestess? It is the Magus who consecrates salt and water, who casts the circle first and is followed around by the Priestess, who hands the Priestess the tools she is to use, who summons the Mighty Ones, and who calls down the Goddess onto the Priestess. That is, we are still in the universe of *High Magic's Aid*, in which the male magician must use the procedures of ceremonial magic to erect the magical circle before the female witch can work her folk magic in it. Yet there are also elements of change here: the uncertainty over whether the arms-crossed position should represent the Goddess or the God; the Magus' kneeling before her in [3] and [6]. These point forward to Gardnerian practice since the mid-1960s (see Farrar 1971, pp. 53-55, for example), in which the Priestess can work the entire ritual by herself. But reading the trend here backward, we can see that before 1957 the coven was presided over by a man, not a woman: and that is what I predicted from my hypothesis that the starting point for Gardner's group in 1939 had been the data in Murray.

Let us, finally, consider dating. Doreen Valiente wrote the quatrain verse form of the Charge after a partial prose form had appeared in *Witchcraft Today*. Hence 5.1 must date to 1954 or later—and, in fact, as we will see below, must be dated in late 1957—and 5.6, 5.10, 7.2, 7.3, and 7.4, which all depend on 5.1, must be later yet (although some elements of the raw material in them date from the period 1948 to 1953). In other words, despite all the explicit and implicit claims made about rituals in *Witchcraft Today*, Gardner had still not established the basic working procedures of his "tradition," and was not yet clear about the relative importances of the Priestess and Priest within the coven, or about which of them should do what in a ritual, even in 1957. This is hardly the situation we would imagine if there had been a coven before 1939 that was organized well enough to hold rituals.

We can see from Tanya Luhrmann's description (pp. 223-4) of the procedure used by the London coven for casting the circle used in the late 1980s that it is still essentially that of "Ye Bok of ye Art Magical," although details have been altered in order to "paganize" it. Her description lists the following steps.

1. A circle is drawn with chalk and a string held down in the center by the High Priestess's athame, just as in 3.1 [1].

2. To begin the ritual, the circle is first cast with the athame in the air, retracing the circle, as in 3.1 [2].

3. The salt is consecrated, as in 3.1 [3].

4. The water is consecrated, as in 3.1 [4].

5. The two are mixed, as in 3.1 [5].

6. The circle is sprinkled, as in 3.1 [6].

7. The quarters are invoked, combining the procedures of 3.1 [9], [11], and [12].

8. Incense is presented to the quarters; this is substituted for the lighting of candles in 3.1 [7].

9. A gate is opened, and the participants, who have been outside the circle so far, are now admitted; then the circle is retraced to close the gate. This agrees with the content of 3.1 [8].

If you compare these steps with the sequence of events in 5.1 here, or in 5.6, 7.3, and 7.4, which all depend on 5.1, you can see that they simply do not match; they all disagree with Luhrmann's description in far more ways than the procedure in "Ye Bok of ye Art Magical" does. In other words, Gardner's original coven was still using the procedures specified in "Ye Bok of ye Art Magical" in the late 1980s, because Gardner did not write the procedures for casting the circle in 5.1, 5.6, 7.3, and 7.4 until *after* Doreen Valiente had stopped working with him in 1957, when he also left the original coven. These later procedures were included in the text of the Book of Shadows given to Gardner's initiates after 1957, and therefore appear in the Farrar's 1981 and 1984 books. In the latter books, although Doreen Valiente supplies commentary about what is in her Texts A, B, and C for everything else, she actually does not say anything about the procedure for casting the circle. As a result, it is not obvious that her book disagrees with the Book of Shadows as used by the great majority of Gardnerian Witches now; and she has confirmed in a recent letter that this is so, and that she did not write the "Conjuration of the Circle" in 7.3. What had happened is that, once she had stopped working with Gerald, he proceeded to rewrite her rituals and much else in the Book of Shadows, and it was this rewritten book that came into the hands of Monique Wilson and Patricia Crowther.

These conclusions also have major implications for the way in which the Craft conducts itself in America, since we can now see that rules about circles being "valid" only if cast by a Third-Degree High Priestess have no basis in Gardnerian practice in England before 1957, as Fred Lamond has been saying loudly for almost a decade now.

5.2. The Prose Charge

[This was included among the Weschcke documents.]

THE CHARGE, to be read while the initiate stands, properly prepared before the Circle.

Listen to the words of the Great mother, who was of old also called among men, Artemis, Astarte, Dione, Melusine, Aphrodite, Cerridwen, Diana, Arianrhod, Bride, and by many other names.

"At mine Altars the youth of Lacedaemon in Sparta made due sacrifice.

" 'Whenever ye have need of anything, once in the month, and better it be when the moon is full. Then ye shall assemble in some secret place and adore the spirit of Me who am Queen of all Witcheries.

" 'There ye shall assemble, ye who are fain to learn all sorcery, yet who have not won its deepest secrets. To these will I teach things that are yet unknown.

" 'And ye shall be free from slavery, and as a sign that ye be really free, ye shall be naked in your rites, and ye shall dance, sing, feast, make music, and love, all in my praise.'

"For mine is the ecstasy of the Spirit, and mine is also joy on earth. For my Law is Love unto all beings.

"Keep pure your highest ideals. Strive ever towards it. Let naught stop you or turn you aside.

"For mine is the secret which opens upon the door of youth; and mine is the cup of the Wine of Life: and the Cauldron of Cerridwen, which is the Holy Grail of Immortality.

"I am the Gracious Goddess who gives the gift of Joy unto the heart of Man.

"Upon Earth I give the knowledge of the Spirit Eternal, and beyond death I give peace and freedom, and reunion with those who have gone before. Nor do I demand aught in sacrifice, for behold, I am the Mother of all things, and my love is poured out upon earth."

Hear ye the words of the Star Goddess, She in the dust of whose feet are the hosts of Heaven, whose body encircleth the universe.

"I who am the beauty of the green earth; and the White Moon amongst the Stars; and the mystery of the Waters; and the desire of the heart of man. I call unto thy soul: arise and come unto me.

"For I am the Soul of nature who giveth life to the Universe; 'From me all things proceed; and unto me, all things must return.'

Beloved of the Gods and men, thine inmost divine self shall be enfolded in the raptures of the infinite.

"Let my worship be within the heart that rejoiceth, for behold: all acts of love and pleasure are my rituals; and therefore let there be Beauty and Strength, Power and Compassion, Honour and Humility, Mirth and reverence within you.

"And thou who thinkest to seek me, know that thy seeking and yearning shall avail thee not unless thou know the mystery, '*That if that which thou seekest thou findest not within thee, thou wilt never find it without thee,*' for behold; I have been with thee from the beginning, and I am that which is attained at the end of desire."

Commentary on 5.2

The last quote is from "Alipilli" on the title page of L. A. Cahagnet, *Magnetic Magic* (privately printed, 1898; 47 pages, paperbound), a book from Gardner's library that I looked at in Toronto. Since we know that this is Doreen Valiente's work after 1954, nothing else needs to be said.

5.3. Cakes and Wine.

[This was included in the pamphlet *Witch*.]

High Priestess seated on Altar, God position.

Magus, kneeling, kisses her feet, then knees, bows with head below her knees, extends arms along her thighs, and adores.

Magus fills cup and offers it to High Priestess, who, holding Athame between palms, places point in cup.

Magus says: "As the Athame is the male, so the cup is the female, and conjoined they bring blessedness."

High Priestess lays Athame aside, and takes Cup and drinks, gives Cup to server, who puts a little in each glass. Meanwhile the Magus presents Pentacle with cakes to High Priestess, saying, "Oh Queen most secret, bless this food unto our bodies, bestowing health, wealth, strength, joy and peace, and that fulfillment of love that is perpetual happiness." High Priestess blesses them with Athame, Takes Cake and eats, while the Magus gives her the Cup again and kisses knees and adores.

All sit as Witches, and invite High Priestess to join them.

Commentary on 5.3

The actions here, and the words in the fifth paragraph, come from Crowley's "Gnostic Mass" in *Magick in Theory and Practice*, pp. 351, 356f, 359f. All my comments about 3.5 still apply here. I believe this is one of the most important times in the working of any coven. This sort of communal eating, drinking, and conversing is intended to be sacramental—and therefore it is so. Another version of this ritual is given by Farrar 1971, pp. 18-19.

5.4. The Sabbat Rituals

[A set of scripts for all eight Sabbats was included among the Weschcke documents; and this is the source for the text here.]

Spring Equinox March 22nd

The symbol of the wheel should be placed on the altar upright, decked with flowers, flanked with burning candles. The Cauldron, containing spirits, is in the east. Magus in west, High Priestess in east with Phallic wand or pinecone-tipped wand, or broomstick, or riding pole, broom upwards.

High Priestess lights Cauldron, saying,

"We kindle fire this day!
In the presence of the Holy Ones:
    Without malice, without jealousy, without envy.
Without fear of aught beneath the sun.
But the High Gods.

Thee we invoke: O light of life:
    Be thou a bright flame before us:
Be thou a guiding star above us:
    Be thou a smooth path beneath us;

Kindle thou in our hearts within,
    A flame of love for our neighbor,
To our foes, to our friends, to our kindred all:
    To all men on this broad Earth.

O merciful son of Cerridwen

From the lowest thing that liveth
To the name that is highest of all."

High Priestess draws pentacle upon Magus with wand, kiss, gives it to him. He does likewise. They lead the dance round the circle, all couples leaping burning fire. The last couple as the fire goes out should be well-purified three times, and each should give Fivefold Kiss to all of opposite sex.

Cakes and wine.

If the people will, the Cauldron dance can be done again, many times, or other games can be played.

The Summer Solstice Midsummer June 22nd

Form circle. Invoke, Purify. Cauldron is placed before altar filled with water, wreathed with summer flowers. The people, men and women alternately, stand round circle.

High Priestess stands in north, before Cauldron, holding wand (which should be Phallic or tipped with a pinecone (anciently the thyrsus) or a riding pole or a broomstick.

High Priestess holding this raised invokes the sun. "Great One of Heaven, Power of the Sun, we invoke thee in thine ancient names, Michael, Balin, Arthur, Lugh, Herne. Come again, as of old, into this thy land. Lift up thy shining spear of light to protect us. Put to flight the powers of darkness, give us fair woodlands and green fields, blossoming orchards and ripening corn. Bring us to stand upon thy hill of vision, and show us the path to the lovely realms of the gods."

High Priestess draws invoking pentacle on Magus with wand.

Magus comes forward sunwise and takes wand with kiss, plunges wand into Cauldron and holds it upright, saying, "The spear to the Cauldron, the lance to the Grail, spirit to flesh, man to woman, sun to earth." He salutes High Priestess over Cauldron, then rejoins people, still bearing wand.

High Priestess takes aspergillum, stands by Cauldron, says, "Dance ye about the Cauldron of Cerridwen the Goddess, and be ye blessed with the touch of this consecrated water, even as the sun, the lord of light, arriveth in his strength in the sign of the waters of life."

The people dance sunwise about the altar and Cauldron, led by Magus bearing wand. High Priestess sprinkles them lightly as they pass her.

Ritual of cakes and wine.

Any other dances, rites, or games as the Priestess and people wish.

Autumn Equinox Sept. 22nd

The altar should be decorated with symbols of autumn, pine cones, oak sprigs, acorns, or ears of corn, and should have fire or burning incense on it as usual. After usual purification, the people stand round, men and women alternately. Magus at west of altar in God position.

High Priestess stands at east of altar, facing him, and reads the incantation.

"Farewell, O Sun, ever returning light. The hidden god, who ever yet remains. He departs to the land of youth, through the gates of death, to dwell enthroned, the judge of gods and man. The horned leader of the hosts of air. Yet, even as stand unseen about the circle the forms of the Mighty Lords of the Outer Spaces. So dwelleth he, *'the lord within ourselves'*. So dwelleth he within the secret seed, the seed of new reaped grain, the seed of flesh, hidden in the earth, the marvelous seed of the stars. *'In him is life, and life is the light of men* [John 1:4],' that which was never born and never dies. Therefore the Wicca weep not, but rejoice."

The High Priestess goes to the Magus with a kiss. He lays aside Athame and scourge, and kisses her. The High Priestess hands him her wand, which should be Phallic, or a branch tipped with a pinecone, or a riding pole, or a broomstick (anciently the thyrsus). They lead the dance, she with a systrum or rattle, he with wand, the people falling in behind them, dancing three times round the altar. Then the candle game is played.

Cakes and wine.

Great Rite if possible.

Dances and games.

The Winter Solstice Dec. 22

Form circle in usual manner, invoking the Mighty Ones.

The Cauldron of Cerridwen is placed in the circle at the south wreathed with holly, ivy, and mistletoe, with fire lighted within it. There should be no other light except for the candles on the altar and about the circle.

After all are purified, the Moon should be drawn down.

Then the High Priestess stands behind the Cauldron in pentacle position, symbolizing the rebirth of the sun. The people, man and woman alternately, stand round the circle. The Magus stands facing the High Priestess with a bundle of torches, or candles, and the book of words of the incantation. One of the officers stands beside him with a lighted candle, so that he may have light to read by.

The people begin to slowly move round the circle sunwise. As each passes him the Magus lights his candle or torch from the fire in the Cauldron, which may be simply a candle, till all have lighted candles or torches. Then the people dance round slowly as he reads the incantation. (A real fire must now be kindled in the Cauldron.)

"Queen of the Moon, Queen of the Sun.
  Queen of the Heavens, Queen of the Stars.
Queen of the Waters, Queen of the Earth.
  Who ordained to us the child of promise:

It is the Great Mother who gives birth to him,
  He is the Lord of Life who is born again,
Darkness and tears are set behind,
  And the star of guidance comes up early.

Golden sun of hill and mountain
  Illumine the land, illumine the world
Illumine the seas, illumine the rivers,
  Grief be laid, and joy be raised.

Blessed be the Great Mother
  Without beginning, without ending,
To everlasting, to eternity,
  I O. Evohe, Blessed be."

The dance commences slowly, in rhythm with the chant, all taking up the call "I. O. Blessed be." The Priestess joins dance and leads them with a quicker rhythm. The cauldron with burning fire is pushed so that the dancers leap or step over it, in couples. Whichever couple is passing it as it goes out, should be well-purified, three times each, and may pay any amusing forfeit as the High Priestess may ordain. Sometimes the cauldron is relighted several times for this purpose.

Commentary on 5.4

I have given here only the four Sabbat rituals that Doreen Valiente wrote, as far as I know, for the quarter days. The four earlier ones, written by Gardner, also remained in the Book of Shadows.

The Farrars (1981, p. 78n2) state that the verse in the Spring Equinox ritual was adapted by Doreen Valiente from two verses in Carmichael's *Carmina Gadelica*, vol. I, on pages 231 and 49; this was the work she had also used as a source for her Yule ritual. Notice that this ritual does not follow the pattern that Gardner used for the four earlier Sabbats, of many scourgings, followed by the Great Rite. Similarly, the Summer Solstice ritual does not follow Gardner's pattern; the Farrars (1981, p. 101n3) state that the material in it from "Great One of Heaven" down to "Waters of Life" was written by Doreen Valiente.

The quote in the autumn equinox ritual is from Crowley's "Gnostic Mass" in *Magick in Theory and Practice*, p. 352. It seems very odd that Valiente would have used this quote, given her normal strategy of getting rid of Crowley; so perhaps Gardner wrote that particular Sabbat ritual. It also is closer to the pattern of the four earlier Sabbats by Gardner, since it calls for the Great Rite.

The winter solstice ritual here has also been thoroughly rewritten from the text that appeared in *Witchcraft Today*. Gardner has done some of this revising, since it is surely he who added the detail that the couple who are leaping over the cauldron when it goes out are to be "purified" with 120 strokes each.

5.5 The Eightfold Path or Ways.

[This was included among the Weschcke documents.]

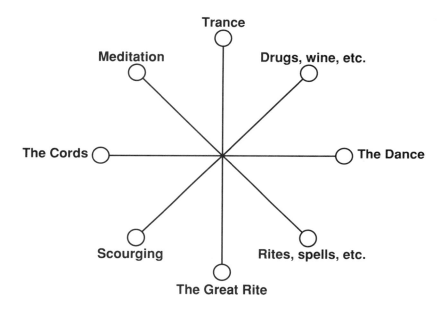

Figure 5.1. The Eightfold Way of the Craft

1. Meditation or concentration, actually by the firm knowledge that you can and will succeed—forming a clear picture in your mind of your requirements.
2. Trance states, Clairvoyance, Projection of the Astral etc.
3. Drugs, Wine, Incense.
4. Dance, Performing Rites with a purpose.
5. Chants, Spells etc.
6. Blood control (Cords etc), Breath control.
7. Scourge
8. The Great Rite
N.B.

The great thing is to combine as many of these paths into the one operation. No. 1 must be in all—for if you have no clear picture of what you wish and no certainty you will not succeed—'tis useless. No. 2 can be combined with this easily. Nos. 3, 4, and 5 are all good preliminaries—also 6 and 7; but No. 3 is dangerous and therefore if possible should be avoided, except for incense, which is harmless if too much is not used.

The best combination is Nos. 1, 4, 5 and 7, for small purposes, with No. 8 if great force is necessary. Also a combination of 1, 6, and 7 is good if more can not be done; this if properly performed leads to No. 2.

Commentary on 5.5

This is a revision of Document 3.14. The "five essentials" (entries 9-13 in Document 3.14) are missing here; perhaps they were on the next page of the Book of Shadows this sheet came from. However, the "N.B." here consists of the material in 3.14.9 combined with that in the last paragraph of commentary in Document 3.14. The long parenthesis about the dangers of drugs in 3.14.4 has here been reduced to a single clause. We noted earlier that Document 3.15 amounts to a rewriting of the concepts in the note to 3.14.4 and in 3.14.9-13. For this reason, I would expect the "essentials" of Document 3.14 to be dissociated entirely from the "Eightfold Path" in most later versions of the Book of Shadows.

Notice that Gardner has here rearranged the contents of paths 3, 4, and 5—since he feels free to rearrange this material, we may suppose he devised the arrangement of it in Document 3.14. We saw no strong reasons to consider anything in Document 3.14 to be derived from an older coven rather than from books; we have even less reason to consider this rewriting of Document 3.14 to be traditional in any way. Since this document, like 5.7, may have been typed by Doreen Valiente, it would fall somewhere in the period 1954 to 1957.

5.6. The First-Degree Initiation

[The text here is based on the Weschcke documents, and on *Witch*, which gives two pages of this ritual not included in the Weschcke documents.]

Draw Circle with Magic Sword or Athame.
Sprinkle with Exorcised Water.
Go round Circle with Magic Sword or Athame, Saying, "I conjure thee, O Circle of Power, that thou beest as a Boundary and a Pro-

tection to contain the magic power which I will raise within thy bounds. So do I bless thee, in the names of Aradia and Cernunnos."

Go round, saying at East, South, West, and North, "I summon, stir, and call thee up, ye Mighty Ones of the East (South, West, North), to witness the rites and to guard the circle."

[According to the Farrars 1984, at this point occurs the rite of Drawing Down the Moon, followed by the "Cabalistic Cross," which is in fact the liturgical prayer, "For thine is the kingdom, and the power, and the glory forever, amen," said in Hebrew. Doreen Valiente confirms that this stood in her Text B. This must have been one of Gardner's revisions, since it does not appear in "Ye Bok of ye Art Magical" or *High Magic's Aid*.]

Read Charge, then say, "O thou who standest on the threshold between the pleasant world of men and the dread domains of the lords of the outer spaces, hast thou the courage to make the assay?" (Place point of the Magic Sword or Athame to Postulant's heart.) "For I say verily it were better to rush on my blade and perish than to make the attempt with fear in thy heart."

Postulant: "I have two perfect words: perfect love, and perfect trust."

Say, "All who have are doubly welcome."

Entering position: "I give you a third to pass you through this dread door." Gives it [kiss].

Leading postulant, proclaim at four quarters, "Take heed, ye Lords of the East (South, West, North), that (name) is properly prepared to be made a priestess and a witch."

Three times round the Circle with Dance step and chant.

Place Postulant in East; say, "In other religions the postulant kneels while the priest towers above him, but in the Art Magical we are taught to be humble, and so we kneel to welcome them, and we say:

"Blessed be the feet that have brought you in these ways [kiss];

"Blessed be the knees that shall kneel at the sacred altar [kiss];

"Blessed be thy womb (or organ of generation), without which we would not be [kiss];

"Blessed be thy breasts, erected in beauty and in strength [kiss];

"Blessed be thy lips, which shall utter the sacred names [kiss].

"Before ye are sworn, art willing to pass the ordeal and be purified?"

Postulant "I am."

Take measure. Secure. Three strokes on bell. Scourge 3, 7, 9, 21.

Say, "Ye have bravely passed the test. Art ready to swear that thou wilt always be true to the Art?"

Postulant "I am."

"Art always ready to help, protect, and defend thy brothers and sisters of the Art?"

Postulant "I am."

"Then say after me: I, (name), in the presence of the mighty ones of the outer spaces, do of my own free will most solemnly swear that I will ever keep secret and never reveal the secrets of the Art, except it be to a proper person, properly prepared, within such a circle as I am in now, and that I will never deny the Secrets to such a person if they be vouched for by a brother or Sister of the Art. All this I swear by my hopes of a future life, and may my weapons turn against me if I break this my solemn oath."

(Assist to rise.)

"I hereby sign thee with the triple sign [the point-down triangle formed by touching the genitals, the right breast, the left breast, and the genitals again.]

"I consecrate thee with oil.

"I consecrate thee with wine.

"I consecrate thee with my lips, Priest (Priestess) and Witch."

Remove Cords [kiss].

"I now present to you the working tools. First the magic sword. With this, as with the athame, thou canst form all magic circles, dominate, subdue, and punish all rebellious spirits and demons, and even persuade angels and good spirits. With this in your hand, you are ruler of the circle." [kiss]

"Next I present to you the athame. This is the true witches' weapon, and has all the powers of the magic sword." [kiss]

"Next I present the white-handled knife. Its use is to form all instruments used in the Art. It can only be used in a magic circle." [kiss]

"Next I present the wand. Its use is to call up and control certain angels and genie to whom it would not be meet to use the sword or athame." [kiss]

"Next I present the pentacle. This is for the purpose of calling up the appropriate spirits." [kiss]

"Next I present the censer of incense. This is used to encourage and welcome good spirits, and to banish evil spirits." [kiss]

"Next I present the scourge. This is a sign of power and domination. It is also used to cause purification and enlightenment, for it is written, 'To learn you must suffer and be purified.' [kiss] Art willing to suffer to learn?"

Postulant: "I am."

"Next and lastly I present the cords. They are of use to bind the sigils of the art, also the material basis. Also they are necessary in the oath." [kiss]

"I now salute you in the names of Aradia and Cernunnos, Newly made Priestess and Witch."

Lead round and proclaim to four quarters, "Hear, ye Mighty Ones, (name) has been consecrated a priestess of the Goddess."

To close circle proclaim to four quarters, "Ye Mighty Ones of the East (South, West, North), I thank you for attending and, ere ye depart for your lovely realms, I say hail and farewell."

Commentary on 5.6

Observe that the procedure for casting the circle at the beginning of this version of the initiation has been influenced by the revised procedure in 5.1. That is, Gardner had rewritten some of the first-degree initiation before he gave the script of it to Olive Green (whom we will meet in Chapter 6) in 1958 or 1959.

5.7. The Second-Degree Initiation

Form Circle in usual manner, invoking the Mighty Ones at the Four Quarters. The Initiate should be properly prepared and bound with the Cords. All are purified, including Initiate.

Circle once, proclaiming at the Four Quarters: "Hear Ye Mighty Ones, . . . (N), a duly consecrated Priestess and Witch is now properly prepared to be made a High Priest and Magus (High Priestess and Witch Queen)."

Circle three times, with dance step and chant.

Initiate then kneels before the Altar and is secured with the Cords.

Priestess or Magus: "To attain to this sublime degree it is necessary to suffer and be purified. Art willing to suffer to learn?"

Initiate: "I am."

Priestess or Magus: "I purify thee to take this great oath

rightly." Strike three strokes upon the bell. Scourge 3, 7, 9, 21.

"I now give thee a new name: . . ." [kiss]

"Repeat thy new name after me, saying, 'I, . . ., swear, upon my mother's womb and by mine honor among men and my brothers and sisters of the Art, that I will never reveal to any at all any of the secrets of the Art, except it be to a worthy person, properly prepared, in the center of a Magic Circle such as I am now in. This I swear by my hopes of salvation, my past lives and my hopes of future ones to come and I devote myself and my measure to utter destruction if I break this my solemn Oath.'"

Kneel. Place Left Hand under Initiate's Knee and Right Hand on Head, thus forming Magic Link, saying: "I will all my power into thee." WILL. Loose, assist to rise.

Consecrate: "I consecrate thee with oil, I consecrate thee with wine, I consecrate thee with my lips, High Priest and Magus (High Priestess and Witch Queen)." Loose remaining cords. [kiss]

"You will now use the working tools in turn,

"First the Magic Sword (Form Circle) [kiss]

"Second the Athame. (Form Circle) [kiss]

"Third the White-Handled Knife (use) [kiss]

"Fourth the Wand. (Wave to 4 Quarters) [kiss]

"Fifth the Pentacle. (Show to 4 Quarters) [kiss]

"Sixth the Censer. (Circle, cense) [kiss]

"Seventh the Cords. (Use) [kiss]

"Eighth the scourge. In witchcraft you must ever give as you receive, but ever triple. So where I gave thee 3 return 9, where I gave 7 return 21, where I gave 9 return 27, where I gave 21 return 63." (Use, 9, 21, 27, 63, i.e., 120 in all [kiss]) "Thou hast obeyed the law. But mark well, when thou receivest good, so equally art bound to return good threefold."

The Priestess or Magus is then loosed from the cords and says: "Having learned thus far you must know why the Wica are called the Hidden Children of the Goddess."

Then the Legend of the Goddess is either read or acted out. If it is possible to act it out, the new Initiate may take one of the parts. One of the Coven should act as Narrator, and another as Guardian of the Portal. The Priestess, or another woman, may act the part of the Goddess, and the Magus, or another man, may act the part of the God. The Priestess—or whoever is taking the part of the Goddess—takes off her necklace and lays it on the Altar. Then she goes outside the circle and is dressed in a veil and jewelry. The Magus—or whoever is taking the part of the God—is invested with a horned crown and girds on a sword, which he draws and stands in the God position with sword and scourge, by the altar.

Narrator: "In ancient times our Lord, the Horned One, was, as he still is, the Consoler, the Comforter; but men knew him as the Dread Lord of Shadows—lonely, stern, and hard. Now our Lady the Goddess <had never loved, but she> would solve all mysteries, even the mystery of Death—and so she journeyed to the Nether Lands. The Guardians of the Portals challenged her."

(The Priestess—or whoever is taking the part of the Goddess—advances to the side of the Circle. Whoever is taking the part of the Guardian of the Portal challenges her with the Sword or Athame.)

Narrator: "'Strip off thy garments, lay aside thy jewels, for nought may ye bring with ye into this our land'. So she laid down her garments and her jewels and was bound, as are all who enter the realms of Death the Mighty One."

(The Priestess takes off the veil and the jewelry and lays them down outside the Circle. The Guardian of the Portal binds her with the Cords and brings her inside the Circle.)

Narrator: "Such was her beauty that Death himself knelt <and laid his sword and crown at her feet> and kissed her feet."

(The Magus—or whoever is playing the part of the God—comes forward and lays the Horned Crown and the Sword at the Priestess's feet and kisses her feet.)

Narrator: "Saying, 'Blessed be thy feet that have brought thee in these ways. Abide with me, but let me place my cold hand on thy heart'. And she replied, 'I love thee not. Why dost thou cause all things that I love and take delight in to fade and die?' 'Lady,' replied Death, ''Tis Age and Fate, against which I am helpless. Age causes all things to wither; but when men die at the end of time, I give them rest and peace and strength, so that they may return. But you—you are lovely; return not—abide with me.' But she answered, 'I love thee not.' Then said Death, 'An you receive not my hand on your heart, you must receive Death's scourge.'"

(The Magus rises and takes up the Scourge from the Altar.)

Narrator: " 'It is fate, better so,' she said, and she knelt."

(The Priestess kneels before the altar, and the Magus uses the scourge 3, 7, 9, 21.)

Narrator: "And Death scourged her tenderly, and she cried, 'I feel the pangs of love'. And Death raised her, and said, 'Blessed be,' and he gave her the Fivefold Kiss, saying, 'Thus only may you attain to joy and knowledge.' "

(The Magus raises the Priestess, gives her the Fivefold Kiss and unties the cords.)

Narrator: "And he taught her all the Mysteries <and gave her the necklace, which is the Circle of Rebirth>."

(The Magus takes the Priestess's necklace from the Altar and replaces it about her neck. The Priestess takes up the Sword and the Horned Crown from the floor, where the Magus placed them, and gives them back to him. Then he stands as before by the Altar, in the position of the God, and she stands by his side in the pentacle position, as Goddess.)

Narrator: "And they loved and were one; and he taught her all the Magics. For there are three great events in the life of man—love, death, and resurrection in a new body—and magic controls them all. To fulfill love you must return at the same time and place as the loved one, and you must remember and love them again. But to be reborn you must die and be ready for a new body; to die you must be born; without love you may not be born—and these be all the magics"

The Priestess or Magus then replaces the Sword, Crown, Scourge, etc., upon the Altar, and taking the new Initiate by the hand and holding the Athame in the other, passes once round the Circle, proclaiming at the Four Quarters, "Hear, Ye Mighty Ones, . . . hath been duly consecrated High Priest and Magus (or High Priestess and Witch Queen)."

Commentary on 5.7

The content of this document probably dates to 1953 or earlier, since it uses terms like Magus and Art that disappear soon after 1953. On the other hand, there are differences in wording that post-date *Witchcraft Today*, and that are given by Farrar 1971, who invariably gives later versions of wordings; and the typing, spelling, and punctuation are much better than in the other Weschcke documents, because this one was typed by Doreen Valiente, some time between 1954 and 1957.

We have all the documents needed to show how this ritual was written. The pre-1949 second-degree ritual in "Ye Bok of ye Art

Magical" does not contain the myth about the descent of the Goddess. The myth first appears in print in 1954 in *Witchcraft Today*, and its language had to be tinkered with in order to fit it into the second-degree ritual; the angle brackets <these things> here flag language that has been added to the earlier version of the "myth" in order to fit it in here.

Notice also that the changes here are in line with Gardner's own agenda. An instruction has been added at the beginning requiring all to be scourged. The "Myth of the Goddess" has also obviously been added; not only is it a theologizing of the scourging, but when acted out it includes another scourging.

5.8. The Third-Degree Initiation

[This was included among the Weschcke documents.]

High Priest gives Fivefold Kiss.
"I beg purification at thy hands."
Priestess scourges High Priest.
He Warlocks [binds] High Priestess.
Circle, Proclaims to 4 quarters, "Take heed ye Mighty Ones, The Lady (name), High Priestess and Witch Queen, is properly prepared to celebrate the Great Rite."
He scourges her.
High Priest kisses her feet. "Ere I dare proceed with this sublime degree, I must again beg purification at thy hands."
She scourges him.
Note: if High Priestess has not performed this rite before, he says, "Here I reveal to you a great mystery. {Kneel and place couch in position so as to face north.}

Assist me to build
    As the Mighty One willed,
An Altar of praise,
    From beginning of days,
Thus doth it lie,
    Twixt the points of the sky,
For thus it was placed
    When the Goddess embraced
The Horned One, Her Lord,
    Who taught her the word,

Which quickened the womb,
   And conquered the Tomb.
Be thus as of yore,
   The Shrine we adore,   [kiss]
The feast without fail,
   The life-giving Grail,   [kiss]
Before it uprear
   The Miraculous Spear,
And invoke in this sign
   The Goddess divine.   [kiss]

Invoke: "Thou who at moon of night doth reign,
   Queen of the starry realm above,
'Not unto Thee may we attain
   Unless Thine Image be of Love.'   [kiss]

By moon-rays silver shaft of power,
   By green leaf breaking from the bud,
By seed that springeth into flower,
   By life that courseth in the blood.   [kiss]

By rushing wind and leaping fire,
   By flowing water and green earth,
Pour us the wine of our desire
   From out Thy Cauldron of Rebirth.   [kiss]

Here may we see in vision clear
   The Secret Strange unveiled at length,
The wondrous Twin-Pillars rear
   Erect in Beauty and in Strength.   [kiss]

Altar of Mysteries manifold,
   The Sacred Circle's central point,
Thus do I sign thee as of old,
   With kisses of my lips anoint.   [kiss]

[Here a pentacle surmounted by a point-up triangle is drawn; see Figure 5.2.]

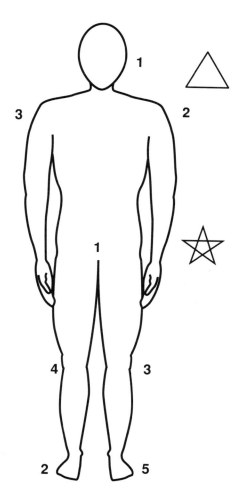

Figure 5.2.

Open for me the Secret Way,
    The pathway of intelligence,
Between the Gates of Night and Day,
    Beyond the bounds of time and sense.

Behold the Mystery aright,
    The Five True Points of Fellowship,
Here where the Lance and Grail unite,
    And feet and knees and breast and lips."

(Exchange Names.)

Anoint 3 points: Lips, 2 Breasts, and back to lips.
Anoint 5 points [as drawn], with oil, wine, and kisses.

Commentary on 5.8

This versified version of the third-degree ritual is given almost verbatim by "Rex Nemorensis"; so it must date from before August 1959. However, it must be later than the version in "Ye Bok of ye Art Magical", whose prose is here being versified. I had deduced by 1981 that Doreen Valiente had written this verse ritual about 1954; so I see no reason to doubt the statements to that effect by the Farrars (1981, p. 92 n3). Notice that a second scourging of the High Priest has been added at the beginning; this would, of course, better enable Gardner to carry out the Great Rite.

5.9. The Witches' Chant or Rune

[This is partly included among the Weschcke documents, and was published in *Witch*.]

Darksome night and Shining Moon,
    East, then South, then West, then North,
Harken to the Witches Rune:
    Here come I to call thee forth.

Earth and Water, Air and Fire,
    Wand and Pentacle and Sword,
Work ye unto my desire,
    Harken ye unto my word.

Cords and Censer, Scourge and knife,
    Powers of the Witches Blade,
Waken all ye into life,
    Come ye as the Charm is made:

Queen of Heaven, Queen of Hell,
    Horned Hunter of the Night,
Lend your power unto the Spell,
    Work my will by Magic Rite.

If chant is used to reinforce a work already begun, end with this:

> By all the power of land and sea
>> By all the might of moon and sun,
> What is my will- *"So mote it be,"*
>> What I do say- "It shall be done."

Witch gives the last two lines as "As I do will, so might it be, Chant the Spell and Be it Done." Doreen Valiente said in *Witchcraft for Tomorrow* (p. 21) that she and Gardner had written this song about 1954 or 1955.

5.10. Consecrating Tools

[This was included among the Weschcke documents.]

CONSECRATING THE SWORD OR THE ATHAME

(Note: if possible lay any new weapon touching an already consecrated one, Sword to Sword, Athame to Athame, etc.)

[1] Prepare Circle and purify. All tools must be consecrated by a man and a woman, both as naked as drawn swords.

[2a] Place sword or Athame on altar. Touching with already consecrated weapon, say, "I conjure thee, O *Sword* (or Athame) of Steel, *that thou servest me for a strength and a defense in all magical operations, against all mine enemies, visible and invisible,* in the names of Aradia and Cernunnos. *I conjure thee anew* by the Holy Names Aradia and Cernunnos, *that thou servest me for a protection in all adversities,* So Aid me." Sprinkle and Cense. Say, "*I conjure thee O Sword of Steel,* by the Great Gods and the Gentle Goddesses, by the virtue of the Heavens, of the Stars, of the Spirits who preside over them. *'that thou mayest receive such virtues that I mayest obtain the end that I desire in all things wherein I shall use thee,'* by the power of Aradia and Cernunnos."

CONSECRATING THE WAND OR ANY OTHER TOOL

[2b] "Aradia and Cernunnos *'Deign to bless and to consecrate this Wand, that it may obtain necessary virtue'* through thee for all acts of love and Beauty." Sprinkle and cense. "Aradia and Cernunnos, bless

this instrument prepared in thine honour." (In the case of the scourge and Cords, add "That it may only serve for a good use and end, and to thy Glory.")

[3] All instruments when consecrated should be presented to their User by giving the [point-down triangle] sign salute (if they are working in the 1st degree, or the sign of the higher degree if they are working that.)

[4] Then it should be placed between the breasts, and the two workers should embrace, it being held in place by their bodies. The new owner should use it immediately, i.e., cast (trace) Circle with Sword or Athame, wave wand to 4 quarters, cut something with white-handled knife, etc. Cords and scourge should be used at once.

Commentary on 5.10

The phrases indicated by italics are from *The Greater Key of Solomon*, pp. 98, 101, 118. Despite the headings, paragraphs [3] and [4] apply to the consecration of the sword or athame as well as to that of the wand; so paragraphs [2a] and [2b] are alternatives within the same procedure. Only two details in this document might conceivably be connected with some sort of pagan magical religious traditions. The first is the idea of touching a new magical tool with an old "charged" tool, in order to transfer some of the "charge" to the new tool. But this is a standard sort of magical procedure, quite in keeping with Frazer's laws of magic, and hence far more likely to have been learned from books than from a previous coven. The second is the male-female embrace, to "charge" the tool with sexual energy; it is another example of the Craft's radical sacramentalizing of sexuality. The use of the cords and scourge at the end has been added in this draft.

Final Comments on the Book of Shadows in 1957

There were apparently a few other paragraphs in the Book of Shadows in 1957 that do not appear in any materials available to me, except in the Farrar's 1984 book. These include:
the paragraph on their pp. 53-54 entitled "Power";
the paragraph on their pp. 54-55 entitled "Properly Prepared";
the paragraph on their p. 55 entitled "The Meeting Dance" (although it is summarized in *Witchcraft Today*, Chap. 13);

the paragraph on their pp. 56-57 entitled "The Cone of Power";
the paragraph on their p. 59 entitled "To Leave the Body";
the paragraph on their p. 61 entitled "The Working Tools"; and
the paragraphs on their pp. 62-63 entitled "Making Tools" and
    "Various Instructions."

I have no doubt that these paragraphs are from Gardner himself, and that they therefore belong in any complete Gardnerian Book of Shadows. But since I have nothing scholarly to add concerning the text of these paragraphs, and since they do not affect my historical argument, I do not think it would be fair for me to give them here. I may already have stolen far more of the Farrar's thunder than I would have liked. So let me compensate for that by recommending that you buy their excellent 1981 and 1984 books, if you haven't already, and copy these passages into your own Book of Shadows.

6. Gardner, 1957-1960

Once Doreen had stopped working with him, Gerald began to rewrite the Book of Shadows rituals as he saw fit. It is these revised rituals, rather than Doreen's versions, that became the authoritative text of the Book of Shadows passed on to the covens in America. Gardner also proceeded to initiate a great many new High Priestesses during the last seven years of his life; these included Patricia Crowther, Eleanor "Ray" Bone, Lois Hemmings, and Monique Wilson, "Lady Olwen." Some of these were well-accepted by his previous initiates; others were not. Doreen Valiente, for example, has always been good friends with Patricia Crowther, but has never had any use for Monique Wilson.

Gardner's activities during these years are in some ways typified by his run-in with the Cardells, who apparently first approached the Gardnerians in early 1958, claiming to be Witches also, and proposing that they all pool their information on the Craft. The earliest reliable information I have been able to find about the Cardells and their relationship to the Gardnerian movement is in a letter in the files in Toronto. It is dated July 17, 1958, and is from Doreen Valiente (using her Craft name of "Ameth") to Dafo.

Dear Dafo,
Enclosed herewith is a copy of the latest edition of "Light", a well-known quarterly which was almost defunct, and has now been revived by Mr. Francis Clive-Ross of the Aquarian Press. You will see that it contains an article by Charles and Mary Cardell, called "The Craft of the Wiccens", and also a full-page ad-

vertisement inviting genuine members of that Craft to get in touch with the advertiser, Charles Cardell.

We are in touch with Cardell, both Ned and myself have had long talks with him, and he has asked us to forward to you a copy of his "Open Letter to Gerald Brosseau Gardner", which I do herewith. He accompanies it with a letter to yourself, which is rather dramatically expressed and calls for some explanation from us.

Firstly, he says that I will vouch for his integrity. I will vouch for the fact that I have seen him once, and had a long talk with him; further than that, I cannot say. I can only repeat what he told me on that occasion.

It appears that, according to him, his mother was a member of the genuine Craft of the Wiccens (he pronounces this word "Witchens"), and that when she died she left her Athame to him and her bracelet to his sister Mary, together with her traditions. I have seen both the Athame and the Bracelet. They are not the same as ours, but bear sufficient resemblance to be worthy of our attention.

His family came from Wales, but he is now living in Surrey, and also has a flat in London. Here he contacted Gerald, and told me that he had proposed to finance the bringing of Gerald's museum to London. However, he became disgusted with Gerald's publicity-seeking and the general behaviour of his followers. . . . He therefore broke with them and wrote to Gerald the "Open Letter" enclosed.

It appears that they [Gardner and his followers] made great play with you, as being the lady from whom originated the link with the old coven. However, when he very much wanted to be put in touch with you, they put him off repeatedly. . . .

Now, there is no doubt of Cardell's enthusiasm for the Craft. I have this morning a letter from Ned, who is a shrewd businessman and nobody's fool generally, as well as having a great deal of experience of the occult, in which Ned says he is convinced Cardell is genuine. I am never convinced of anything nor prepared to vouch for anything on the strength of one meeting; however, I personally liked Cardell, and his sister. I will go so far as to say that I have a completely open mind on the subject.

What the proposal is at the moment is that we get together with Cardell and pool our respective traditions. As you will remember, I wrote to you some time ago and told you very frankly of our feelings with regard to what we had received from Gerald. Your reply was so cautious that I could make neither head nor tail of it! So what we have been doing has been to try to get as close as we could to the spirit of the old beliefs, and try to feel intuitively what was right and real, and embody it in our rituals. We were engaged on this task when our contact came with Cardell.

Incidentally, we now have a good meetingplace which we are busy getting into the shape we want it; a matter I am very pleased about, though it will mean a lot of hard work.

Well, my dear, such are the latest developments. I trust you and yours are all well. "Blessed be ......"

Yours sincerely,
Ameth

Consider the second-from-last paragraph. The mention of traditions to be pooled reminds Doreen of her dissatisfaction with the "traditions" learned from Gerald, as well as with Dafo's cautiousness when questioned. Hence, during the 18 months since she and Ned had begun their coven, they have been trying to get close to the spirit of the old beliefs (there is a contrast implied with getting close to the letter; although Doreen believed such beliefs existed, they were unwritten), discover what was real about those beliefs by means of intuition, and then embody those discoveries in their rituals. Doreen's phrase about trying "to feel intuitively what was right and real" means that they really were trying to reconstruct and recreate what they believed to be an older religion, by means of intuition and imagination. This is typical of a search for religious authenticity.

Doreen did not believe then, nor does she believe now, that Gardner, Dorothy, and the other members of the original coven had simply made up everything about the Craft; instead, she believed that there had been some sort of religious tradition preserved by an older coven. Hence her initial response, and that of the other initiates in the 1950s, to Cardell's claims was to hope that the claims were true, because they would then provide independent evidence that some sort of religious tradition had existed before 1939.

All the statements about Cardell I have seen indicate that he had used a trick common among con artists: he had simply taken the data in *Witchcraft Today*, augmented it with his own inventions, and taken it back to Gerald and Doreen, claiming to have learned it from his mother. Doreen reported to me in a recent letter that Mary was, in fact, not Charles' sister, that they had been living together for thirty years as "brother and sister"; this shows that his story about what they had inherited from "their" mother was a fabrication. Gardner must, of course, have known that Cardell was spinning a tall tale, but he could not have said so without damaging his own credibility. Instead, he allowed Doreen and the others to believe that

Cardell might indeed represent an independent witness to the existence of the Old Religion.

However, Doreen has written me, "the more both Ned and I saw of Cardell, the less favourably we viewed him. I was invited to his 'consulting-rooms' in Queen's Gate, London. They were quite splendidly appointed as a sort of private temple; but when Cardell showed me a bronze tripod which was obviously nineteenth-century and tried to tell me that it had been dug up from the ruins of Pompeii, I became rather unhappy. When he showed me a bronze statue of Thor and tried to tell me that it was of a Celtic horned god, I couldn't help myself pointing out that Thor was not a Celtic god—and then he became rather unhappy. There were a number of other things like this. And then Cardell crowned the performance by making a ham-handed and unsuccessfull attempt to hypnotize me. Well, I knew a trick worth two of that, and he didn't get anywhere. . . .

"Now, give old Gerald his due, he never went in for that sort of 'deviousness'; so I was not favourably impressed. However, I kept on friendly terms with Cardell in order to find out what he was up to. And, of course, we eventually learned just how nasty he could be when he was thwarted."

It thus became obvious to Doreen and the others that the Cardells had no independent information to pool, and were instead engaging in a ruse in order to get their hands on a Gardnerian Book of Shadows. When this ruse failed, the Cardells turned to another strategy, which is recorded (although in a strange way) in the pamphlet *Witch*, of which I have a xerox (kindly sent me by Margot Adler) of the second edition, dated December 1964. It is typewritten and self-published. The name on the title page is "Rex Nemorensis"—that is, the "King of the grove at Nemi" who guards Diana's sacred bough in Frazer's 13-volume work—but a notice about Gardner's recent death on the next page is signed "Charles and Mary Cardell."

The first section is given the grandiose title, "Nemesis: Rex Nemorensis Draws His Sword." It begins,

> It was a wild night, the rain was lashing down with the wind blowing it fiercely . . . in my sound-proof consulting rooms in London . . . I sat in peace. For over forty years I have been a confidential Psychologist, specialising in trying to unravel the tangle and jumble created in the minds and emotions of unfortunate people who have dabbled in the occult in some form or other.

In what follows he continues to paint himself as a sort of occult Sherlock Holmes. Out of the storm, there arrives a young woman who informs "Rex" that she has been initiated by Gardner and a woman, because of whose "beastliness, superstition, and sheer downright roguery" (which are not explained by any further details), her "sensitive nature" has suffered a "complete breakdown." So next we read,

> on that stormy night in 1957, Rex Nemorensis woke from his sleep and, drawing the Sword of the Water City, set forth to do battle with one more slimy serpent of the bogus occult world, leading a small band of people who dedicate their time and money to protecting the innocent from these money grubbing ghouls, who pretend to occult powers.

(This sort of grandiosity appears many times in this brief pamphlet. It seems to be not merely literary, but a symptom of poor mental health.) He gives some opinions (which I will discuss later) about Gardner and Doreen Vlachopoulos, whose marriage certificate is reproduced and whom he identifies as "Ameth." (Doreen commented to me, "Cardell's venom against me was occasioned by the fact that he tried very hard to recruit me into his coven, and I wasn't having any. Neither was Ned.") Cardell next says, if I may paraphrase, that he sent in "Florannis" (whose name was actually Olive Green) as a ringer to be initiated, so that she could get her hands on Gardner's rituals.

In Section 2 of the pamphlet, Cardell prints those rituals. (He also used them to set himself up in business teaching witchcraft classes in exchange for hefty fees, as Gardner's friends immediately reported to him.) The rituals are virtually identical to the Weschcke documents, and so are of some help in understanding the chronology of the various drafts of Gardner's rituals.

In her statement in Section 3 of the pamphlet, Florannis describes her initiations in some detail. She attempts to paint Gardner as a simple-minded old pervert, but instead manages to portray him as a rather kindly and gullible eccentric. Doreen has written to me, "I was told some years later by Jack Bracelin that all the business about Florannis having a 'private initiation' was occasioned by the fact that the others had never liked her and never wanted her in Gerald's coven; but poor old Gerald was so infatuated with her that he wouldn't listen to any warnings. I can believe this. It was typical of him, unfortunately, and just the sort of thing that our 'Proposed Rules' had been intended to prevent."

In Section 1 of the pamphlet, we find a letter from Gardner. It reads,

> Castletown 28.8.59.
> My dear Olive
>   Now, the main thing I have to say is, "You say I stink."
> Well, I do not think that this is so, and I do not think I am fright-
> ened·either. But if you think "I STINK," I do not think it is worth
> saying anything more.
>   Yours sincerely
>   May you be blessed.
>   Gerald [handwritten]
>   "I SENT A LETTER TO MY LOVE"!

If the letter to which Gardner is replying is anything like the letters from Olive Green in the files in Toronto, then it was evil-tongued indeed. (I do not have specialized knowledge of "poison-pen" letters, but certainly Ms. Green's letters are the most malevolent and vicious writing I have ever seen. Doreen has written me, "Gerald showed me some specimens of Florannis's letters, after we got together again. It takes something to shock me; but I was genuinely shocked. It is possible, however, that they were actually dictated by Cardell.") Gardner's letter is rather calm and compassionate for a man who has been betrayed by a young woman whom he had loved and trusted. It certainly does not square with the story Florannis tells in her statement, nor with Cardell's claim that the Gardnerians proceeded to cast curses at him—something that is strictly against Gardnerian ethics in any case. Why was this letter included at all? Apparently Cardell could not see that it damaged his claims. Fortunately for my purposes, the letter gives us a "last possible date" for these events, and so for the documents reproduced in Section 2, and therefore for the Weschcke documents to which they correspond.

The story Cardell tells here is contradicted on most points by Doreen's letter to Dafo, and by the fact that the Cardells were teaching Witchcraft classes for money during this period. I see no reason to doubt the veracity or authenticity of Doreen's letter; so I must suppose that Cardell is untrustworthy, as is also indicated by his grandiosity. This casts a pall of dubiousness over everything else he says, even those things that I would tend, for independent reasons, to think are true.

For example, on p. 4 he says that Gardner had begun searching for witches in 1944, but had not found any by 1951. When he met Doreen Vlachopoulos [Valiente],

> realising that there were not any witches in Britain, they hit on the idea that people might be persuaded that there were. So together they wrote and compiled ... *Witchcraft Today*, in which ... Gardner ... stated that he had discovered witches in Britain. ... Our own investigations ... have proved conclusively that there was no suggestion of modern witchcraft in Britain prior to the advent of Gerald Brosseau Gardner and Doreen Vlachopoulos. Until then, witches were merely characters in children's fairy tales. ... [p. 7] the complete witchcraft ritual, with its initiations and ceremonies, has been pieced together by [G.B.G and D.V.] from ... many different sources ... Masonry, Aleister Crowley, Kabbalistic magic, odds and ends of Folklore, Barrett's "Magus", Rites of Isis, and much actual [quoting] and paraphrasing of "Aradia" ... There are even ideas from the Catholic Mass.

To some extent Cardell was clearly on the right track, but he knows nothing about *High Magic's Aid*, Dorothy, Dafo, and Gardner's work during the decades before he met Doreen. Cardell then goes on to claim that the Gardnerian covenstead at the nudist club near St. Albans was merely for "hoaxing the National Press." Having heard a history of that covenstead from Fred Lamond, who has met with his coven in it regularly for the last thirty-odd years, I know better. Cardell also calls almost all of Gardner's followers "psychologically unbalanced," but that, I suspect, is projection. Cardell's desire to get his hands on Gardner's Book of Shadows in order to teach classes for a profit seems to provide a simple and sufficient explanation for the facts related by Doreen, and for those inadvertently revealed in his own pamphlet.

Witch included the "Warning," that is, the document given here in 3.12, but the wording is closer to that in the Craft Laws. Since this passage from *Witchcraft Today* was incorporated into the Craft Laws, and would not have been included separately in a Book of Shadows after the Craft Laws had been promulgated, we can see that Gardner did not begin giving out the Craft Laws as part of the Book of Shadows until after September 1959.

7. The Book of Shadows in 1961

The changes here resulted from Gardner's additions of new material, especially the "Craft Laws," and his revisions of the basic casting procedure.

7.1 The Old Laws

[This was included among the Weschcke documents, as two separate documents, in which I have assigned line numbers separately, beginning with 1 again in Section [J]. In the commentary in the right-hand column, I indicate the sources of the materials that Gardner rewrote into the Craft Laws.]

[A] The Law was made and Aredan of old. The law was made for the Wica, to advise and help in their troubles. The Wica should give due worship to the Gods and obey their will, which they Aredan, for it was made for the good of the Wica, As the [5] Wica's worship is good for the Gods, For the Gods love the Wica. As a man loveth a woman, by mastering her, so the Wica should love the Gods,

Meaning of Witchcraft, pp. 26 and 136: "They think that the God and the Goddess assist them in making their magic, as they assist the God and the Goddess in their turn by raising power for them by their dances and by other methods ... the 'Sacred Marriage' was not merely for the satisfaction of those who took part; their powers were dedicated to . . . giving great power to the

145

by being mastered by them.

And it is necessary that the Circle, which is the Temple of the Gods, should be truly cast and purified, that it [10] may be a fit place for the Gods to enter. And the Wica should be properly prepared and purified, to enter into the presence of the Gods.

With love and worship in their hearts they shall raise power from their bodies to give power to the Gods, as has been taught us of old, [15] For in this way only may man have communion with the Gods, for the Gods cannot help man without the help of men.

[B] And the High Priestess shall rule her Coven as representative of the Goddess, and the High Priest shall support her as the representative of the God, And the High Priestess shall choose whom she [20] will, if he have sufficient rank, to be her High Priest.

For the God himself, kissed her feet in the fivefold salute, laying his power at the feet of the Goddess, because of her youth

Gods, . . . bringing the Gods into communion with their worshippers."

Witchcraft Today, p. 28: "When drawn the circle is carefully purified, as also are all who celebrate the rites. Witches attach great importance to this, for within the circle is the gods' domain." [Note that being bound and scourged has thus been made part of the Craft Laws.]

High Magic's Aid, p. 83: "'We witches have our gods also, and they are good, at least to us, but they are not all-powerful, and so they need our aid. They desire fertility for man, beast, and crops, but they need our help to bring it about, and by our dances and other means they get that help.'"

Witchcraft Today, p. 154: "Now the god is represented by the high priest (if there is one) and . . . 'He is whoever the high priestess appoints to take this position.' In practice she always appoints her husband if he has sufficient rank; but she may appoint anyone who is eligible."

[This is a reference to, and rewriting of, the "Myth of the Goddess" in *Witchcraft Today*, pp. 45-46.]

and beauty, her sweetness and kindness, her wisdom and Justice, her humility and generosity. So he resigned his lordship to her.

But the Priestess should [25] ever mind that all power comes from him. It is only lent when it is used wisely and justly. And the greatest virtue of a High Priestess is that she recognizes that youth is necessary to the representative of the Goddess, so that she will retire gracefully in favour of a younger woman, Should the Coven so decide in Council, For the true [30] High Priestess realizes that gracefully surrendering pride of place is one of the greatest of virtues, and that thereby she will return to that pride of place in another life, with greater power and beauty.

Meaning of Witchcraft, pp. 128-9: "Among the virtues she must have is the realization that youth is among the requisites necessary for the representative of the Goddess, and that she must be ready to retire gracefully in favour of a younger woman in time. . . . So a true Priestess realizes that gracefully surrendering pride of place now is one of the greatest virtues, and she will return to that pride of place the next time, in another incarnation, with greater power and beauty."

[C] In the days when Witchdom extended far, we were free and worshipped in Alther Greatest Temples, but in these unhappy times [35] we must hold our sacred mysteries in secret. So it be Aredan, that none but the Wica may see our mysteries, for our enemies are many, And torture looseth the tongues of many. It be aredan that each Coven shall not know where the next Coven bide, or who its members

Witchcraft Today, p. 129: "witches . . . deliberately never know where the next coven is. If they do not know, they cannot tell, for who knows when the persecution may break out again?" *High Magic's Aid*, p. 214: "In the old days all knew where the Sabbath was to be held, and who would attend it, so when a few were taken and tortured, it was easy to find out all who went to the meetings, their

are, save the Priest and Priestess, [40] That there shall be no communication between them, save by the Messenger of the Gods, or the Summoner. Only if it be safe, may the Covens meet, in some safe place, for the great festivals.

And while there, none shall say whence they come, or give their true names, to the end that, if any are tortured, in their agony, they can [45] not tell if they know not. So it be Aredan that no one may tell any not of the Craft who be of the Wica, nor give any names, or where they bide, or in any way tell any thing which can betray any to our foes, nor may they tell where the Covenstead be, or where is the Covendom, [50] or where be the meetings or that there have been meetings.

And if any break these laws, even under torture, The Curse of the Goddess shall be upon them, so that they are never reborn on earth, And may

leaders and priests, and often even who represented the God Himself. . . . only officers must know who are the leaders of the covens, and especially, who is our God."

Rule 9. Members will meet upon the traditional occasions, or as near to them as possible, and such meetings will be arranged by the Elders, or such Officers as the Elders authorise to do so.

Rule 2. No affairs of the Craft will be discussed by members in the presence of uninitiated persons, or in places where conversation is likely to be overheard.

Rule 5. No member of the Craft will give any information or interview about the Craft to any journalist or writer, or cause any such information to be published in any way, without the approval of the Elders. . . .

Rule 8. No member will disclose the name and address or telephone number of any other member to any person whatsoever, without the said other member's previous permission.

Witchcraft Today, p. 86: "the curse of the goddess may be on any who break this law."

<they> remain where they be-long, in the Hell of the Christians.

[D] Let each High Priestess govern her Coven with Justice and [55] love, with the help of the advice of the elders, always heeding the advice of the Messenger of the Gods, if he cometh. She will heed all complaints of brothers, and strive to settle all differences among them, but it must be recognized that there be people who will ever strive to force others to do as they will. [60] They are not necessarily evil, and they often do have good ideas, and such ideas should be talked over in council. And if they will not agree with their brothers, or if they say, "I will not work under this High Priestess," it hath always been the old law to be convenient for the brethren, and to void disputes, any of the Third [65] may claim to found a new Coven because they live over a league from the Covenstead, or are about to do so. Anyone living within the Covendom wishing to form a new Coven, to avoid strife, shall tell the Elders of his intention and on the instant void his dwelling and remove to the new Covendom.

Members of the old Coven may join the New one when it be

Rule 4. As it is essential for the successful working of ritual by a group that there should be unity of purpose and an harmonious psychic atmosphere, members who create dissension and discord within the Craft will be asked to resign. Should they fail or refuse to do so they will be informed in writing by the Elders that they have been expelled.

Rule 6. If any member of the Craft feels that he or she has reason to complain of the conduct of any other member in matters affecting the Craft, or of any misdemeanour towards any member whilst on Craft premises, he or she will bring the said complaint to the notice of the elders as soon as possible. The Elders, after considering all available evidence, will, if they find the complaint justified, take appropriate action.

Rule 9. Members will meet upon the traditional occasions, or as

formed, but if they do, must utterly void the old Coven. The Elders of the New and the Old Covens should meet in peace and brotherly love, to decide the new boundaries. Those of the Craft who dwell outside both Covendoms may join either indifferent, but not both, though all may, if the Elders [75] agree, meet for the Great Festivals, if it be truly in peace and brotherly love. But splitting the coven oft means strife, so for this reason these laws were made of old, And may the curse of the Goddess be on any who disregard them. So be it aredan.

near to them as possible, and such meetings will be arranged by the Elders, or such Officers as the Elders authorize to do so. If the Elders be not present at such meetings, they will receive a report of them.

[E] <If you would> Keep a book <let it be> in your own hand of write. [80] Let brothers and sisters copy what they will, but never let the book out of your hands, and never keep the writings of another, for if it be found in their hand of write, they <well may> be taken and <Engined.> Each should guard his own writings and destroy it whenever danger threatens. Learn as much as you may by heart, and when danger is [85] past, rewrite your book <an> it be safe. For this reason, if any die, destroy their book if they have not been able to, for <an> it be found, 'tis clear proof against them, <And our op-

[Sections E and G are the "Warning" that appeared on the first page of "Ye Bok of ye Art Magical", and in *Witchcraft Today*. In neither place was there any suggestion that it was an excerpt from a larger body of traditional laws. I have put angle brackets <these things> around words that have been added to the earlier text, and around the archaic words that have been substituted here for the common words used in the earlier text. This is obviously not how someone treats genuinely old material.]

pressors well know>, "Ye may not be a witch alone" So all their <kin and> friends be in danger of torture. So ever destroy anything not necessary.

[90] If your book be found on you, 'tis clear proof against you <alone>. You may be <engined>. Keep all thoughts of the <Craft> from your mind.

Say you had bad dreams; a devil caused you to write it without your knowledge. Think to yourself, "I know nothing. I remember nothing. I have forgotten everything." Drive this [95] into your mind. If the torture be too great to bear, say, "I will confess. I cannot bear this <torture>. What do you want me to say? Tell me and I will say it." If they try to make you speak of the brotherhood, Do NOT, but if they try to make you speak of [100] impossibilities, such as flying through the air, consorting with the <Christian> Devil, or sacrificing children, or eating men's flesh, to obtain relief from torture, say, "I had an evil dream. I was not myself. I was crazed."

Not all Magistrates are bad. If there [105] be an excuse they may show mercy. If you have confessed aught, deny it afterwards; say you babbled under

[Where "cult" was used in "Ye Bok of ye Art Magical" and *Witchcraft Today*, it has been replaced by "Craft," which began to be used as a name for the religion only rather late in the 1950s.]

["Dwale" is defined by the *Oxford English Dictionary* as being either nightshade or a soporific drink made therefrom; the examples run from the tenth to

torture, you knew not what you did or said. If you are condemned, fear not. The Brotherhood is powerful. They may help you to escape, if you stand steadfast, but if you betray aught, there is no <hope> for you, in this [110] life, or in that which is to come. <Be sure>, if steadfast you go to the pyre, <Dwale> will reach you. You will feel naught. You go but to Death and what lies beyond, the ecstasy of the Goddess.

[F] 'Tis probable that before you are engined, Dwale will reach you. [115] Always remember that Christians fear much that any die under torture. At the first sign of swoon, they cause it to be stopped, and blame the tormenters. For that reason, the tormenters themselves are apt to feign to torment, but do not, so it is best not to die at first. If Dwale reaches you, 'tis a sign that you have a friend somewhere. [120] You may be helped to escape, so despair not. If the worst comes, and you go to the pyre, wait till the flames and smoke spring up, bend your head over, and breath in with long breaths. You choke and die swiftly,

the nineteenth centuries. Here is another archaic word, intro-introduced where Gardner had first used "drugs." Gardner mentions "dwale" specifically in *Meaning of Witchcraft* (p. 74) as a word peculiar to the Craft, in a passage that means he was busy finding archaic words in 1957 to 1958.] 3.9 [8]: Remember the Words of the Goddess "I give unimaginable joys, on Earth certainty not faith while in life and upon death, peace unutterable, Rest and Ecstasy." [Notice that this is a quote from Crowley.]

3.9: "command them that if they are ever questioned about Witchcraft or Witches to immediately fall asleep." {Section [F] was not in *Witchcraft Today*, nor in the copy that went to Patricia Crowther and thence to Sanders and Lady Sheba. This late insert is concerned with using the archaicizing terms "dwale" and "engined." Like Sections [E] and [G] in general, it is conceptually based on material from 3.9.}
Witchcraft Today, p. 151: "In the old days many witches went to the flames laughing and singing; they had a joy of life and of beauty, and the Peace of Death with the

and wake in the arms of the Goddess.

[G] <To void discovery, let> the working tools [125] be as ordinary things that any may have in their houses. Let the Pentacles be of wax, so they may be broken at once. Have no sword unless your rank allows you one. Have no names or signs on anything. Write the names and signs on them in ink before consecrating them and wash it off immediately after. <Do not Bigrave them, [130] lest they cause discovery. Let the colour of the hilts tell which is which.>

[H] <Ever remember, ye are the Hidden Children of the Gods. So never do anything to disgrace them.> Never boast, Never threaten, Never say you would wish ill to anyone. If <you or> any <not in the Circle> speak of the Craft, [135] say, "Speak not to me of such. It frightens me. 'Tis evil luck to speak of it."

For this reason: the Christians have spies everywhere. These speak as if they were well affected, as if they would come to Meetings, saying, "My mother

promise of return, so they braved the fires, for they believed that they were going to a better world, and they died happy."

[The material in lines 124-129 that was in *Witchcraft Today* has been heavily rewritten here, in order to create a better transition within this larger document. (Here the earlier text read, "The same with the working tools. Let them be." I pointed out the importance of this in discussing 3.12.) Again, this is not how a person treats genuinely traditional writings. Lines 129-130 expand material in *Witchcraft Today*, to create a bridge to Section H; they could not have stood alone.]

["Hidden Children of the Gods" is a reference to the post-1953 version of the second-degree ritual, and "not in the Circle" is a reference to the oath of the first or second degree; so this passage could not have been written before the initiation rituals had been.]

3.9 [5]: "Ever remember if tempted to admit or boast of belonging to the cult you be endangering your brothers, for though now the fires of perse-

used to go to worship the Old Ones. I would that I could go myself."* To these ever deny all knowledge.

cution may have died down <but> who knows when they be revived? . . . if we take many recruits, we may loose the fires of persecution against us again. So ever keep the secrets." Here combined with concepts in Rules 2, 5, and 8.

[140] But to others ever say, "'tis foolish men talk of witches flying through the air; to do so they must be light as thistle down," and "Men say that witches all be bleared-eyed old crones, so what pleasure can there be in witch meetings such as folk talk on?" Say, "Many wise men now say there be no such creatures." Ever [145] make it a jest, and in some future time, perhaps the persecution will die, and we may worship safely again. Let us all pray for that happy day.

{Section [H] is woven together from *High Magic's Aid*, p. 214 (see section [C] above), *Witchcraft Today*, pp. 151-2 (see section [F] above; and *Meaning of Witchcraft*, p. 150 (see section [L] below). Lines 145-147 are a "prediction after the fact" that allow an "earliest possible date" to be assigned to this document. The document wishes us to think of the late eighteenth century; in fact, what it actually refers to is the repeal of the last witchcraft law in 1951.}

[I] May the blessings of the Goddess and the God be on all who keep these laws which are Aredan.

[This closing exhortation for the document could not have stood alone. I think the first draft that Gerald sent to Doreen and the rest in 1957 ended here.]

[J] If the Craft hath any Appanage, let all brothers guard it, and help to keep it clear and good for the Craft, and let

[According to the *Oxford English Dictionary* (p. 95), this French word came into English in the late sixteenth century.

---

* My Lady Epona points out that this is precisely what Charles Cardell had claimed; that is, this paragraph is a response to Cardell, and so it was probably inserted into the Craft Laws after the run-in with the Cardells and Olive Green in 1959. This again is an indication that Gardner did not promulgate the Craft Laws as a document for the Book of Shadows until about 1960, when Mr. Q. was initiated.

all justly guard all monies of the Craft.

But if some brothers truly wrought it, 'tis right that they have their pay, an it be just, an this be not taking [5] money for the use of the Art, but for good and honest work. And even the Christians say, "A labourer is worthy of his hire." But if any brothers work willingly for the good of the craft without pay, 'tis but to their greater honour. So it be Aredan.

[K] If there be any disputes or quarrels among the brethren, the [10] High Priestess shall straight convene the Elders and enquire into the matter, and they shall hear both sides, first alone, then together, and they shall decide justly, not favouring the one side or the other, ever recognizing that there be people who can never agree to work under others, but at the same time there be some people who [15] cannot rule justly. To those who ever must be

Not only is this archaic word being used here in its precise and original sense of "land possessed to provide one with the means of subsistence," but the first sentence has been written specifically to use it. "Coven" would make more sense than "Craft" here; what is being discussed is the affairs of a small group, not of a large religious movement.]

{Lines 4-9 make little sense unless you have already read section [M], where these lines should have been inserted. This is a late gemara that happened to get attached to the front, rather than the rear, of this second batch of laws. Since it is dependent on section [M], for which there are ample parallels, it cannot be traditional in this form.}

{Section [K] duplicates Section [D], and is likewise based on Rules 4 and 6. I presume that in the wording here Gerald is responding to Doreen's desire to split the coven in 1957.}

chief, there is one answer, "Void the Coven and seek another, or make a Coven of your own, taking with you those who will to go." To those who cannot rule justly, the answer be, "Those who cannot bear your rule will leave you," for none may come to meetings with those with whom they are at [20] variance; so, an either cannot agree, get hence, for the Craft must ever survive. So it be Aredan.

[L] In the olden days when we had power, we could use our Arts against any who ill-treated any of the Brotherhood, but in these evil times, we may not do so, for our enemies have devised a burning [25] pit of everlasting fire, into which they say their God casteth all the people who worship him, except it be the very few who are released by their priests' spells and Masses, and this be chiefly by giving money and rich gifts to receive his favour, for their Alther Greatest God [Greatest God of all] is ever in need of Money. [30] But as our Gods need our aid to make fertility for men and crops, So the God of the Christians is ever in need of man's help to search out and destroy us.

High Magic's Aid, p. 83: "In the Christian belief you have a good God ... all-powerful, and who greatly desires worshippers ... yet you ... must give money or other rich gifts before you can hope to receive favor. . . We witches have our gods also, and they are good, at least to us, but they are not all-powerful, and so they need our aid. They desire fertility for man, beast, and crops, but they need our help to bring it about, and by our dances and other means they get that help ... your god so loved the world he made that he devised a burning purgatory of everlasting fires, into which he casteth all the peoples he had created for many thousands of years, except a few of a chosen race. Then, it seems, he changed his mind, and casteth all that chosen race into this fiery pit, all save a few who embraced a new faith which he had made!"

[This passage has clearly been created to link the preceding passage with the following one. It would have no point if it stood in isolation.]

Their priests tell them that any who get our help or our cures are damned to the Hell forever, so men be mad for the terror of it. But they make men [35] believe that they may scape this hell if they give victims to the tormenters. So for this reason all be forever spying, thinking, "An I can but catch one of the Wica I will scape this fiery pit." But we have our hidels, and men searching long and not finding say, "there be none, or if they be, they be in a far country."

[40] But when one of our oppressors die, or even be sick, ever is the cry, "This be Witches Malice," and the hunt is up again. And though they slay ten of their people to one of ours, still they care not; they have many thousands, while we are few indeed. So it is Aredan that none shall use the Art in any way to do ill [45] to any, howevermuch they have injured us. And for long we have obeyed this law, "Harm none" and nowtimes many believe we exist not. So it be Aredan that this law shall still continue to help us in our plight. No one, however great an injury or injustice they receive, may use the

Meaning of Witchcraft, p. 150: "if witches could kill their enemies so easily, why was there not a notable number of deaths among their opponents? . . . I think that when first attacked they hit back, but the actual 'initiated witches' as distinct from the 'Congregation' were few. . . . It is a tradition among witches that thousands of people were tortured and burnt for every one witch . . . The witches met and decided, 'We can't fight against this terror; every time we strike, so many thousands were massacred, the only way any of us can survive, is to go underground. Never hurt any, however much they

Art in any to do ill or harm any. [50] But they may, after great consultations with all, use the Art to prevent or restrain Christians from harming us and others, but only to let or constrain them and never to punish, to this end. Men say, "Such an one is a mighty searcher out and persecutor of Old Women whom he deemeth to be Witches, [55] and none hath done him Skith [harm], so this be proof they cannot, or more truly, that there be none," For all know full well that so many folk have died because someone had a grudge against them, or were persecuted because they had money or goods to seize, or because they had none to bribe the searchers. And many have died [60] be cause they were scolding old women, so much so that men now say that only old women are witches, and this be to our advantage, and turns suspicion away from us.

In England 'tis now many a year since a witch hath died the death,

but any misuse of the power might raise the Persecution again; so never break this law, [65] however much you are tempted, and never consent to its being broken. If you know it is being broken in the least, you have wronged you, then in time we will be forgotten.' They did so, and with a bit of skilfull propaganda, made witchcraft a figure of fun, an old woman with a black cat, flying on a broomstick, and so, slowly, they were forgotten, all laws against them having been repealed, as soon as it was known how harmless they were."

[That is, this is being written long after the end of the persecutions.]

{Rule 13. "It will be understood by all members that these rules are equally binding upon all Grades of the Craft, including the Elders, and that serious and/or persistent breach of these rules will be

must work strongly against it, and any High Priestess or High Priest who consents to it must be immediately deposed, for 'tis the blood of the Brethren they endanger. Do good, an it be safe, and only if [70] it be safe, for any talk may endanger us.

[M] And strictly keep to the Old Law, never accept money for the use of the art. It is Christian priests and sorcerers who accept money for the use of their Arts, and they sell Dwale and evil love spells and pardons to let men scape from their sins. [75] Be not as these. *Be not as these.* If you accept not money, you will be free of temptation to use the Art for evil causes.

[N] You may use the Art for your own advantage, or for the advantage of the Craft, only if you be sure you harm none. But ever let the Coven debate the matter at length. Only if all are

grounds for expulsion." 3.9 [6]: "Ever remember if tempted to admit or boast of belonging to the cult you be endangering your brothers, for though now the fires of persecution may have died down {but} who knows when they [may] be revived? . . .we may loose the fires of persecution against us again." Doreen Valiente, in the Farrars 1984, p. 63, gives a line that stands in her Text B: "All are brothers and sisters, for this reason, that even the High Priestess must submit to the scourge."}

[The second "Be not as these" is underlined. Apparently Gardner thought it worth emphasizing, no doubt because the Cardells were charging money to teach the Gardner/ Valiente material. *Meaning of Witchcraft*, pp. 25-6: "there is a strong witch tradition that they may never take money for practising their art; that is, they may not work for hire." P. 205: "Witchcraft . . . is a religion . . . and no genuine practitioner will perform its rites for pay."]

Meaning of Witchcraft, p. 127: "They believe a certain law to be important, 'You must not use magic for anything which will cause harm to anyone, and if, to prevent a greater wrong

satisfied that none may be harmed [80] may the Art be used. If it is not possible to achieve your ends one way without harming any, perchance the aim may be achieved by acting in a different way, so as to harm none. May the Curse of the Goddess be on any who breach this law. So it be Aredan.

[O] 'Tis adjudged lawful an anyone need a house or land, an none will [85] sell, to incline the owner's mind to be willing to sell, provided it harmeth him not in any way, and that the full worth is paid, without haggling. Never bargain or cheapen anything which you buy by the Art. So it be Aredan.

[P] It is the Old Law and the most important of all Laws [90] that no one may do or say anything which will endanger any of the Craft, or bring them in contact with the law of the land, or the Law of the Church or any of our persecutors. In any disputes between the brethren, no one may invoke any laws but those of the Craft, or any Tribunal but that of the Priestess and the Priest and the [95] Elders. And may the Curse of the Goddess be on any who so do. So it be Aredan.

[Q] It is not forbidden to say as

being done, you must discommode someone, you must do it only in a way which will abate the harm.' This involves every magical action being discussed first, to see that it can do no damage, and this induces a habit of mind to consider well the results of one's actions, especially upon others."

[This is a gemara based on the preceding laws against harmfulness, for which the parallels are ample. As is typical of gemara, it cites an applicable precedent, a magical one, on line 87, which is apparently based on Crowley, *Magick*, p. 64: "buy whatever may be necessary without haggling."]

Based on Rules 2 and 6, and on *High Magic's Aid*, p. 214: "In the old days all knew where the Sabbath was to be held, and who would attend it, so when a few were taken and tortured, it was easy to find out all who went to the meetings, their leaders and priests, and often even who represented the God Himself. . . . only officers must know who are the leaders of the covens, and especially, who is our God."

{Again, "of old" reveals that

Christians do, "There be Witch craft in the Land," because our oppressors of old made it Her-esy not to believe in Witchcraft, and so a crime to deny it, which thereby put [100] you under suspicion. But ever say "I know not of it here, perchance they may be, but afar off. I know not where." But ever speak so you cause others to doubt they be as they are. Always speak of them as old crones, consorting with the Devil and riding through the air. But ever say, "But how may men ride through the air an they be not [105] as light as thistledown?" But the curse of the Goddess be on any who cast any suspicion on any of the Brotherhood, or speaks of any real meeting place, or where any bide. So it be Aredan.

[R] Let the Craft keep books with the names of all Herbs which are good for man, and all cures, that all may learn. But keep [110] another book with all the Banes [poisons] and Ap-ies, and let only the elders and trustworthy people have this knowledge. So it be Aredan.

[S] And may the Blessings of the Gods be on all who keep these Laws and the Curses of both God and Goddess be on all who break them. So it be Aredan.

the time of writing is after the time of persecution; so lines 97-100 are discussing a past situation. But then lines 100-107 attempt to speak as if persecution were a present danger. Section [Q] duplicates Section [H], and is based on the same materials, especially *Meaning of Witchcraft*, p. 150.}

[The text of the Old Laws in the Weschcke documents ends here—and this closing exhorta-tion could not have existed in isolation. Everything beyond this point was added after about 1960.]

Gardner apparently felt that the first draft, sent to Doreen and the others in 1957, was not long enough; so he worked on expanding it during 1958 and 1959, by writing sections J to S. This addition duplicates the first draft in both content and structure; but the overall effect is very much like that of traditional documents. Four more sections were also added during Gardner's last few years, canonizing the early paragraphs that I pointed out in discussing 3.10 [2] and 3.15 [5].

The preceding analysis, by setting the text of the various "Craft Laws" next to their sources, ought to be more than adequate as proof that Gardner wrote this document during the years 1957-1959. (I provide an even more detailed argument and analysis in the footnoted version of this book.) I am well aware that there are "orthodox" members of the Craft who are going to refuse to believe this argument, because it conflicts with what they want to believe. For example, members of the New Wiccan Church, Inc., believe that their original copy of the "Ordains" (as they call the Craft Laws) was brought to California by a British war bride in the 1940s. This is simply historically impossible, and is as ridiculous as believing that in about 1300 B.C.E. Moses invented monotheism and wrote the Torah, including the account of his own death and the summary of Israelite history down to about 600 B.C.E. I frankly find it difficult to understand why people with this sort of ultraconservative mindset wanted to be Witches in the first place. Doreen Valiente's response to my telling her about this was, "I have been very saddened by what you and others have told me about what is happening to the Old Religion in the USA. 'Orthodoxies' springing up—ye Gods! We'll be having heresy hunts and holy wars next." Yes, that is unfortunately starting to be possible.

7.2. The Verse Charge

[This was included in the Weschcke documents, and was also published in *Witch*, though the two versions disagree in many places, and thus show that the rewriting of it was on-going during 1958 and 1959. This quintain form of the Charge is apparently Gerald's rewriting of Doreen's quatrain form, since he in many places worsens the scansion and punctuation. However, overall it reads somewhat better (simply as narrative) than the quatrain form; so I would suppose that Gerald may have had some help with this revision. I am not going to show all the minor differences in wording, but I will include the alternative lines in the two versions.]

THE CHARGE

I the Mother, darksome and divine,
Say to thee, Oh children mine
(All ye assembled at mine Shrine),
    Mine the scourge and mine the kiss
    The five-point star of love and bliss
Here I charge ye in this sign. (Assume Goddess position.)

All ye assembled here tonight
Bow before my spirit bright
    Aphrodite, Arianrhod,
    Lover of the Horned God,
Mighty Queen of Witchery and night

Astarte, Hecate, Ashtaroth, Dione,
(Morrigan, Etain, Nisene),
Diana, Brigid, Melusine,
    Am I named of old by men,
    Artemis and Cerridwen,
Hell's dark mistress, Heaven's Queen.

(Whene'er trouble comes anoon)
All who would learn of me a Rune
Or would ask of me a boon,
    Meet ye in some secret glade
    Dance my round in greenwood shade,
By the light of the full moon.

(In a place wild and lone)
With the comrades alone
Dance about my altar stone.
    Work my holy Magistry,
    Ye who are fain of sorcery,
I bring ye secrets yet unknown.

(Whate'er troubles come to thee),
No more shall ye know slavery
Who give due worship unto me,
    Who tread my round on Sabbat-night.

Come ye all naked to the rite,
In token ye be truly free.

I teach the mystery of rebirth,
Keep ye my mysteries in mirth
    Heart joined to heart, and lip to lip,
    Five are the points of fellowship
That bring ye ecstasy on Earth.

I ask no offerings, do but bow,
No other law but love I know,
    By naught but love I may be known,
    All that liveth is mine own
From me they come, to me they go.

7.3. Casting and Charging

[This was included among the Weschcke documents, and was also published in *Witch*. It dates to about 1958.]

[1] Forming Circle. Light candles.

1. Draw Circle with Magic Sword or Athame.
2. Sprinkle with consecrated water.
3. Cense.
4. Say, "I conjure thee, O Circle of Power, that thou be a Boundary and a Protection and a meeting place between the world of men and the realms of the Mighty Ones, A Guardian and a Protection that shall preserve and contain the Power which we shall raise within thee, Wherefore do I Bless and Consecrate thee."
5. Say "I summon, Stir, and Call Thee up, Ye Mighty Ones of the (East, South, West, North) To witness the Rites and to guard the Circle."

[2] Closing Circle.

Say, "Mighty Ones of the (East, South, West, North), I thank you for attending, and ere you depart for your lovely realms, I say Hail and Farewell."

[3] Consecration of Water and Salt.

Touch water with Athame, saying, "I exorcise thee, O Creature of Water, that thou cast out from thee all the impurities and uncleannesses of the spirits of the World of Phantasm, In the names of Aradia and Cernunnos."

Touching Salt with Athame, say, "Blessings be upon this creature of Salt. Let all malignity and hindrance be cast forth hencefrom and let all good enter herein. Wherefore I bless thee that thou mayest aid me, In the names of Aradia and Cernunnos."

[4] Drawing Down the Moon.

"I invoke Thee and call upon Thee, Oh Mighty Mother of us All, Bringer of all Fruitfulness. *By Seed and Root, by Stem and Bud, by Leaf and Flower and Fruit, by Life and Love, Do We invoke Thee to descend* upon the body of Thy servant and Priestess (name)."

High Priest and other men give Fivefold Kiss. Women all bow.

Commentary on 7.3

This version of the basic Gardnerian ritual is intermediate between the versions in 5.1 and 7.4. It is directly dependent on 5.1, because we still have the sequence introduced in 5.1 of censing the circle, followed by the redundant second casting of the circle, and then the invoking of the quarters. This is obviously not a full ritual, but merely notes on a few specific procedures, which would occur in the order [3, 1, 4, 2] during an actual ritual, as can be seen from 7.4 and from the published sources. The reasons why we can be sure this is still a working draft will appear in 7.4. The writing of the document must date before August 1959, probably sometime in 1957 or 1958; but this revised typing of it dates to about 1960.

7.4. Forming the Circle.

[This was included among the Weschcke documents.]

FORMING THE CIRCLE.
[1] Must have a man and a woman, properly prepared, i.e., naked.
[2] Mark a circle nine feet across on the floor with chalk, etc. The best way is to get a string. Tie 2 loops four foot, six inches apart. Put one loop over a nail or something in the center. Put chalk in the other

and run it round. If you can't make marks on the floor, put furniture, etc., round to form it. Have a table, etc., as an Altar, with all tools, etc., on it. Have a bowl of water, and some salt.

[3] Place Athame on the bowl of water. Say, "I exorcise thee, O creature of Water, that thou cast out from Thee all the impurities and uncleannesses of the Spirits of the World of Phantasm in the name of Aradia and Cernunnos. But ever mind that Water purifies the body, but the scourge purifies the soul."

[4] Then place Athame on the salt. Say, "Blessings be upon this creature of Salt. Let all malignity and hindrance be cast forth hencefrom, and let all good enter herein. Wherefore I bless thee that thou mayest aid me, in the name of Aradia and Cernunnos."

[5] Then trace Circle on the lines you have marked out, starting at the East and returning to the East. (Always go round the circle with your Right hand to the Altar. Never go Widdershins.) Then put the Salt into the water, and go round the circle again, sprinkling it to purify it. Then go round again censing it. (Everyone in the circle must be sprinkled and censed.)

[6] Then go to the East, Sword or Athame in hand. Draw an invoking pentacle in the Air, starting at the top and going to the lefthand corner, saying, "I summon, and call thee up, O Ye Mighty ones of the East, to guard the Circle and witness our rites." Then holding the point of sword or Athame upwards, do the same to the south, west, and north, and return to the center, to the south of the Altar.

[7] Then each girl should bind her man, hands behind back and Cable Tow to neck. He should kneel at altar, and be scourged. When all men are thus "purified," they purify the girls in turn. No one may be in the circle without being thus purified.

[8] Then do whatever work wanted.

[9] When closing the Circle, the High Priestess, or whoever she tells to do it, saying, "Hail, ye mighty ones of the East. I thank you for attending, and ere ye depart for your lovely realms, We say, Hail and Farewell."

Commentary on 7.4

I have already identified the sources of this ritual in *The Greater Key of Solomon* in the commentary on earlier versions of this procedure, and see no reason to repeat all that yet again. However, we may note that the final line in paragraph [3] occurs as a separate line of dialogue in *High Magic's Aid*; it is added here to bolster the theological status of the scourging. Also, the instruction in paragraph [7], requiring all in the circle to be bound and scourged, has been added.

A careful comparison of the sequence of events here with that in the procedure for casting the circle given by the Farrars (1981, pp. 37-40; 1984, pp. 295-6) shows that the Farrars' procedure, and hence the procedure used by Patricia Crowther, is based on the one given here. The two differ in only three details, and the overall sequence is the same. In contrast, the Farrars' procedure differs from the one in "Ye Bok of ye Art Magical" and from the one described by Tanya Luhrmann (pp. 223-4) in many specific details, and the overall sequences are quite different.

That is, this procedure—the first to include the instruction about "Always go round the circle with your Right hand to the Altar. Never go Widdershins"—was not written until about 1960, and was never used by Gardner's original coven. Hence decisions made by "orthodox" American Gardnerians about what is a valid circle need to be placed in a somewhat more realistic perspective.

8. Gardner's Last Years, 1960-1964, and the Enduring Significance of the Craft

Gardner's wife, Donna, died in 1960. Her health had been failing for some time, and so at some time in the late 1950s two of Gardner's initiates, Monique and Campbell Wilson, took over the fulltime tasks of housekeeping for him and running the museum. (Doreen Valiente informs me that "Monique Wilson was no more old Gerald's niece than I am! . . . I don't know where the 'niece' story came from.") When he died in 1964, they inherited his museum and his library of books and manuscripts.

From 1960 to 1963, now operating entirely on his own (not that Donna appears ever to have cramped his style), Gardner initiated a great many people, probably many more than have ever been publicly heard of. The most prominent of these late initiates, aside from the Wilsons, included, as I have already said, Arnold and Patricia Crowther, Eleanor "Ray" Bone, and Lois Hemmings.

Fred Lamond told me that the biography titled *Gerald Gardner: Witch* was actually written by Idries Shah, who, in addition to being a Sufi, is an expert on ceremonial magic. However, by the time he had finished the project, Shah seemed to be extremely puzzled and uncomfortable. In talking about why he had done the project, Shah said, "I have it from the highest authority [that is, on the inner planes] that this will be one of the most significant religions of this century." And then, Fred said, Shah got this bewildered look on his face, and said, "Personally, I can't see it"—and so he decided that he didn't want his name on the book, and instead let it be published under Jack Bracelin's name. (This story makes sense, since Bracelin's letters in the Toronto collection show that he was even more dyslexic than Gardner.) Perhaps another reason may be that the book is certainly not up to Shah's usual standards, since he had no way to check up on Gardner's stories.

Doreen Valiente records (1989, p. 80) that "I have to recognize that it was really the events when the old coven run by Gerald Gardner and myself split open like a ripe seed-pod and many people went their separate ways, which caused the dispersion of many new covens and many new ideas. Good therefore eventually came out of evil; and I am glad . . . that, after a period of not being on speaking terms, Gerald and I met again and were reconciled. We continued friends until his death. Gerald . . . did a great work in bringing back the Old Religion to many people. I am glad to have known him."

Gardner died while on a sea voyage in February 1964, and was buried in Tunis, Africa. Doreen Valiente (1989, p. 44) relates that some years later Eleanor Bone discovered that the cemetery he was buried in was about to be redeveloped; so she raised a collection among Britain's witches, and succeeded in having him reburied in a different cemetery, where he could "rest in peace."

In May 1964, the first edition of Cardell's *Witch* was published, and in it Cardell published the names Aradia and Cernunnos as the secret names of the deities used by the Gardnerians. (This is certainly correct, else why would these names have been written in "Ye Bok of ye Art Magical" at the point in the third-degree initiation where the names are given?) I had thought when I first saw Cardell's *Witch* that the Gardnerians must have been forced by it to "change the locks" and so they have. Monique Wilson apparently did choose a new pair of names, and Raymond and Rosemary Buckland, who were initiated in 1963, were among the first to receive them. The Bucklands brought these new names back to Long Island, where they founded the New York coven, which became the center of the Gardnerian Craft in America for the next two decades, and from which almost all Gardnerians in America are now descended. (Doreen Valiente has confirmed, in a letter to Judith Harrow, that these two names were never used in the coven when she was in charge.)

Neither Gardner nor anyone else planned things to work out this way, but it is nevertheless unjust that the Craft in America traces its ancestry back, not to Doreen Valiente, but to Monique Wilson, "Lady Olwen," who contributed nothing of any importance to the

Craft, as far as I can tell, and who disappeared from public view after selling the museum to Ripley's in 1971. The Alexandrians, we now know, trace their ancestry, via Pat Kopanski, to Patricia Crowther, who at least is one of Doreen's friends. I do not offhand know how this bit of injustice might be cleared up, but I think the Craft community ought to think about acknowledging Doreen Valiente's creative genius rather more clearly than has ever been done so far.

"Lugh" and Disinformation

I must also deal with some data that I know will be appealed to by those who want to resist my conclusions. These are the claims about George Pickingill raised by a writer known only as "Lugh," in a series of articles that appeared in two British Craft periodicals, *The Wiccan*, and then later in *The Cauldron*, in the 1970s. (Doreen Valiente has written me that, as Lugh's "stories became more and more preposterous . . . Michael Howard, the editor of *The Cauldron*, eventually stopped publishing them.") These have since been reissued as a pamphlet, and the pamphlet has been republished, along with other short Craft writings, in two volumes of the Garland Publishing series on new religions edited by J. Gordon Melton (I had the honor to write the introductions to these two volumes). Lugh has meanwhile disappeared from public view entirely.

In order to evaluate Lugh's claims, we need to place them in the perspective of what at least *looks* like a purposeful policy of disinformation instituted by Gardner and carried on by some of his successors in the leadership of the Craft movement. Doreen Valiente says there was never any such policy, and certainly there is no evidence that she ever had anything to do with such a policy. However, I still must conclude from the available evidence that Old Gerald was much more devious than Ms. Valiente has ever wanted to believe, and that Lugh, for whatever reasons, was pursuing a course built on foundations laid down by Gerald.

Norman Moss's *The Pleasures of Deception* discusses the theory of hoaxes proposed by R. V. Jones, a physicist who was one of the most important members of British Intelligence during the Second World War, and indeed into the 1960s. In his paper "The Theory of Practical Joking," Jones proposed that the key to perpetrating a hoax is to gain control of all channels of communication, use them to feed false information to the audience, and thus distort their picture of reality enough that they make the desired false assumption and then the desired false move. This is easiest to do if there is only one possible channel of communication.

The application of his theory to the Gardnerian movement is this. Gardner, by writing his books, had created essentially a single channel of communication: the only possible source of information about "the Craft" was what he himself had devised. Since the religion had not previously existed, there was no need to worry about contradictory information coming from any other source, except perhaps from religious scholars—but then scholars do not get interviewed on TV at Hallowe'en, and have no audience comparable in size to the one Gardner was aiming for.

Another technique used by Gardner is that of misdirection. He had claimed in *Witchcraft Today* that there was an earlier coven, that some information had come from it, that an older religious tradition had existed all along—that is, he used the sole channel of communication to create a false but plausible history. The misdirection then consisted in pointing backward to that history. As long as scholars and other curious people were looking back—to the 1930s or 1920s, or the 1890s or the 1880s, or any date at all—and trying to find information relevant to the Gardnerian claims, the misdirection was successful: because no such information had ever existed, it could not turn up; and Gardner could continue to claim that there was no evidence to disprove his story. Once I had discovered that I could account for absolutely everything in the documents as being devised by Gardner, Valiente, and whoever else might have helped, there was no longer any reason to suppose there had been any earlier information, or coven, or sect at all—and then I realized that this misdirection was the key to the trick: it was the stage magician's technique of gesturing dramatically with his right hand, to grab your attention, while the left hand carries out the substitution that later seems so mysterious. Therefore, to accept the claim that there was any earlier tradition is epistemologically equivalent to buying the Gardnerian claims in full. Gardner could not have cared less what questions were asked, so long as attention was directed away from the 1950s.

For example, Elliot Rose, after considering the Book of Shadows material that is "quoted" in *Witchcraft Today*, goes on to say (pp. 204ff):

I would not like to exclude the possibility that the myth [of the descent of the Goddess] was originally composed . . . about the eighties; . . . A *terminus a quo* for the text quoted would be supplied by the first translation of the cuneiform tablets; but . . . the nearest one could say is "about 1880." This is to put it at the earliest . . . I should ascribe the texts quoted, merely on literary flavour, to about the nineties; . . . I think we have someone raised on the last of the pagan Romantics [e.g., Swinburne] as the most recent Magus, not necessarily of the whole of British witchcraft, but of that part of it with which Mr. Gardner has come in contact.

Rose makes the strategic error of believing Gardner's claim that there had been an earlier coven, and so becomes lost in speculations about what sort of person might have been creating covens around the turn of the century, a point on which there can be no evidence *if there was no such person*—and it is Gardner who was obviously raised on Swinburne. But it does not seem strange that so able a scholar as Elliott Rose could have been thus misled when we realize that he was misled by precisely the techniques devised by the geniuses who worked in British Intelligence during the Second World War to mislead the Nazi war machine and make the Normandy invasion possible.

I don't think Gardner intentionally set out to deceive anyone; that's not how religious people think. He probably hit on the disinformation techniques by accident, while trying to make *Witchcraft Today* sound plausible, and only gradually realized how useful they were for getting the new religion accepted. However, I think "Lugh" was purposely creating a phony history in order to throw researchers off the trail.

Lugh claims that "Old George" Pickingill was from a Hereditary "persuasion" of the Craft, had founded nine covens, had helped write the original rituals of the Hermetic Order to the Golden Dawn, and had initiated Aleister Crowley. He claims further that the coven into which Gardner had been initiated in 1939 was descended from a Pickingill coven, that Gardner had a copy of their Book of Shadows, that Crowley had written out from memory a second draft for Gardner of the Book of Shadows used by the Pickingill covens, and that Gardner had used these as a basis for his reform.

It seems to me that this story about Pickingill and Crowley is an extrapolation on a paragraph in Chapter 4 of *Witchcraft Today*; in fact, Lugh mentions this passage specifically in his first letter.

The only man I can think of who could have invented the rites was the late Aleister Crowley. When I met him he was most interested to hear that I was a member, and said he had been inside when he was very young, but would not say whether he had rewritten anything or not. But the witch practices are entirely different in method from any kind of magic he wrote about, and he described very many kinds. . . . certain expressions and certain words. . . smack of Crowley; possibly he borrowed things from the cult writings, or more likely someone may have borrowed expressions from him.

Having looked at drafts of Gardner's documents from 1946 to 1960, we can see how very devious Gardner is being here: Crowley, being dead, cannot deny any of this; the witch practices are based directly on Crowley's methods; Gardner himself borrowed wholesale from Crowley; and Valiente rewrote this material to disguise the borrowing. If Gardner had had a Book of Shadows that had been written for him by Crowley (as Francis King claimed), he would not have needed to undertake the drafts and rewritings that we have been looking at.

I presume that Gardner simply made up the claim that Crowley had been a witch when young. There is no corroboration of this anywhere in Crowley's writings, and Crowley kept no secrets about anything.

Lugh's claim that Crowley wrote Gardner's original Book of Shadows—he is no doubt building on the similar claim by King (p. 180)—cannot possibly be true: nothing that could be called a Book of Shadows existed while Crowley was alive. Furthermore, Lugh seems to be ignorant (or is pretending to be ignorant) of the true role of Doreen Valiente in writing the Book of Shadows.

But there is a way to demonstrate directly that the letter is a scarlet herring. At one point it states:

> The Pickingill-led covens have commemorated a cardinal tenet of the Old Religion. All of our rites are conducted in toto by a woman. This derives from the Scandinavian and French models,

which are purely imaginary. As we saw in Section 5.1, before 1957, the dominant figure in Gardner's coven had been the High Priest, Gardner himself, just as we expected for a "re-creation" of witchcraft based on Margaret Murray's descriptions. Lugh's argument is specious, since it is based on the Gardnerian party line, adopted only after 1959, that only the priestess could conduct the circle. Lugh goes on:

> The Horned God was always served and honoured by women in Scandinavia. The Mother Goddess could only be served and honoured by men. . . . only the priestess approved by the God could call upon him to descend into the body of a man chosen as his living representative. Only a priest consecrated to the Goddess could call upon her to descend into the body of a woman chosen as Her living representative. . . . In many Traditionalist covens the Lady calls down the sun on the Magister, and the Magister reciprocates by Drawing Down the Moon on the Lady.
>
> I can find no published reference to substantiate our claim that "Old George" Pickingill devised the basic format of the Gardnerian rituals.

We have also seen the ritual of "Drawing Down the Moon" evolve through several stages; but even in 1957 Gardner was not clear on whether the arms-crossed position represented the God or the Goddess.

We can see that Lugh is proposing an elegant bit of theologizing: the Priest is the Priest *of* the Goddess, but incarnates the God; the Priestess is the Priestess *of* the God, but incarnates the Goddess. But none of this could have predated the rituals that we now know were created in the 1950s; so all of Lugh's statements are similarly groundless. Hence I had wondered why Doreen Valiente, who helped write these rituals in the 1950s, quotes Lugh (in her 1978 book on pp. 15-20, and in Chapter 12 of *Rebirth of Witchcraft*) as if he were a reliable source of historical information; it seemed to me that she, of all people, must know better. (She has written to me, "I really don't know what to think about him. As I said in [*The Rebirth of Witchcraft*], nothing checks out. At the same time, I didn't like to call the man a complete imposter. I tried to take a charitable view—did he have some hidden motive in telling all these years? If so, what was it?") Ms. Valiente's wanting to be charitable to Lugh goes along with her continuing to believe that there was some sort of Craft tradition before 1939. My own answer to her question is, yes, he did have a hidden motive: the covert purpose of his letters was to take advantage of Rose's speculations about someone at the turn of the century, and to give a name and a face to the person Rose had guessed at, in order to divert attention away from the 1940s and 1950s.

To confirm this, notice that Chapter 4 of *Witchcraft Today*, just after the passage about Crowley quoted above, goes on to mention the founders of the Hermetic Order of the Golden Dawn (ca. 1885), Napoleon, Francis Barrett (ca. 1800), and Sir Francis Dashwood, the Hellfire Club, and the Cabalists of the 1790s as possible authors of the rituals; all of these are dismissed as unlikely, but the misdirection consists in the suggestion that the true carriers of the witchcraft tradition during this period were not well-known public figures.

George Pickingill is a historical figure, mentioned by Eric Maple, but all the evidence is that he was a garden-variety folk-magic witch and a home-grown Satanist. Such persons can be found in the working-class neighborhoods of any metropolitan area; they are not evil, but they are also not very sophisticated by middle-class standards. Lugh seems to be aware that the argument about Pickingill is flimsy, and insists that a "conspiracy of silence" has for 125 years suppressed the true status of a man who, Lugh also asserts, gloried in publicity and extravagant public statements. A private detective who was a member of a NROOGD coven tried to track down some of these statements, and could find no trace of them, nor of any of the supposedly published articles Lugh cites as evidence. I think we are being fed a tall tale that is simultaneously a conspiracy theory and an argument from silence—impressive in its way.

At the point in my thinking (about 1974) when I thought that Gardner might have had two separate, original documents on which the Craft Laws were based, I found Lugh's assertions, that Gardner had two different Books of Shadows from two covens that he had been initiated into, to be quite exciting: here was a possible source for those documents—and I went to Toronto hoping to find those original books. But they weren't there. Having now concluded that Gardner compiled the Craft Laws himself, I see that this argument, unlike a string, can be pushed as well as pulled. Suppose we ask, "What information must Gardner have gotten from these alleged Book of Shadows rather than from somewhere else?" The answer is, "None." It merely complicates life to suppose that Gardner had gotten the Masonic, Golden Dawn, magical, etc., raw material that he worked with at second hand, via these supposed Pickingill covens, rather than directly from the available sources.

Lugh also alleges that Crowley had used bits and pieces of Pickingill's rituals in his own writings. He apparently wants his readers to think that the passages from Crowley which Gardner quotes are the ones that Crowley was quoting from Pickingill. Likewise, his allegation that Pickingill was the source for various unspecified elements of the Golden Dawn rituals is intended to encourage his readers to think that the identifiable Golden Dawn elements in Gardner's rituals may therefore instead be from the Pickingill tradition. Hence this is all special pleading.

Lugh also capitalizes on statements by Buckland and others that they had seen a Book of Shadows (purported by some to have been in Crowley's handwriting) on display in Gardner's museum. Doreen Valiente says that, to the contrary, there was no such book in Gardner's collection, and that the Book of Shadows in question is in fact "Text A," which she owns.

What about Lugh's claim that Pickingill devised the basic format for rituals that was inherited and used by Gardner? As we have seen, the order of events in a basic Gardnerian ritual are:

(1) casting the circle;
(2) invoking the guardians of the four quarters;
(3) invoking the Goddess or the God;
(4) working magic, or an initiation, or both;
(5) having the "little feast" of cakes and wine;
(6) dismissing the guardians, and breaking and
     grounding the circle.

We have seen that Gardner was painfully working his way through drafts of (1), (2), and (6) in the 1940s, working directly from such sources as *The Greater Key of Solomon*, and again in the late 1950s. No doubt he would have been happy to have ready-made procedures for all this—but he didn't. Any number of sources could be suggested for (5), but Gardner clearly didn't know a standard procedure for this.

What this "format" boils down to, then, is that you meet in a circle presided over by a priestess, invoke the deity, work magic or other business, and finish up with some refreshments. Except for the formal circle, this is quite close to what Murray describes, as we saw in Chapter 2, or to the folklore about witches, for that matter. The only thing left that Pickingill could have contributed, therefore, is the basic idea of combining the working circle of the magicians with the shamanistic procedures of witches—and as I argued in Chapter 2, that idea was apparently the contribution of the New Forest group in 1940. If there is any closer similarity between the Gardnerian rituals and those of Lugh's "persuasion," this merely proves that Lugh's are dependent on Gardner's, not vice versa.

This situation might also explain why Gardnerians appear to have done very little over the years to dispute the claims of interlopers, no matter how blatant. As the Farrars also argue in their 1981 and 1984 books, Alex Sanders' copy of the Book of Shadows was derived from that written by Gardner and Valiente; he certainly did not inherit it from his grandmother. There is also a letter in the Ripley's files, to Gardner from Pat Kopanski, giving the date and other details of Sanders' initiation in 1963; this correlates with Sanders' admission to Johns (p. 62) that he was unaware of the existence of any other witches before 1963.

I have tended in the past to suppose that the Gardnerians did not bother to prove Sanders a liar (which they could have done several times over without detracting anything of significance from the general Gardnerian story) because the annoyance caused by Sanders' grandiose claims was more than offset by the usefulness of his claim to descend from the "old religion" independently of the Gardnerians. After all, if you have two cousins, then their common grandparent must really have existed. That is, Sanders' claim blurs the trail to the 1950s, and reinforces the misdirection tactic, by also pointing back to the 1920s. However, Doreen Valiente points out to me that I am being unfair, and am unaware of some of the facts. She writes in a recent letter, "To my knowledge, various Gardnerians did try to expose Sanders as a phony, but as I said in *The Rebirth of Witchcraft*, the media simply didn't want to know. For instance, Pat Crowther sent a letter to one newspaper attacking Sanders' claims— and the newspaper sent it back to her, saying that they couldn't publish it because Sanders might sue them for libel! Actually, in my opinion, the situation was that Sanders was supplying the media with colorful stories that sold newspapers, and that was all they cared about. . . . On another occasion certain Gardnerians, again to my personal knowledge, agreed to appear on a television programme only on condition that Sanders was not on it. They were given verbal assurances to this effect; but when the programme appeared, there was Sanders strutting his stuff as usual. They protested, only to meet with the usual bland reply that 'it had been a misunderstanding.' What could they do about it?"

I agree that it must have been a difficult situation. It's hard to see from this side of the Atlantic how radically different British journalistic standards are from American ones—British tabloids, for example, make the *National Enquirer* and other rags sold with the Twinkies look pompous and conservative. The fact is that the newspaper Pat Crowther sent her letter to could have gotten away with saying anything it liked about Sanders, and its declining to publish her letter for fear of being sued was simply an astonishing piece of bare-faced mendacity. We have a similar situation here with clowns like Geraldo Rivera and other journalists who are too stupid (or pretend to be too stupid) to understand that Witchcraft has nothing to do with Satanism, no matter how often they are told.

What we have seen in this book is that Gerald Gardner, with occasional help from others, invented a plausible history for his new religion, and created documents to support that history. If he had been doing this for the sake of fame, wealth, or power, we could call what he did forgery—but he was not. It is (or at least ought to be) notorious that the Gardnerians have from the beginning refused to allow their movement to be used to make money for anyone. This sort of ethical stance is taken only by persons whose motivations are genuinely religious. Gardner was engaging in what is actually a well-known sort of religious behavior: the inventing of a new history for one's community is a way of searching for meaning and authenticity. What he did is not so very different, after all, from what the scribes of the school of Ezra did in assembling legends and fragments of history into the new, unified history of Israel we have in the Law and the Earlier Prophets.

The new magical religion that Gardner, Dorothy Clutterbuck, and Doreen Valiente helped to create is utterly different in nature from the kind of folk-magic witchcraft that we looked at in Chapter 1 and from which they may have started. As a viable system, it began to grow, to take on a life of its own, and to display the assimilative voracity typical of living systems. (Folk religions, in contrast, are continuing to die out.)

One body of information the Gardnerian movement began to assimilate was the "White Goddess theology" invented by Robert Graves, although this only becomes visible in the late 1950s. Murray emphasizes the Horned God, not the Goddess; and so the New Forest coven did also at first. I think Gerald was responsible for introducing the Horned God and Goddess as *equals*, but even in *Witchcraft Today* that is often obscured by references to "the Gods" in general, since that sounds like a reference to the Greco-Roman pantheon, rather than to this "duotheistic" concept. It was only gradually that the Goddess came to be more important in practice than the Horned God (and later came to be of sole importance in some covens in the USA), and that the High Priestess came to be more important than the High Priest. The period of this shift in emphasis apparently coincides roughly with the period of Doreen's tenure as High Priestess of the London coven; so I have tended to think that she must have had something to do with forcing Gardner to see the importance of Graves' White Goddess concept, and to make it the focus of the reform. However, she insists that she cannot take the credit for that. Whoever was responsible for this, it was a stroke of genius, for it is the Goddess concept that seizes the hearts of those who are drawn into the Craft movement.

No one before now has given Gardner, or especially Valiente, credit for what measure they have of creative genius—but, then, they could not claim such credit as long as they maintained the stance that they were merely reviving and carrying on an older tradition. The critical perspective I introduced in Chapter 1, of understanding the Craft as a new religion, and hence as evolving according to the same laws that apply to any other social institution, means that we can apply the same standards to it as to any other movement. Especially, if we understand the creating of a new religion to be a creative activity, then we can think about such activity in terms of artistic criteria. That is, we don't have to consider all new religions, or all versions of the Craft, to be equally "good," any more than we must with art: there is both good art and bad art—and yet this is not a moral category. It is not an accident that Starhawk teaches a course on the creating of rituals as an artform in the Institute for Culture and Creation Spirituality at Holy Names College. It is not an accident that the New, Reformed, Orthodox Order of the Golden Dawn began as a project for a course on creating rituals taught by the poet James Broughton in the Creative Arts department at San Francisco State. All of the reforms made in the Roman Catholic liturgy since the Second Vatican Council look incredibly stodgy compared with the ritual and liturgical discoveries made, and still being made, by the current Neopagan movement.

I am aware that most people—certainly most practicing Christians—react to the idea of creating a ritual that is intended to have genuinely religious effects, with something approximating horror:

"How can you do that? That's tampering with people's lives! That's irresponsible!" I think this sort of vehemence results from assuming a Golden Age model: if the rituals or liturgies we have now were instituted by God himself, then any change, any innovation, must be for the worse. But, of course, our present liturgies must have been created by people at some time and some place. A Golden Age model, with its tendency toward dualistic interpretations, tends to overblow the ethical dimension. In contrast, an evolutionary model (and a strict monotheism) help keep ethics in perspective. If a new ritual works better for some people than the old one did, if it gives them a religious experience or dimension they had been lacking, then it represents a step in the right direction, and is a gift of the spirit. How great the step is, is a different question. Note that this implies that current Witches can follow in Gardner's footsteps only by exercising as much creativity as he did, and so by eliminating anything in the Craft that doesn't work for them, such as, and especially, the scourging.

When I apply aesthetic criteria to new religions, I find the Gardnerian Witches to be far more interesting than many other new religions. In saying this, I am not stating a simple preference. Rather, I am making a complex judgment about the quantity and quality of the creativity that has gone into the movement and that its members routinely display, about how accurately its founders assessed needs that the established churches were not meeting, about how effectively the movement has been structured to meet those needs, about how its peculiar perspective reorganizes the raw materials of theology into a coherent and novel worldview, about how well it enables its members to proceed with their own maturation, and so on. It is fair, and not very subjective at all, to compare religions in general in these terms. In contrast, I find a "new religion" that is merely another literalistic, elitist Christian sect, or merely an Eastern religion transported wholecloth to America, to be not very new, not very creative, and therefore not very interesting.

Moreover, my intuition tells me that the Gardnerian movement is far more important than most other new religions, far more important than perhaps any of us now realize. Why? I keep turning back to study the movement, trying to explain that intuition to myself, trying to justify it to others. I will, of course, be discussing this issue at length in Volume II of this history, but let me deal with it briefly here.

I can suppose that someone might be stubborn enough to say at this point, "Well, if this witchcraft movement is a new religion, then you are admitting that Gardner did just make it all up, that he was some sort of well-meaning fraud." No, that is not what I am saying, because that is not how religion works. Can you say, "The Buddha just made it all up"? Or "Homer just made it all up"? Or on the other hand, can you give me an example of a religion that was not made up by human beings? If that mysterious factor, creativity, is needed in order to write a poem, it is very much more needed to found a religion. Gardner could be written off as a charlatan if his work had been unsuccessful—but then who would ever have heard of him? The fact that the Craft movement has grown so rapidly in a few decades is proof enough, indeed, the only relevant proof, that Gardner was doing something right.

It may well be that Gardner, even though he appears to be a first-class dissembler, and even though he was also trying to meet his own sexual needs, did in fact think that what he was doing was reforming an older religion—because founders of new religions usually seem to think that they are merely putting an old religion on a firmer foundation by introducing a few new elements into it. Zoroaster began his reform of Iranian religion at almost the same time that Gotama was reforming what was still almost the same religion in India, and at the same time that Hilkiah was reforming Israelite-Canaanite religion. Christianity began with what was, I think, an attempt to establish a reform movement in Judaism. Mohammed intended to reform not only native Arab religions, but also Judaism and Christianity as he understood them. Numerous less-famous religions—Jainism, Manichaeism, those of the Druse and the Sikhs, Bahá'í, to name just a few—have resulted from this same process.

Anyway, whatever Gardner's intentions may have been, he did found a new religion, entirely different in structure and functioning from what had gone before it. That the Gardnerian Craft still shares many elements with the Old Religion of Europe as described by Murray and others, and with other folk religions, does not change the situation. The sharing results merely from the fact that human creation is never *ex nihilo*; it begins from the available materials. A poet may sometimes coin a new word, but he does not invent a new language; he uses the resources of the language that everyone around him speaks. Likewise, a religious reformer starts from the religion that he knows; Gotama, by an extraordinary feat, could invent

Buddhism, but he could not have invented Christianity.

In fact, the Gardnerian Craft is so different from the kinds of religions, past and present, that have been called witchcraft that it is not very logical to call the members of these very different religions by the same name. If Gardnerians are Witches, then they are the first true Witches in history; if those other people back then were Witches, then Gardnerians are not.

Anthropologists, medieval historians, and various other scholars generally agree that in their fields the term "witch" refers to a person believed to worship the principle of evil, to work malevolent magic against enemies, and generally to lack all redeeming social qualities. If so, why do the members of the Gardnerian movement choose to call themselves Witches? Why do they choose to explain over and over again to cub reporters, weekend TV announcers, and graduate students in religious studies, that they, like all the witches in the past, worship only a pleasant goddess of bunny rabbits and flowers, perform only faith healing and fortunetelling, and have regular nature walks and dances in field and grove to the sound of pipe and timbrel?* Why? Well, for one thing, calling yourself a Witch gets you free publicity at Hallowe'en; calling yourself a Goddess-worshipper would not. But there is a far more important reason for the choice. To see it, we need to look briefly at the nature of the movement.

Gardner's claim that in September 1939 he had been initiated into one of the last surviving covens in England, a coven whose ancestry went back through the Burning Times and ultimately to the Stone Age, serves, as I have said, as the foundational myth of the Gardnerian movement. It establishes continuity, and therefore solidarity, with all those persons—as many as 9 million, in some estimates—who died in the first Holocaust. The meaning of a myth, after all, does not depend on its historicity. Why is this important?

Only during and after the Second Vatican Council has the Roman Catholic Church offered an apology, and the beginnings of an attempt at amends, to the Jewish community at large for its slander and persecution of Jews during the preceding 1640 years. The world Jewish community seems to still be deciding whether the apology is sincere, and whether the amends proposed might be adequate. I

---

* The Craft generally does have an innocuous "party line" like this to be given out to the media. The Craft's actual activities are far more serious, and not nearly so innocuous; else it would not have much to offer its adult members, of whom there are many.

mention this only so that I can go on to make the point that neither the Roman Catholic Church, nor any other Christian church, has ever offered any apology, or attempted to make any amends, for the murder of those millions of "witches" and "heretics" from the 12th through the 17th century. Worse yet, the office of the Inquisition still exists! That it still exists is a scandal. That its name has been changed, to the "Congregation for the Doctrine of the Faith," but not its nature, is an insult. The man who holds the position of the Grand Inquisitor, Joseph Cardinal Ratzinger, is responsible for the harassing of Fr. Charles Curran, and of Fr. Matthew Fox, whom he has accused of heresy. Why? Because Fox hired Starhawk (and Luisah Teish, a Voudun priestess) to teach at Holy Names College in Oakland, California.

This is not the place to review the evidence that the Roman Catholic Church is politically corrupt or, in another vocabulary, suffering from systemic sinfulness. Nevertheless, when Starhawk or Gardner or anyone else says, "I am a Witch," that says, "You Catholics did not stop persecuting people until we took the power to persecute people away from you by force. You claim, in your Vatican II documents, that you do not intend to persecute anyone again. *So why do you still own all the machinery of the Inquisition?*" And in 1987 I realized that I had no answer. It was and is a scandal, and I was ashamed for my church.

"Your church?" my Witch friends asked. "Why do you still think it is your church?"

"Because," I answered, "I will not allow the Grand Inquisitor to decide whether I am truly a Christian. I cannot do that to you."

"Ah," said the Witches. "Perhaps you really are one of us."

And I realized that I was—because I also realized that from the Witches I was hearing the same voice of prophecy that cried out against injustice, against corrupt power, against privilege that destroys our ability to feel compassion, that cried out through Amos, and Hosea, and Jeremiah, and Jesus. And that voice is the gift of the Spirit. This is not the place for me to explain my theology, which is broad enough to include Neopagan Witchcraft and a very liberal form of Catholic Christianity as special cases. Let me merely extend an invitation: if you, dear reader, can no longer stomach being in communion with Cardinal Ratzinger—or whoever the Chief Son-of-a-Bitch of your particular persuasion may be—then come circle with the Witches. We offer you liberty, fraternity, and equality.

Bibliography

This bibliography includes: books to which I refer; books that are essential for understanding Gardnerian Witchcraft; and books that are useful for understanding new religions in general. I hope it is comprehensive, but I have not attempted to make it exhaustive. For some books, I list the original date of publication, but any page numbers that I give are for the editions listed here. [I use square brackets to indicate authors of works that were published anonymously or pseudonymously.]

Adler, Margot. *Drawing Down the Moon*. Viking, 1979. Beacon Press paperback, 2d ed., 1987.

[Bell, Jessie W.] *The Grimoire of Lady Sheba*. Llewellyn, 1972.

Bonewits, P. E. I. *Real Magic*. Weiser, 3d ed., 1988.

Bracelin, Jack. *Gerald Gardner: Witch*. Octagon House, 1960. Fred Lamond told me that this was actually written by Idries Shah, who then decided he didn't want his name on it.

Buckland, Raymond. *Witchcraft from the Inside*. Llewellyn, 1971.

Burland, C. A. *Echoes of Magic: A Study of Seasonal Festival Through the Ages*. Peter Davies, 1972. Burland was a member of the Gardnerian inner circle in the late 1950s.

Cardell, Charles [Published under the pseudonym "Rex Nemorensis."] *Witch*. London: Privately published, 1964.

Carmichael, Alexander. *Carmina Gadelica*. Edinburgh: Oliver & Boyd, 1900.

Cavendish, Richard. *The Black Arts*. Putnam's, 1967.
_____. *A History of Magic*. London: Weidenfeld and Nicolson, 1977.

Colquhoun, Ithell. *Sword of Wisdom: MacGregor Mathers and the "Golden Dawn."* Putnam's, 1975.

Crowley, Aleister. *Magick in Theory and Practice*. Castle, n.d. [ca. 1930].

Dewar, James. "Masonic Ceremony." In Tiryakian, pp. 101-109.

Eliade, Mircea. "Some Observations on European Witchcraft." *History of Religions*, 14, no. 3 (Feb. 1975), 149-172.

Ellwood, Robert S., Jr. *Religious and Spiritual Groups in Modern America*. Prentice-Hall, 1973.
_____. *Alternative Altars: Unconventional and Eastern Spirituality in America*. University of Chicago Press, 1979.

Farrar, Stewart. *What Witches Do: The Modern Coven Revealed*. Coward, McCann, 1971.
_____, and Janet Farrar. *Eight Sabbats for Witches*. London: Robert Hale, 1981.
_____. *The Witches' Way*. London: Robert Hale, 1985. (These two volumes are available in the U.S. in paperback, under the title *A Witches Bible*, from Magickal Child.)

Farren, David. *The Return of Magic*. Harper and Row, 1973.

Galbreath, Robert. "The History of Modern Occultism: A Bibliographical Survey." *Journal of Popular Culture*, v, no. 3 (Winter 1971), 98-126.

Gardner, Gerald B. "Ye Bok of ye Art Magical." Unpublished MS., written between about 1945 (or earlier) and 1953, formerly owned by Ripley's International, Ltd., now owned by Richard and Tamara James of the Wiccan Church of Canada, Toronto.
_____. *High Magic's Aid*. Michael Houghton, 1949.
_____. *Witchcraft Today*. Rider, 1954. Jarrolds reprint, 1968 (this edition has 192 pages; page numbers can be found in other editions roughly by proportion).

_____. *The Meaning of Witchcraft*. Aquarian Press, 1959.

Gibson, Ian. *The English Vice: Beating, Sex, and Shame in Victorian England and After*. London: Duckworth, 1978.

Glanvil, Joseph, and Henry More. *Saducismus Triumphatus: Or, Full and Plain Evidence Concerning Witches and Apparitions*. London: Lowndes, 3d ed., 1689. Scholar's Facsimiles, 1966. One of Murray's major sources of information.

Grant, Robert. *Gnosticism and Early Christianity*. Columbia University Press, 1966.

Graves, Robert. *The Greek Myths*. Pelican, 2 vols., 1955.
_____. *The White Goddess: A Historical Grammar of Poetic Myth*. 1948. Noonday, 3d, rev. ed., 1966.
_____. "Witches in 1964." *Virginia Quarterly Review*, XL (1964), 550-559.

Iron Mountain: A Journal of Magical Religion. Edited by Charles Clifton and Mary Currier-Clifton. Artemisia Press.

Johns, June. *King of the Witches: The World of Alex Sanders*. Coward McCann, 1969.

Kelly, Aidan A. "Textual Criticism and the Craft Laws." *Gnostica*, Sept. 1974. [Published under pseudonym C. Taliesin Edwards.]
_____. "The Invention of Witchcraft: Uses of Documentary and Oral-Historical Materials in Reconstructing the History of the Gardnerian Movement." Paper given to the Religion and Social Science Section of the AAR, in San Francisco, December 1981. *Zetetic Scholar*, #10, 1982.
_____. "An Update on Neopagan Witchcraft in America." Paper given to the Group on New Religious Movements of the AAR, Boston, Dec. 1987.
_____. "Witchcraft and the Techniques of Disinformation." Paper given to the Group on New Religious Movements of the AAR, Anaheim, CA., Nov. 1985.

Kenyon, Theda. *Witches Still Live*. 1928.

King, Francis. *Ritual Magic In England, 1887 to the Present*. Spearman, 1970.

Leland, Charles Godfrey. *Aradia: The Gospel of the Witches of Tuscany.* Scribner's, 1897. Many recent reprints.

Lethbridge, T. C. *Witches: Investigating an Ancient Religion.* 1962. Citadel, 1968.

Luhrmann, T. M. *Persuasions of the Witch's Craft: Ritual Magic in Contemporary England.* Cambridge, Mass.: Harvard University Press, 1989.

Marty, Martin. "The Occult Establishment." *Social Research,* XXXVII (Summer 1970), 212-230.

Mathers, S. L. MacGregor, ed. and trans. *The Greater Key of Solomon.* De Laurence, Scott, 1914.

Melton, J. Gordon. *Encyclopedia of American Religions.* Detroit: Gale Research, 3d, rev. ed., 1989.
_____. "Modern Alternative Religions in the West." In J.R. Hinnells, ed., *A Handbook of Living Religions* (Viking/Penguin, 1984), pp. 455-474.
_____. *Magic, Witchcraft, and Paganism in America: A Bibliography.* Garland, 1982.
_____. "Origins of Modern Sex Magick." Paper delivered to the Society for the Scientific Study of Sex, Midcontinent Region, Chicago, June 7-9, 1985.

Metzger, Bruce M. *The Text of the New Testament: Its Transmission, Corruption, and Restoration.* Oxford University Press, 1964.

Midelfort, H. C. Erik. "Recent Witch Hunting Research, or Where Do We Go from Here?" *Papers of the Bibliographical Society of America,* LXII (1968), 373-420. Lists 509 items, almost all published since 1940, and some of which are relevant to the Gardnerian Craft.

Miller, David L. *The New Polytheism: Rebirth of the Gods and Goddesses.* Harper and Row, 1974.

Moore, Virginia. *The Unicorn: William Butler Yeats' Search for Reality.*

Moss, Norman. *The Pleasures of Deception.* Reader's Digest Press, 1977.

Murray, Margaret A. *The Witch-Cult in Western Europe.* Oxford University Press, 1921. Oxford paperback, 1962.

_____. *The God of the Witches*. Oxford University Press, 1934. Doubleday Anchor, 1960.

Nugent, Donald. "The Renaissance and/of Witchcraft." *Church History*, XL (March 1971), 69-78.
_____. "Witchcraft Studies, 1959-1971: A Bibliographic Survey." *Journal of Popular Culture*, V, no. 3 (Winter 1971), 82-97.

The Oxford English Dictionary. Oxford University Press, 2 vols. (compact ed.), 1971.

Randolph, Vance. *Ozark Superstition*. Columbia University Press, 1947. Dover reprint, under title *Ozark Magic and Folklore*, 1964.

Regardie, Israel. *The Golden Dawn: An Account of the Teachings, Rites, and Ceremonies of the Order of the Golden Dawn*. 1937-1940. Hazel Hills, 2d ed., 1969.
_____, ed. *Gems from the Equinox: Selected Writings of Aleister Crowley*. Llewellyn, 1974.

Robbins, Rossell Hope. *The Encyclopedia of Witchcraft and Demonology*. NY: Crown, 1959. Lists virtually everything published about any kind of witchcraft up to 1958.

Rose, Elliott. *A Razor for a Goat: A Discussion of Certain Problems in the History of Witchcraft and Diabolism*. University of Toronto Press, 1962.

Russell, Jeffrey B. *A History of Witchcraft: Sorcerers, Heretics, and Pagans*. Thames and Hudson, 1980.

Ryall, Rhiannon. *West Country Wicca: A Journal of the Old Religion*. Custer, WA: Phoenix Publishing, 1989.

Schad-Somers, Suzanne P. *Sadomasochism: Etiology and Treatment*. Human Sciences Press, 1982.

Shah, Sayed Idries. *The Secret Lore of Magic: Books of the Sorcerors*. Muller, 1957; Citadel paperback, 1970.

Seth, Ronald, ed. *In the Name of the Devil: Great Witchcraft Cases*. Jarrolds, 1969; Arrow paperback, 1970.

Starhawk [Miriam Simos]. *The Spiral Dance: A Rebirth of the Ancient Religion of the Great Goddess*. Harper & Row, 1979.

_____. *Dreaming the Dark: Magic, Sex, and Politics*. Beacon Press, 1982.

Tiryakian, Edward A., ed. *On the Margin of the Visible: Sociology, the Esoteric, and the Occult*. Wiley, 1974.

Truzzi, Marcello. "The Occult Revival as Popular Culture: Some Random Observations on the Old and the Nouveau Witch." Paper presented to the Ohio Valley Sociological Society, Akron, May 1, 1970. *Sociol. Quarterly*, 13 (Winter 1972), 16-36. Excerpted in Tiryakian, pp. 215-222.
_____. "Towards a Sociology of the Occult: Notes on Modern Witchcraft," in Zaretsky and Leone.

Valiente, Doreen. *Where Witchcraft Lives*. Aquarian Press, 1962.
_____. *An ABC of Witchcraft Past and Present*. St. Martin's, 1973.
_____. *Witchcraft for Tomorrow*. St. Martin's, 1978.
_____. Letter to the Editors, *Iron Mountain*, vol. 1, no. 3 (Fall 1985), pp. 3-6.
_____. *The Rebirth of Witchcraft*. London: Robert Hale, 1989.

Zaretsky, I. J., and M. P. Leone, eds. *Religious Movements in Contemporary America*. Princeton University Press, 1974.

STAY IN TOUCH

On the following pages you will find listed, with their current prices, some of the books and tapes now available on related subjects. Your book dealer stocks most of these, and will stock new titles in the Llewellyn series as they become available. We urge your patronage.

However, to obtain our full catalog, to keep informed of new titles as they are released and to benefit from informative articles and helpful news, you are invited to write for our bi-monthly news magazine/catalog. A sample copy is free, and it will continue coming to you at no cost as long as you are an active mail customer. Or you may keep it coming for a full year with a donation of just $2.00 in U.S.A. ($7.00 for Canada & Mexico, $20.00 overseas, first class mail). Many bookstores also have *The Llewellyn New Times* available to their customers. Ask for it.

Stay in touch! In *The Llewellyn New Times'* pages you will find news and reviews of new books, tapes and services, announcements of meetiongs and seminars, articles helpful to our readers, news of authors, advertising of products and services, special moneymaking opportunities, and much more.

The Llewellyn New Times
P.O. Box 64383-Dept. 370, St. Paul, MN 55164-0383, U.S.A.

• • •

TO ORDER BOOKS AND TAPES

If your book dealer does not have the books and tapes described on the following pages readily available, you may order them directly from the publisher by sending full price in U.S. funds, plus $2.00 for postage and handling for the first book, and $.50 for each additional book. There are no postage and handling charges for orders over $50. UPS Delivery: We ship UPS whenever possible. Delivery guaranteed. Provide your street address as UPS does not deliver to P.O. Boxes. UPS to Canada requires a $50 minimum order. Allow 4-6 weeks for delivery. Orders outside the U.S.A. and Canada: Airmail—add retail price of book; add $5 for each non-book item (tapes, etc.); add $1 per item for surface mail.

FOR GROUP STUDY AND PURCHASE

Because there is a great deal of interest in group discussion and study of the subject matter of this book, we feel that we should encourage the adoption and use of this particular book by such groups by offering a special "quantity" price to group leaders or "agents."

Our Special Quantity Price for a minimum order of five copies of *Crafting the Art of Magic* is $32.85 cash-with-order. This price includes postage and handling within the United States. Minnesota residents must add 6% sales tax. For additional quantities, please order in multiples of five. For Canadian and foreign orders, add postage and handling charges as above. Credit card (VISA, Master Card, American Express) orders are accepted. Charge card orders only may be phoned free ($15.00 minimum order) within the U.S.A. or Canada by dialing 1-800-THE-MOON. Customer service calls dial 1-612-291-1970. Mail orders to:

LLEWELLYN PUBLICATIONS
P.O. Box 64383-Dept. 370 / St. Paul, MN 55164-0383, U.S.A.

BUCKLAND'S COMPLETE BOOK OF WITCHCRAFT
by Raymond Buckland, Ph.D.

Here is the most complete resource to the study and practice of modern, non-denominational Wicca. This is a lavishly illustrated, self-study course for individuals or groups. Included are rituals, exercises for developing psychic talents, and information on all major "sects" of the Craft, sections on tools, beliefs, dreams, meditations, divination, herbal lore, healing, ritual clothing and much, much more. This book unites theory and practice into a comprehensive course designed to help you develop into a practicing Witch, one of the "Wise Ones." It is written by Dr. Ray Buckland, a very famous and respected authority on Witchcraft who first came public with "the Old Religion" in the United States. Large format with workbook-type exercises, profusely illustrated and full of music and chants. *Buckland's Complete Book of Witchcraft* takes you from A to Z in the study of Witchcraft.

Never before has so much information on "the Craft of the Wise" been collected in one place. Traditionally, there are three degrees of advancement in most Wiccan traditions. When you complete studying this book you will be the equivalent of a "Third Degree Witch." Even those who have practiced Wicca for years find useful information in this book, and many covens are using this for their textbook. If you want to become a Witch, or if you merely want to find out what Witchcraft is really about, you will find no better book than this.

0-87542-050-8, 272 pgs., 8 1/2 x 11, illus., softcover $12.95

WITCHCRAFT: YESTERDAY & TODAY
by Raymond Buckland, Ph.D.

This is a fascinating video by recognized Witchcraft authority Raymond Buckland, whose purpose is to straighten out the popular misconceptions about the Wiccan religion. For the approximately 70,000 to 75,000 people in the United States who consider themselves Wiccans or Pagans, this is the only completely factual "how-to" depiction of the rites and practices of their religion in the world.

This video details the origins and history of Witchcraft, and discusses the resurgence of Wicca in our own day. Wiccan priests and priestesses dramatize the ancient rites and rituals. For the merely curious, there is no better way to experience the inner beauty and strength of the Craft of the Wise than from seeing a teacher in action. For students, this is better than a book; and it makes an excellent tool for coven leaders and teachers.

0-87542-089-3, VHS, running time: approx. 60 min. $29.95

WICCA: A GUIDE FOR THE SOLITARY PRACTITIONER
by Scott Cunningham

Wicca is a book of life, and how to live magically, spiritually, and wholly attuned with Nature. It is a book of sense and common sense, not only about Magick, but about religion and one of the most critical issues of today: how to achieve the much needed and wholesome relationship with out Earth. Cunningham presents Wicca as it is today—a gentle, Earth-oriented religion dedicated to the Goddess and God. This book fulfills a need for a practical guide to solitary Wicca—a need which no previous book has fulfilled.

Here is a positive, practical introduction to the religion of Wicca, designed so that any interested person can learn to practice the religion alone, anywhere in the world. It presents Wicca honestly and clearly, without the pseudo-history that permeates other books. It shows that Wicca is a vital, satisfying part of twentieth century life.

This book presents the theory and practice of Wicca from an individual's perspective. The section on the Standing Stones Book of Shadows contains solitary rituals for the Esbats and Sabbats. This book, based on the author's nearly two decades of Wiccan practice, presents an eclectic picture of various aspects of this religion. Exercises designed to develop magical proficiency, a self-dedication ritual, herb, crystal and rune magic, recipes for Sabbat feasts, are included in this excellent book.
0-87542-118-0, 240 pgs., 6 x 9, illus.   **$9.95**

THE TRUTH ABOUT WITCHCRAFT TODAY
by Scott Cunningham

The Truth About Witchcraft Today, is the first real look at the facts about Witchcraft and the religion of Wicca. For centuries, organized religions have perpetrated lies about the ancient practice of Witchcraft, and to this day, many misinformed people think Wicca involves worship of the Devil, sex orgies, and drug use—it just isn't so! As Cunningham plainly states, the practice of magic is not supernatural or Satanic—Witches and folk magicians are only utilizing, through timeless rituals, *natural energies* found within the Earth and our bodies to enrich life by creating positive change.

If you are completely unfamiliar with Witchcraft, and have wondered exactly how magic works, this book was written for you! In a straightforward, easy-to-understand manner, Cunningham explains the differences between folk magic, ritual magic, ceremonial magic, and religious magic. He describes the folk magician's "tools of power"—crystals, herbs, candles, and chants—as well as the ritual tools of the Wiccan: the athame, cauldron, crystal sphere, and pentacle, among others. He also provides an excellent introduction to the practice of magic by delineating two simple folk magic spells, a circle-casting ceremony, and a complete Wiccan ritual.
0-87542-127-X, 224 pgs., mass market   **$3.95**

ANCIENT MAGICKS FOR A NEW AGE
by Alan Richardson and Geoff Hughes

With two sets of personal magickal diaries, this book details the work of magicians from two different eras. In it, you can learn what a particular magician is experiencing in this day and age, how to follow a similar path of your own, and discover correlations to the workings of traditional adepti from almost half a century ago.

The first set of diaries is from Christine Hartley and shows the magick performed within the Merlin Temple of the Stella Matutina, an offshoot of the Hermetic Order of the Golden Dawn, in the years 1940-42. The second set is from Geoff Hughes, and details his magickal work during 1984-86. Although he was not at that time a member of any formal group, the magick he practiced was under the same aegis as Hartley's. The third section of this book, written by Hughes, shows how you can become your own Priest or Priestess and make contact with Merlin.

The teachings of Christine Hartley and Geoff Hughes are like the poles of some hidden battery that lie beneath the Earth and beneath the years. There is a current flowing between them, and the energy is there for you to tap.

0-87542-671-9, 320 pgs., illus., 6 x 9   **$12.95**

EARTH GOD RISING:
THE RETURN OF THE MALE MYSTERIES
by Alan Richardson

Today, in an age that is witnessing the return of the Goddess in all ways and on all levels, the idea of one more male deity may appear to be a step backward. But along with looking toward the feminine powers as a cure for our personal and social ills, we must remember to invoke those forgotten and positive aspects of our most ancient God. The Horned God is just, never cruel; firm, but not vindictive. The Horned God loves women as equals. He provides the balance needed in this New Age, and he must be invoked as clearly and as ardently as the Goddess to whom he is twin.

The how-to section of this book shows how to make direct contact with your most ancient potentials, as exemplified by the Goddess and the Horned God. Using the simplest of techniques, available to everyone in any circumstance, *Earth God Rising* shows how we can create our own mystery and bring about real magical transformations without the need for groups, gurus, or elaborate ceremonies.

0-87542-672-7, 256 pgs., illus., 5-1/4 x 8   **$10.95**